"Nothing hits the connecting point between our individual daily stories and God's great story like *Story Thru the Bible*. What a provocatively simple way to experience that intersection in our own lives and be equipped to encourage others toward its Author!"

—RICH LELAND, senior pastor, Summer Street Church, Nantucket, Massachusetts

"This book is a breakthrough for humanity. It will encourage many people to read, learn, and enjoy the Bible. The fact that it is for oral learners—which describes 50 percent of people in the Middle East—is brilliant."

—WAHID WAHBA, founder and president, Middle East Leadership Training Institute, Cairo, Egypt

"*Story Thru the Bible* is interesting, important, and applicable to every nation and culture. Story grabs people, connects family members together, touches hearts, and transforms lives. It's simple, understandable, systematic, and practical for all ages. This book will echo with beauty in many lives."

—YURI SHELESTUN, regional director, WorldTeach Ukraine, Kiev

"Our people loved *Story Thru the Bible*. I have led small groups in various forms and places for a number of years, yet rarely have I seen the interest and interaction I found as we simply retold the Bible story in our own words and then discussed how it applied to our lives. From week one, our group bonded as we focused on the story of God's love found in the stories of His Word."

—TERRY SEAMON, associate pastor, West Cabarrus Church, Concord, North Carolina

"*Story Thru the Bible* is an unforgettable adventure. It follows biblical chronology, which is often neglected. We discover the real-life experiences of people who heard God's voice, encountered His presence, and experienced His work. The format of *Story Thru the Bible* is seamless and generates an interest that results in changed lives."

— VALLAB SATHYABAL, regional director, WorldTeach
South Asia, Hyderabad, India

"I expect to see our small groups use *Story Thru the Bible* with great joy. I also believe that our dads and moms can use it in their families to train and disciple their children. What an awesome tool this will be!"

— STEVE KEYES, founding pastor, CrossRoads Community Church,
Simpsonville, South Carolina

Story Thru the Bible

An Interactive Way to Connect with God's Word

WALK THRU THE BIBLE

By Chris Tiegreen

NavPress is the publishing ministry of The Navigators, an international Christian organization and leader in personal spiritual development. NavPress is committed to helping people grow spiritually and enjoy lives of meaning and hope through personal and group resources that are biblically rooted, culturally relevant, and highly practical.

For a free catalog go to www.NavPress.com
or call 1.800.366.7788 in the United States or 1.800.839.4769 in Canada.

ISBN-13: 978-1-61521-820-2

Cover design by Faceout Studio, Jeff Miller
Cover images by iStock and Art Bible–Anthony Van Dyck

Unless otherwise identified, all Scripture quotations in this publication are taken from the *Holy Bible, New International Version*® (NIV®). Copyright © 1973, 1978, 1984 by International Bible Society. Used by permission of Zondervan. All rights reserved. Other versions used include: The New King James Version (NKJV). Copyright © 1982 by Thomas Nelson, Inc. Used by permission. All rights reserved; and the New American Standard Bible® (NASB), Copyright © 1960, 1962, 1963, 1968, 1971, 1972, 1973, 1975, 1977, 1995 by The Lockman Foundation. Used by permission.

Library of Congress Cataloging-in-Publication Data

Tiegreen, Chris.
  Story thru the Bible : an interactive way to connect with God's word
Walk thru the Bible / By Chris Tiegreen.
    p. cm.
  "Walk thru the Bible."
  Includes bibliographical references.
  ISBN 978-1-61521-820-2
  1. Bible stories, English. 2. Bible--Study and teaching. I. Walk
Thru the Bible (Educational ministry) II. Title.
  BS550.3.T54 2011
  220.5'2097--dc22

                              2010045156

Printed in the United States of America

1 2 3 4 5 6 7 8 / 15 14 13 12 11

Other Books from Walk Thru the Bible

The Seven Laws of the Learner
Closer Walk
The Daily Walk Bible
Family Walk
Talk Thru the Bible
Your Daily Walk
Youth Walk
Youth Walk Bible
WALK THRU DISCUSSION GUIDES (series)

Other Books by Chris Tiegreen

The One Year at His Feet Devotional
The One Year Walk with God Devotional
The One Year Wonder of the Cross Devotional
The One Year Worship the King Devotional

To Avery T. Willis Jr. (1934–2010),
whose vision of reaching the oral learners of
this world inspired the development of
this book.

NOTE FROM THE PUBLISHER

Avery Willis has been a friend and mentor to me over the past twenty years. I am personally challenged to give the rest of my life to helping people discover how to live as Christ followers. NavPress owes unending gratitude for Avery's partnership on this project. Through this resource Avery yet speaks though he is now in heaven. I believe this book is God-directed and will be a great blessing to your church.

Sincerely,
MICHAEL D. MILLER
President of NavPress

CONTENTS

INTRODUCTION

The Bible is a book of stories. God could have given us an instruction manual or a religious textbook, but instead He chose to give us a collection of real-life experiences of people who heard His voice, encountered His presence, or experienced His works. We aren't just told that God is a deliverer, for example; we learn the story of how He miraculously delivered His people out of Egypt. We aren't just told that God is a healer; we are shown those who received His healing and the circumstances in which they were healed. In His Word, we see how people met Him and followed Him, we read their poems and songs and letters, and we learn deep truths from these glimpses into their lives.

Why did God give us a book of stories? Because that's how human beings learn most naturally. When words create pictures that we can understand and remember, the truth behind those pictures sinks in and sticks with us. This is one reason Jesus told so many parables. Stories express powerful truth much more effectively than long explanations could, which is clear by the impact the Bible's stories still have on us today.

This book of fifty-two stories from Scripture is based on this concept that we learn best through stories. It is designed for anyone to be able to learn a story, remember it, and pass it on to others. This process is a key aspect of discipleship—we multiply ourselves by allowing God to use us to bear fruit in others. Biblical stories are highly transferable from one person to another and always have been. The storytelling method has been one of God's primary means for spreading truth and passing it from one generation to the next.

Storying through the Bible is a highly effective and natural way to communicate key truths, concepts, and values. It is practical and culturally sensitive, and it works with all ages. About two-thirds of the world's people prefer an oral communication style of learning. Though this is largely due to low literacy rates in many areas, the postmodern generation is returning to this learning lifestyle as well, preferring an oral and visual approach to education rather than a literary one. The story approach to biblical truth is not only engaging, it also encourages the process of spiritual reproduction because the listener is able to pass the truth on to others. This is especially important with cultures or age groups in which oral learning is the primary means of learning, but it's a compelling way for everyone to learn.

The stories in this book were chosen because of their ability to present a biblical worldview. Most people in most cultures—even traditionally Christian cultures—do not see the world from a biblical perspective. In many societies, statistics related to divorce, pornography, ethical behavior, and other moral indicators hardly differ between Christians and non-Christians. This is largely due to the influence of a secular worldview. To change our worldview, we need to immerse ourselves in biblical truth regularly and repeatedly. These stories will help accomplish that and, when taken to heart, can powerfully reshape one's worldview.

For the most part, the stories are presented in chronological order—the primary exceptions being in the Gospels, where chronology isn't clear. But in general, participants will get a sense of the flow of Scripture as each story further develops God's overall plan for His people.

HOW TO USE THIS BOOK

The intent of *Story Thru the Bible* is to help people tell biblical stories effectively. The stories are accurately retold as they are presented in Scripture, with room for listeners to discern the implications of each. We've provided some helpful guidelines for telling biblical stories, but *Story Thru the Bible* is designed for flexibility. You can follow the pattern closely, or you can adapt it to your group's needs. You may find that different approaches work for different participants. The main goal is to faithfully retell the story as it's given in Scripture and discuss its implications. That's how lives are changed by God's Word.

Because storytelling is a natural and universal way to learn truth and shape one's worldview, this guide can be used in a variety of settings and across cultures. While it's possible to use this book effectively for personal growth, it's even better (and specifically intended) for use in a group or family context. That group can be as small as two or three people or as large as a formal class—any size that allows for meaningful discussion. Level of education or Bible knowledge is not a major issue; the story approach works well among highly literate people as well as with a nonliterate population or a culture that emphasizes storytelling as a vital part of its traditions. All that's required is at least one leader who can read or listen to the story and learn it well.

In a group that meets regularly, try rotating leaders week to week or periodically throughout the study, if possible. You may want to start with one leader who has experience or feels comfortable in that role, but this kind of study is a great opportunity to encourage and cultivate new leaders. Anyone can tell a Bible story. Learn to see everyone as a potential storyteller and take turns. Making disciples involves more than just passing on information or teaching truth. It includes giving hands-on experience and developing spiritual gifts in others. This is how God's people multiply—by bearing fruit in people who can then bear fruit in other people, and on and on. The story approach provides a great context and a great opportunity to do that.

In each session, we've included a section specifically geared toward families. That's because passing on God's Word to future generations is a vital part of His plan and a key emphasis in Scripture. Getting truth and an accurate worldview into young hearts and minds is important to God and a necessary aspect of discipleship. This is one of the strengths of the story approach; it is easily grasped by even the youngest minds. It powerfully communicates values without having to specifically describe or explain them. The most important thing we can do for our children is set them up to encounter God and lead them into a relationship with Him. We share life-changing truth with those we love.

FORMAT AND STRUCTURE

Each chapter (story) contained in *Story Thru the Bible* follows this structure:

- Theme
- Scripture reference
- Background information
- Pre-story comments
- The story
- Discussion questions for adults
- Discussion questions for families
- Memory verse option(s)
- Key takeaway application
- Appendix notes

Every section begins with a **theme**—a one-sentence summary—and the **Scripture reference** from which the story is derived. These are followed by any relevant **background information** (history, culture, society, and so on) necessary to understand the story. If you're using this material in a small group, the leader will need to have read the story in the Bible and be aware of these brief background comments.

In the session itself, the leader will want to begin with the **pre-story dialogue**—a short introductory comment that includes some questions or observations that are important for listeners to consider while the story is being told. Some questions are suggested in this section, but feel free to adapt them for your group's needs. It's helpful to keep this part of the discussion *short* so the story itself becomes the main focus of the session. The primary point is simply to prepare to listen—to put on "ears to hear," as Jesus often said.

The leader then **tells the story**. Remember that the goal is not to recite the story word for word or even to remember every minor detail. In preparation, read or listen to the story as it is written in Scripture and also read the reworded summary offered in this book. But remember that the summaries we've provided are just a guideline. You'll want to know the story well enough to cover all the main points in an engaging way, but use your own words and know your audience. The story may be told somewhat differently to children than to adults, or to people more unfamiliar with Christianity than to longtime church members. The point is to communicate truth, not to repeat a formula from memory. Just enjoy the plot, the characters, and the interesting details that make the stories compelling.

A series of **discussion questions** follow the story. Some of them are short-answer prompts to remember details of the story, but others may require some more thought. You may find that your group lingers on one or two questions much longer than others; this is fine, as long as the discussion doesn't carry the group on a tangent that misses the point of the story. Some groups cover all the discussion questions, and others prefer to focus on a few, allowing time to deal with them in greater depth. This is simply a matter of the group's needs and preferences.

Questions for families and children have been provided so *Story Thru the Bible* can be used at home or in children's classes. Adult small-group members may want to use these questions with their children in the time between sessions. This not only unites the family around the same biblical truth each week, it can also reinforce what the adult has learned with the group. Feel free to adapt these questions to the needs and ages of your children.

An optional **memory verse** (or verses) has been included at the end of each session. Memorizing Scripture may seem simply to be a mental exercise at first, but it's a very effective way to get God's truth into your heart. God's Spirit will bring these verses to mind in key situations in life if they are "on file" in your spirit.

Finally, each session concludes with what we've called the **key application**, by which we mean the key point or conclusion listeners should derive from the story and discussion.

In the appendix at the end of this book, you'll find some leader's notes for each session. These include **key points** that should be covered at some point in the session, either in the story or in the discussion before and after the story. This allows the leader to refer to a good summary view of the session. The leader's notes also contain some **additional information**, interesting facts about the story, or other Scripture references that supplement the story's points. These facts and insights can be used wherever helpful in the discussion but are not necessary to include unless the leader wants to.

DURING THE WEEK

If you're using this resource in a weekly small-group setting, encourage participants to increase the impact of each story in their lives by doing some exercises and activities between sessions. One of the best ways to reinforce the message is to **retell the story** to others—family, friends, and anyone else you can think of. Even people you think aren't interested may be willing to let you "practice" on them. The retelling process not only helps you get God's truth into your heart, it might open theirs as well.

You can also **dramatize the story** with family or friends, make up a song with the memory verse or the story's theme, draw a scene from the story in order to help you retain a visual memory of it, or come up with any other experiential activity you can think of. Feel free to be creative. God has given us five senses and a variety of learning styles, and the more of them we use, the more we learn. In a small-group setting, these activities could be collaborative and of the moment, assigned as homework to bring back to the class in the next meeting, or simply suggested for each participant to use as he or she chooses.

During the week is a good time to **practice any verses you've**

chosen to memorize. You can write the verses on index cards or type them into a handheld device and carry them with you wherever you go. That's a great way to maximize downtime that would otherwise be lost standing in line or waiting for appointments. Review your verses as often as possible; even a brief look can help establish them in your memory.

Another great way to dive deep into a biblical story is to **look at that story from a variety of different angles**. Put on a specific set of "lenses" through which you will view the week's story each day, and you'll be amazed at how many insights and applications open up to you. You can use the suggested patterns below or come up with one of your own.

THROUGHOUT THE WEEK

Until your next session, reflect on the story you heard and discussed this week. One way to do that is to consider the story from a different angle each day. Following are five suggestions to help you see a story's theme through different lenses. Depending on the story, some of these questions may not apply, and your answers to questions on one day may overlap with your answers on another day. But thinking through them this way will broaden your understanding and help you apply God's Word to your life in practical ways.

Look Upward

▶ How does this story apply to your relationship with God?

▶ What does it teach you about Him — His will and His heart?

▶ What aspect of His character is He inviting you to experience and enjoy?

▶ How will you benefit by applying the truths of this story in your relationship with God? How will God benefit?

▶ What practical steps can you take to live out these truths in your relationship with God?

Look Inward

- ▶ How does this story apply to your heart and your own spiritual growth?
- ▶ What does it teach you about yourself, your needs, or your goals in life?
- ▶ In what aspects of your personal life is God inviting you to grow and mature?
- ▶ How will you benefit by applying the truths of this story inwardly? How will those around you benefit?
- ▶ What practical steps can you take to allow these truths to help you grow spiritually?

Look Around

- ▶ How does this story apply to your relationship with others?
- ▶ What does it teach you about how to see others and relate to them?
- ▶ What is God inviting you to do differently in your relationships?
- ▶ How will you benefit by applying the truths of this story in your relationships? How will others benefit?
- ▶ What practical steps can you take to live out these truths in your relationships?

Look Outward

- ▶ How does this story apply to your ministry and mission in life — to your role in God's kingdom, in society, and in the world?
- ▶ What does it teach you about God's purposes for the world?
- ▶ What part of His mission is He inviting you to participate in?
- ▶ How will you benefit by applying the truths of this story in your ministry? How will the world benefit?
- ▶ What practical steps can you take to live out these truths in the world?

Look Forward

▶ How does this story apply to your future, both in this age and in eternity?

▶ What does it teach you about God's plan for your life, now and forever?

▶ What aspect of eternity is God inviting you to participate in?

▶ How will you benefit in the future by applying these truths now? How will God's kingdom benefit?

▶ What practical steps can you take to impact eternity now with these truths?

1

CREATION
In the Beginning

THEME

God creates everything, and it is good.

PASSAGE/REFERENCE

Genesis 1–2

BACKGROUND

From ancient times to today, people have asked life's big questions: How did this world begin? What is the meaning of life? Where is it all headed? Why am I here? While plenty of answers for these questions have been suggested by scientists, philosophers, and anyone else with a sense of curiosity, most human beings still consider these questions a mystery.

PRE-STORY DIALOGUE

Today we want to talk about the answers given by the One who was there at the beginning. We want to talk about Creation—where everything came from and how our world began. Before we start, think about some of the answers people give for these big questions. What are some of the ideas people have about how the world began? What do they say is the meaning of life? Who are considered the experts on this topic?

Now as you listen to the story, think about the following questions: What was there in the beginning? Where did everything that was made come from? Where do human beings fit into the story of Creation?

TELL THE STORY

In the very beginning, God made the heavens and the earth. The earth was shapeless and empty and dark, but God's Spirit hovered over the waters. When God said, "Let there be light," there was light. (That's how He created everything—by speaking. He would say, "Let there be . . ." and then it was there.) He separated light from darkness and called it "day" and "night." That was the first day of creation. Then on the second day, God stretched out an expanse above the waters and called it "the heavens," or sky. Then on the third day, He separated the waters by creating dry land, and He called the land "earth" and the waters "seas." He looked at all He had made and said it was good.

God said, "Let the earth bring forth plants," and plants began to grow—grass and trees and all kinds of seed-bearing vegetation so the plants could reproduce themselves. On the fourth day, He made the sun and moon and stars to give light during the day and the night. He set the sun and moon in the sky and planned their times and seasons to give us days, months, and years. On the fifth and sixth days, He began creating animal life the same way He had created everything else, just by speaking them into existence: first creatures of the sea and birds in the air, then land animals of all kinds. He blessed them all to "be fruitful and multiply," and they all reproduced according to their own kind.

Finally, but still on the sixth day, God made human beings in His own image—designed to be just like Himself. He made both male and female and blessed them to "be fruitful and multiply," just as He had blessed the animals. He formed the man out of dust, but the man was alone so God made the woman out of the man. He united them together and said they were "one flesh." He made man to have authority over all the other creatures and over the earth itself, and He gave the man and woman a command to "fill the earth and subdue it." He gave them a beautiful place to live: a garden they would work in and take care of.

Every step of the way, God looked at what He had made and said it was good. But after He made human beings, when He had finished everything, He looked at it all and said it was "very good." Then on the seventh day God rested, and He blessed that seventh day and set it apart for rest.

DISCUSSION QUESTIONS

- What existed "in the beginning"?
- In this story, does the world seem to be an accident or a well-planned design? What evidence is there in the story for your answer?
- Why do you think the Spirit hovered over the waters? What was He doing?
- Do you think creation is still good? How do you think it is different now than it was when God first made it?
- In what ways are human beings made in God's image? How are we different than everything else He created? Why do you think He designed us to be like Him? What does this say about our value to God? How does that make you feel?
- What does it mean for human beings to subdue the earth or have dominion over it? In what ways do you think we could abuse this assignment? How can we carry it out responsibly?
- What does this story tell us about God's design for marriage?
- What does this story tell us about God? What is He like? How powerful is He? What is valuable to Him? What characteristics of His do we see in this story?

- How does it affect our lives if we believe that God made everything we can see?

QUESTIONS FOR FAMILIES/CHILDREN

- Who made everything?
- Did God do a good job when He made the world? How do we know? In what ways did He show how creative He is?
- How do you think we should treat the world God made?
- How did God make us different from the animals?
- Why do you think God made each of us able to know Him and talk with Him?
- How does this story show us that each of us is extremely special to God?
- What do we know about God from this story? What do we know about ourselves?

MEMORY VERSES

So God created man in his own image, in the image of God he created him; male and female he created them.

GENESIS 1:27

God saw all that he had made, and it was very good.

GENESIS 1:31

KEY APPLICATION

We are to value all the people and things God has created.

2

FALL

Paradise Lost

THEME

God sees His people fall away from Him by sinning.

PASSAGE/REFERENCE

Genesis 3

BACKGROUND

God put the man and woman in the Garden of Eden, and He placed two trees in the center of the garden: the tree of life and the tree of the knowledge of good and evil. God gave Adam and Eve specific instructions—they could eat from any tree in the garden except for one: the tree of the knowledge of good and evil. The consequences of eating from that tree would be death.

PRE-STORY DIALOGUE

In our last story, we saw that God created a very good world, placed the man and woman in a beautiful garden, and gave them clear instructions about what He expected of them. They had everything they needed, including fellowship with God. As you listen to today's story, think about what life was like in that garden and about the decisions the people made. What privileges did they have? Why did Adam and Eve choose to disobey God? What were the consequences of their disobedience?

TELL THE STORY

When God placed Adam and Eve in Eden, He told them they could eat of any tree in the garden *except* the tree of the knowledge of good and evil. If they ate of that tree, they would die. But one day a serpent came to Eve and asked her, "Did God really say, 'You must not eat from any tree in the garden'?" Eve explained that they could eat the fruit of any tree, but they must not eat or touch the tree in the middle of the garden. The serpent then told her that the reason God did not want them to eat from that tree is because He knew their eyes would be opened and they would be like Him. The serpent said they wouldn't die.

Eve looked at the fruit of the forbidden tree and saw that it was desirable, so she ate it. Then she gave some to Adam, and he ate it too. When they had eaten, their eyes were opened, and they realized they were naked and tried to cover themselves. When they heard God walking in the garden later, they tried to hide from Him because they were afraid.

"Have you eaten from the tree that I commanded you not to eat from?" God asked. Adam confessed but blamed Eve for giving him the fruit, and then Eve confessed but blamed the serpent for deceiving her. Then God cursed the serpent to crawl on his belly as a snake and declared that there would forever be hostility between humans and snakes. He also foretold a time when the woman's offspring would crush the serpent's head, though the serpent would bite his heel.

Then God declared that, as a consequence of sin, the woman would have greater pain in childbirth and her husband would rule over her. And because Adam listened to his wife and disobeyed, God cursed the ground and declared that it would produce food only through the hard labor of mankind. And, as God had warned them, they would now die; as Adam had been made from dust, they would return to dust. Then God made clothes for Adam and Eve out of animal skins, banished them from Eden, and set an angelic guard to keep people from eating from the tree of life.

DISCUSSION QUESTIONS

- What kind of life did Adam and Eve have in the Garden of Eden?
- Who did Adam and Eve choose to believe about the forbidden tree—God or the serpent?
- How did the serpent tempt Eve to eat what had been forbidden? In what ways did he deceive her?
- Why do you think Eve trusted the serpent's words instead of God's? Why do you think Adam trusted Eve's words instead of God's?
- Do you think this seemed like a major decision to them? Why or why not?
- What were the consequences of their decision? How did it affect their relationship with God? Their relationship with each other? Their quality of life?
- Why did God cover Adam and Eve with clothes? What does this say about His nature?
- Why do you think God kept Adam and Eve from returning to Eden? What do you think would have been the consequences if they ate from the tree of life in their fallen condition?
- In what ways are we tempted to disbelieve God today?
- What are the consequences when we do? How does disobedience affect our relationship with God and with each other?

QUESTIONS FOR FAMILIES/CHILDREN

- What was the Garden of Eden like? Did Adam and Eve have all they needed?
- What instructions did God give Adam and Eve?
- Why do you think Adam and Eve didn't obey the instructions God gave them?
- How did the serpent trick Eve into eating the fruit? How did Eve get Adam to eat it?
- What happened when Adam and Eve disobeyed God?
- Why is it important for us to follow God's instructions?

MEMORY VERSE

I will put enmity between you and the woman, and between your offspring and hers; he will crush your head, and you will strike his heel.

GENESIS 3:15

KEY APPLICATION

Our sin alienates us from God.

3

FLOOD
Regrets and a Rescue

THEME

God righteously judges the world's sinful people.

PASSAGE/REFERENCE

Genesis 6:5–9:17
Focus: Genesis 6:11–8:21; 9:11-13

BACKGROUND

After Adam and Eve had been expelled from Eden and raised two sons, one of their sons killed the other. Then Adam and Eve had other children. Human nature did not improve; in fact, it only got worse. Although a few righteous people lived and served God, wickedness increased on the earth. God's beautiful creation had become very corrupt.

PRE-STORY DIALOGUE

In our last session, we saw how human beings were exiled from the paradise God had made for them. One of Adam and Eve's sons was named Seth. Our story this session is about one of Seth's descendants, a righteous man named Noah who lived during a time when God was very displeased with humanity and its immorality and disobedience. As you listen to this story, think about these questions: Why do you think God was so grieved about the corruption of humanity? Why didn't God just wipe out the human race or destroy the earth?

TELL THE STORY

Humanity had become very corrupt, and the world was full of violence. God was grieved that He ever made people, so He decided to wipe mankind off the face of the earth and start over. But Noah found favor in God's eyes, so God decided to spare him and preserve humanity through Noah's family. He told Noah to build a huge ark and gave him very specific instructions with exact dimensions. God warned Noah that He was about to send a flood to destroy everything alive on the earth. God told Noah to bring into the ark two of every kind of animal, a male and a female, and to stock the ark with plenty of food. So Noah began building and did everything just the way God had told him to do it.

Finally, when Noah had finished building the ark, it was time. Noah, his wife, and his three sons and their wives all got on the boat along with all of the animals God had told him to bring. The rains began to fall, and water sprang up from the oceans and lakes. It rained for forty days and forty nights. The flood rose, and the ark floated on the surface of the water. Every living creature on the land was wiped out. Water covered the earth for 150 days, until the ark settled on a mountain; the water continued to recede until the tenth month after the flood had begun.

To see how far the flood had subsided, Noah sent out a raven, but the raven never returned. Then he sent out a dove, but the dove found no place to land and returned to the ark. Noah waited another week and then sent the dove out again. This time, the dove came back with a freshly plucked olive leaf, and Noah knew the waters had subsided.

God told Noah to leave the ark, so he and his family and every living creature on the ark left. Noah built an altar to God and made sacrifices. God answered him with a promise never to curse the ground and destroy the earth with a flood again, and He symbolized the promise with a rainbow.

DISCUSSION QUESTIONS

- Why do you think God was so grieved about the world? What does this tell you about His nature?
- Why did God decide to spare Noah and his family?
- Do you see the story of the Flood more as a story of judgment or of rescue and salvation? Why?
- In what ways did Noah have to demonstrate faith in order to be saved?
- What does God's judgment against mankind's sin tell us about His attitude toward sin? What does God's desire to save Noah tell us about His attitude toward those who serve Him?
- What did God want Noah and his family to do after the Flood? How did He want them to live?
- Why did God make a covenant with Noah? What did God promise? In what ways does that promise comfort us today?

QUESTIONS FOR FAMILIES/CHILDREN

- Why was God grieved about the world? What did people do to make Him sad?
- What did God tell Noah to do? Do you think it was hard for Noah to obey God's instructions? Why or why not?
- Why did God choose Noah to save?
- Do you think God wants us to be obedient today? Do you think God punishes disobedience?

- What should we think of when we see a rainbow today? How does a rainbow remind us of God?

MEMORY VERSE

Never again will I curse the ground because of man, even though every inclination of his heart is evil from childhood. And never again will I destroy all living creatures, as I have done.

GENESIS 8:21

KEY APPLICATION

God judges the world's sin and disciplines us as His children.

4

NATIONS
The Tower of Babel

THEME

God orders humanity's distinctions.

PASSAGE/REFERENCE

Genesis 11:1-9

BACKGROUND

The history of man-made religions is the story of humanity trying to grasp the divine however we can—perhaps by becoming holy or righteous enough by our own efforts, or even by trying to tap into supernatural powers. Though God would show throughout the Bible that the only way to know Him is through the ways He has revealed Himself to us, the building of the tower of Babel was an attempt by human beings to exalt themselves. It took place "in the land of Shinar" in ancient Mesopotamia (Genesis 11:2, NASB)—in the area where Babylon would one day become a dominant empire.

PRE-STORY DIALOGUE

Long ago, God had given Adam and Eve a mission to "fill the earth and subdue it" (Genesis 1:28). After the Flood, God told Noah's family to be fruitful, multiply, and fill the earth (see 9:1). Noah's sons had many sons who would become the fathers of many nations, and they would scatter throughout the earth; but they did not always do so willingly. As you listen to the following story, see if you can answer these questions: What did the people do that was opposite of God's instructions? How did God reverse the effects of their disobedience?

TELL THE STORY

As people began to spread across the earth, they had only one language. Everyone could understand each other. And as they migrated, they found a plain in Shinar and settled there. They found a way to make bricks and mortar, so they decided to build a city. And in the city, they decided to build a very tall tower that would reach into the skies. They wanted to make a name for themselves, and they also wanted to stick together and not be scattered.

God saw the efforts of the people to build a city and a tower and saw that it was just the beginning of what people would attempt as long as they had the ability to speak the same language and be united. "Then nothing they plan to do will be impossible for them," He said. So He confused their language so they would not be able to understand one another, and then He dispersed them over the face of the earth. They abandoned their building project, and the place was called Babel because that's where God confused their language. (The word *babel* sounds like the Hebrew word for "confusion.")

DISCUSSION QUESTIONS

- What mission on the earth had God given Adam and Eve? What had He told Noah and his sons to do in the world?
- How did the people who tried to build the city and tower disobey God's mission?
- What do you think they were really trying to accomplish?
- Why do you think God thought it necessary to prevent their work?
- How did confusing their language cause them to give up their project?
- In what ways do diverse languages cause us difficulty today? Do you think there's any benefit in today's world having a diversity of languages?
- Do you think God was opposed to anyone's building a city? Why or why not? If not, what was offensive about this particular city and the desire to build a tower into the heavens?
- How do you think God wanted them to relate to Him?

QUESTIONS FOR FAMILIES/CHILDREN

- How many languages did people speak after the Flood?
- What had God told them to do about spreading out across the earth? What did they do instead?
- Why did the people want to build a huge tower?
- Why did God want to stop them? How did He do it?
- What happened when they all started speaking different languages?

MEMORY VERSES

The Lord said, "If as one people speaking the same language they have begun to do this, then nothing they plan to do will be impossible for them. Come, let us go down and confuse their language so they will not understand each other."

Genesis 11:6-7

KEY APPLICATION

We honor God by appreciating the differences in those He has made.

5

ABRAHAM
A Promised Blessing

THEME

God calls Abraham as the model of faith.

PASSAGE/REFERENCE

Genesis 12:1-8

BACKGROUND

Many years after the tower of Babel, God led a family from the city of Ur in Mesopotamia toward the land of Canaan. Up until then, God's dealings with people had applied to everyone alive, but when He called Terah's family out of Ur, He was beginning to develop a special relationship with a specific group of people. Terah's family only made it halfway, however; the family settled in Haran, far north of Canaan.

PRE-STORY DIALOGUE

Though humanity had departed from God's purposes in many ways, God did not forget His mission. In this story, we will see how God was working through a man named Abram (later named Abraham) to set apart a people to cultivate for special purposes. As you listen, put yourself in Abram's place and think about what it would be like to do what he did. Consider these questions: Why did God tell Abram to do what he did? How did Abram respond to what God wanted him to do?

TELL THE STORY

While Terah's family was in Haran, God spoke to Terah's son, Abram. "Leave your country, your people and your father's household and go to the land I will show you," He said. Then God made some amazing promises: He would make Abram into a great nation, bless him, make his name great, bless his friends and curse his enemies, and cause him to be a blessing to all the nations of the earth. So at the age of seventy-five, Abram did what God said and left his home, along with his wife, Sarai, and his nephew Lot.

When Abram arrived in Canaan, God told him this was the land He would give to Abram and his descendants, even though many Canaanites were already living in the land. So Abram built an altar and worshipped God there. Then he moved to another area in Canaan east of Bethel. He built an altar and worshipped God there, too.

DISCUSSION QUESTIONS

- What did God tell Abram to do? Why do you think He told him to do that?
- How did Abram respond to God? Do you think it was hard for him to respond that way? Why or why not?
- How much did God tell Abram about his future when He told him to leave home? What risks did Abram take to obey God? How much did he have to lose? What did he give up?
- What did God promise Abram? How did His promises fit His mission for the world? How did it relate to the instructions He had given Adam and Eve?

- How old was Abram when God made those promises? How difficult do you think it was for Abram to believe those promises? Why?
- What did Abram do when he got to Canaan?
- In what ways is God's guidance for us similar to the way He guided Abram? In what ways are Abram's faith and obedience examples for us?

QUESTIONS FOR FAMILIES/CHILDREN

- How old was Abram when God spoke to him?
- What did God tell Abram to do?
- What do you think it would be like to leave home without knowing exactly where you are going? Would that be scary? Why or why not?
- Do you think God wants us to trust Him like Abram did? How can we show God that we do trust Him?
- Why do you think it was important for Abram to worship God when he arrived in his new land? How can we worship God like Abram did?

MEMORY VERSES

I will make you into a great nation and I will bless you; I will make your name great, and you will be a blessing. I will bless those who bless you, and whoever curses you I will curse; and all peoples on earth will be blessed through you.

GENESIS 12:2-3

KEY APPLICATION

God calls us to follow Him and to be models of faith to others.

6

ISAAC
A Promise Fulfilled

THEME

God provides a substitute sacrifice.

PASSAGE/REFERENCE

Genesis 15–22
Focus: Genesis 18:1-15; 21:1-7; 22:1-18

BACKGROUND

Abram knew that God's promise depended on his having descendants, yet he remained childless. When Abram questioned God about this, God reaffirmed His promise (see Genesis 15:1-6), and Abram believed. Later, Abram and Sarai tried to accomplish God's promise by having Abram father a child through Sarai's servant (see Genesis 16). The result was a son named Ishmael, but this was not how God intended to give Abram descendants. Again, God reaffirmed His promise, and to signify that they would become the parents of many nations, He changed their names to Abraham ("father of many") and Sarah ("princess").

PRE-STORY DIALOGUE

Abraham faced an impossible situation. God had told him he would be the father of many nations, yet he still had no children. How could this be? Much of Abraham's story involves his struggle with this impossibility. Yet as we will see in this session, nothing is impossible with God. As you listen to Abraham's story, think about these questions: Why would God wait so long to fulfill His promise to Abraham? Why did God choose to work through an impossible situation rather than just giving Abraham and Sarah a child at a more normal stage of life? What does this story show us about God and His ways?

TELL THE STORY

The Lord appeared to Abraham one day—as three men. When Abraham saw the three men, he bowed down and then offered them water and something to eat. He ran to tell Sarah to prepare a feast. As Abraham and the three men were eating, they asked him where Sarah was. "In the tent," Abraham answered. Then the Lord said that Sarah would have a son within a year.

By this time, Sarah and Abraham were very old. When Sarah heard the Lord say this—she had been listening from inside the tent—she laughed. So the Lord asked Abraham why she laughed. "Is anything too hard for the LORD?" He said. Sarah denied laughing, but the Lord knew that she had.

Soon, the Lord did what He promised, and Sarah became pregnant. She and Abraham had a son and named him Isaac, as the Lord had instructed them. (*Isaac* means "he laughs.") They also had him circumcised, as the Lord had instructed. Abraham was one hundred years old when Isaac was born, and Sarah was ninety. Sarah said, "God has brought me laughter, and everyone who hears about this will laugh with me." And they marveled at the miracle God had done by giving them a son in their old age.

Years later, God tested Abraham by telling him to sacrifice Isaac as an offering. Abraham obeyed God and took Isaac with him to a mountain in Moriah, where Abraham would build an altar and sacrifice the boy. Near the mountain, Abraham told the servants to wait behind as he and Isaac climbed the mountain. "We will worship and then we will come back to you," he told them. As they went forward, Isaac noticed that there was wood and fire but no lamb for the offering. Abraham told him, "God himself will provide the lamb for the burnt offering, my son." When they arrived, Abraham built an altar and laid Isaac on it. He raised his knife to slay his son, but an angel appeared and stopped him. The Lord told Abraham, "Do not do anything to him. Now I know that you fear God, because you have not withheld from me your son, your only son." Then Abraham looked up and saw a ram caught in a thicket, so he took the ram and offered it as a sacrifice to God. He called that place "The LORD Will Provide." Because Abraham had not withheld his own son from God, God again promised to bless him, to give him a multitude of descendants, and to bless all the nations of the earth through his descendants.

DISCUSSION QUESTIONS

- How did God appear to Abraham? How did Abraham react when he saw the visitors?
- What did God promise Abraham? What made God's promise to Abraham impossible by human standards? How would you respond if God gave you such an unlikely promise?
- What impossibilities do you face in your life? How do you think God might want to deal with them? How hard is it for you to wait for Him to fulfill His promise?
- Why did Sarah laugh when God reminded Abraham of His promise? Why did she laugh after Isaac was born?
- Why do you think God waited so long to give Abraham and Sarah the promised son? Why do you think He tells us to

"wait on Him" so often in Scripture?

- What did God tell Abraham to do when Isaac had grown older? Why do you think He gave such a hard command?
- How did Abraham respond to God's instructions? What do you think Abraham thought of this command?
- What does this story show us about God? What does it show us about Abraham's faith and obedience?
- In what ways does the story of Abraham sacrificing Isaac give us a picture of Jesus and the Cross?
- In what ways does God relate to us as He did to Abraham?
- Which is easier for you: believing God's promises or obeying His commands? Why are both important in our relationship with God?

QUESTIONS FOR FAMILIES/CHILDREN

- What promise did God give to Abraham? Why did Abraham and Sarah think it was impossible?
- How would you feel if God did an amazing miracle in your life? Do you think He wants us to believe He can do anything?
- God let Abraham and Sarah wait a long time before He fulfilled His promise to them. Do you think He lets us wait for His blessings too? Why is it important for us to be patient?
- God gave Abraham a very difficult command. Does He ever expect you to do anything that's hard for you to do? Why is it important for us to trust Him enough to obey Him even when it's hard?

MEMORY VERSES

Is anything too hard for the LORD?

GENESIS 18:14

"The fire and wood are here," Isaac said, "but where is the lamb for the burnt offering?" Abraham answered, "God himself will provide the lamb for the burnt offering, my son."

GENESIS 22:7-8

KEY APPLICATION

God provides our perfect sacrifice in Christ.

7

JACOB

Encounters with God

THEME

God wrestles with His reluctant follower.

PASSAGE/REFERENCE

Genesis 25:21–33:20
Focus: *Genesis 28:10-22; 32:3-30; 33:1-11*

BACKGROUND

Isaac married Rebekah, a woman from the country Abraham's family had come from. They had two children, twin boys named Esau and Jacob. Esau had been born moments before Jacob, but over the years Jacob became like the firstborn by bargaining for Esau's birthright and then deceiving his father into giving him the firstborn's blessing. Esau was furious, so Jacob fled to the home country, where he married Rachel and Leah, the daughters of the relative he worked for. Through these two wives and their two servants, Jacob fathered twelve sons who would become the fathers of the twelve tribes of Israel.

PRE-STORY DIALOGUE

As Jacob fled from Esau and journeyed toward the family's original homeland, he had a dream in which he saw angels and heard God's voice. Many years later, as he was returning to the land God had promised Abraham's descendants, he encountered God again. The stories in this session are about these two encounters with God. As you listen, consider these questions: Why were these events important in Jacob's life? How are Jacob's encounters with God important in God's big-picture plan?

TELL THE STORY

Jacob left his home and went toward Haran, where Abraham had once lived. When night came, he lay down and put his head on a stone. While he was asleep, he had a dream about a stairway reaching from earth to heaven; angels were going up and down on it. The Lord was above the stairway, and He promised to give Jacob the land he was on and a multitude of descendants and to bless all peoples of the earth through him and his offspring. Then God added, "I am with you and will watch over you wherever you go, and I will bring you back to this land. I will not leave you until I have done what I have promised you."

When Jacob woke up, he realized God had been there. He was afraid and called that place the "house of God" and the "gate of heaven." He set up the stone he had been lying on as a monument and poured oil on it. Then he called the place Bethel ("house of God") and made a vow there. He promised that if God would be with him, watch over him on the journey, give him all he needed, and bring him back safely, then the Lord would be his God and the stone would be God's house. And of all God gave him, Jacob would give a tenth back to God.

Years later, after Jacob had been married and had many children, God told him to return to Canaan. Jacob was afraid to see his brother, Esau, again, so he sent messengers ahead of him to promise Esau gifts of much livestock and many servants. But when the messengers returned, they told Jacob that they had seen Esau and that he was coming out to meet Jacob along with four hundred men.

This made Jacob very anxious and worried, so he divided up all of his people and possessions into two groups, thinking that if Esau attacked one group, the other could escape. Then he prayed. He reminded God of His special relationship with Abraham and Isaac, and that God was the one who told him to return to Canaan. He expressed humility and gratitude, remembering that he had left Canaan with only his staff but was returning with many family members, servants, and possessions. Then he pleaded with God to save him from Esau and reminded God of His promise to cause Jacob to prosper and give him many descendants.

Jacob selected extravagant gifts for Esau and sent his servants ahead with them to meet Esau. He was hoping to pacify Esau and avoid a battle. Then Jacob sent his family across a stream ahead of him and spent the night alone.

During the night, Jacob had a strange experience. A man wrestled with him all night until daybreak. The man saw that he could not overpower Jacob, so he touched Jacob's hip socket and wrenched it. The man told Jacob to let him go, but Jacob said, "I will not let you go unless you bless me." The man asked Jacob his name, and when Jacob told him, the man said, "Your name will no longer be Jacob, but Israel, because you have struggled with God and with men and have overcome." Then Jacob asked the man's name, but the man wouldn't tell him. He blessed Jacob, and Jacob called the place Peniel ("face of God") because, as he said, "I saw God face to face, and yet my life was spared."

The next day, when Jacob saw Esau coming, he bowed down seven times to Esau. But Esau ran to Jacob and embraced him, and they wept together. None of Jacob's gifts had been necessary, and Esau didn't even want to keep them. But Jacob insisted, so Esau accepted them.

DISCUSSION QUESTIONS

- Why did Jacob leave home? Was everything going well in his life? Had he done anything wrong? What attitudes might he have had as he fled?
- In what way did God encounter Jacob? What was Jacob's dream about? What did God say to him? Was this the first time God had given these promises to someone? Who else received these promises from God?
- What does God's willingness to meet Jacob in his distress tell us about God's nature?
- How did Jacob respond to God? What did he promise? Can we make agreements like this with God too?
- What attitudes did Jacob have when he returned to Canaan years later? Why? What did he expect Esau to do?
- How did Jacob pray to God when he was afraid? In what ways did he base his prayer on God's covenant with him?
- How did God encounter Jacob during the night? Why do you think God chose to encounter him this way?
- What did Jacob say to the man who wrestled with him? In what ways did Jacob demonstrate faith during this encounter with God? What did God say in response to Jacob's persistence? Why did He change Jacob's name?
- Have you ever had a "wrestling match" with God? How do you think God feels about that? What have you learned about faith in the process?
- What did Jacob do when he finally saw Esau? What did Esau do?
- In these two encounters with God, how do we see God taking care of Jacob? What problems did Jacob have? How did God address Jacob's problems?
- How should we approach God when we have problems and worries and messes in our lives? What can we expect God to do about our problems?

- Do you think God is faithful to keep His promises to Abraham? To Jacob? To us today?

QUESTIONS FOR FAMILIES/CHILDREN

- Why was Jacob running from his brother, Esau? Why was he afraid?
- What kind of dream did Jacob have? How did God encourage Jacob? What did Jacob say in answer to God?
- God made a lot of promises to His people. Do you think He always keeps them? Do you think He keeps His promises to you?
- Why was Jacob afraid to go back home years later? What did he think Esau would do? What did Jacob do to try to make Esau happy?
- Who was the man who wrestled with Jacob during the night? What did Jacob ask the man to do? What did the man say to Jacob?
- When Jacob finally saw Esau, what did Esau do? Was he still angry? How did God show that He was taking care of Jacob?
- Do you think God takes care of you when you have trouble? How does Jacob's story encourage us that God is always with us?

MEMORY VERSE

I am with you and will watch over you wherever you go, and I will bring you back to this land. I will not leave you until I have done what I have promised you.

GENESIS 28:15

KEY APPLICATION

We often wrestle with God, but ultimately we should yield to Him.

8

JOSEPH
A Painful Providence

THEME

God strengthens Joseph to flee temptation, endure hardship in faith, and forgive others.

PASSAGE/REFERENCE

Genesis 37; 39–50
Focus: Genesis 37; 39; 41:1–42:22; 45–46

BACKGROUND

Jacob had children through his two wives, Leah and Rachel, and through their two maidservants, Bilhah and Zilpah. Rachel, his beloved wife, was the last to have children. She gave birth to Joseph, Jacob's eleventh son, and then died giving birth to Benjamin, the twelfth son. Jacob had a special affection for these two sons of the wife he loved.

PRE-STORY DIALOGUE

Remember what we have seen from God's dealings with Abraham, Isaac, and Jacob: He made a covenant with a family and was establishing them, leading them, and watching over them. In this story, we will see how one of Jacob's twelve sons received a dream from God and how God preserved the family through him. As the story is told, notice particularly how God's ways with Joseph seemed for a long time to contradict His promises—and how the setbacks in Joseph's life were actually used to further God's plan.

TELL THE STORY

Jacob loved Joseph more than all his other sons and made an expensive robe for him. This favoritism caused Joseph's brothers to hate him. When Joseph was seventeen, he had two dreams. In one dream, he and his brothers were out in the fields harvesting grain, and suddenly Joseph's sheaf of grain stood upright while his brothers' sheaves bowed down to his. In the next dream, the sun and moon and eleven stars bowed down to him. His brothers understood that this meant Joseph thought he would someday rule over the rest of the family. This made them very jealous; even his father rebuked him.

One day when Joseph went to deliver a message to his brothers out in the fields, they saw him coming and plotted to kill him. One of them convinced the others not to kill him, so they threw him in an empty well instead. When some traders came by, Joseph's brothers decided to sell him as a slave. So the traders bought Joseph and took him to Egypt; the brothers dipped Joseph's fancy robe in goat's blood, took it back to their father, and let him believe that Joseph had been killed by an animal. Jacob said he would grieve for Joseph the rest of his life.

In Egypt, one of Pharaoh's officials, a man named Potiphar, had bought Joseph. Potiphar trusted him and put Joseph in charge of his household. But Potiphar's wife came to Joseph day after day and tried to seduce him. "How then could I do such a wicked thing and sin against God?" Joseph said, which made her angry. One day when he went into the house to attend to his duties, Potiphar's wife grabbed him by his cloak and tried again to tempt him. Joseph ran out of the house but left his cloak. When Potiphar came home, his wife accused Joseph of attacking her and said she had screamed. So Potiphar had Joseph put in the prison where the king's prisoners were confined.

Even in prison, God caused Joseph to prosper. The warden put Joseph in charge of other prisoners. Later, two of Pharaoh's officials — the cupbearer and the baker — were put in prison, and when they had dreams they didn't understand, Joseph interpreted the dreams for them, and the dreams came true.

Two years later, Pharaoh had two disturbing dreams. One was about seven fat, healthy cows that came out of the Nile and were eaten up by seven skinny, ugly cows that also came up out of the river. The second dream was about seven good and healthy heads of grain that were swallowed up by seven thin and scorched heads of grain. Pharaoh asked all the wise men and magicians of Egypt to help him understand his dreams, but no one could interpret them. Then the cupbearer, who had been released from prison two years earlier, remembered Joseph and told Pharaoh how Joseph had accurately interpreted the prisoners' dreams. So Pharaoh sent for Joseph.

Joseph explained that the dreams meant that God was showing Pharaoh what He was about to do. There would be seven years of plenty followed by seven years of famine. Joseph suggested that Pharaoh save a portion of the harvest during each of the years of plenty so there would be enough food to eat during the famine. Pharaoh saw the wisdom in this plan and put Joseph in charge of it. "Since God has made all this known to you, there is no one so discerning and wise as you," he said. So at the age of thirty, Joseph rose to great power and was given an Egyptian wife with whom he would have two sons.

Things happened just as Joseph had said. He stored up huge quantities of grain during the seven years of abundance. Then when the famine struck, people came from all around to buy grain from Egypt's storehouses.

Even Joseph's family back in Canaan was hungry. Jacob sent Joseph's brothers — all except Benjamin, the youngest — to Egypt to buy grain. When Joseph saw them, he pretended to be a stranger and spoke harshly to them. He accused them of being spies, and when they told him their story—that they were ten of twelve sons, and that the youngest was still at home—Joseph insisted that they go get Benjamin and bring him back. In the meantime, he would hold Simeon as a prisoner until they returned. He filled their sacks with grain and secretly hid their money in the sacks, too. When they returned home, they discovered the money in their sacks and worried that they would be seen as thieves. They told Jacob all that had happened, but Jacob did not want to send Benjamin to Egypt.

Because they were desperate for food, Jacob eventually allowed his sons to take Benjamin to Egypt. They were very worried that Joseph would punish them for stealing and that Simeon might already be dead. But Joseph welcomed them back, asked how their father was, and was deeply moved to see Benjamin again. He put his brothers through some more tests to see if they were still the kind of people who had long ago betrayed him. He also set up an opportunity for them to be jealous of Benjamin and betray him to see if they would do to Rachel's other son what they had once done to him. But they proved themselves to be honorable.

Finally, Joseph revealed himself. His brothers were terrified when they recognized him, but Joseph reassured them: "Do not be distressed and do not be angry with yourselves for selling me here, because it was to save lives that God sent me ahead of you," he told them. And they embraced and cried and talked.

When Pharaoh heard that Joseph's brothers had come, he urged Joseph to have his entire family move to Egypt to survive the famine. So Joseph sent his brothers back to get Jacob and their wives and children. Jacob could hardly believe that Joseph was alive after all these years—and that he was a ruler in Egypt. He was stunned, but they finally convinced him. And Jacob and all the rest of Joseph's family moved to Egypt where Joseph could provide for them throughout the famine.

DISCUSSION QUESTIONS

- What did Joseph dream when he was young? How did his family respond to his dreams?
- Why did his brothers not like him? What did their jealousy and anger toward him cause them to do?
- Why did Potiphar trust Joseph and put him in charge of his entire household?
- What did Potiphar's wife try to get Joseph to do? How did Joseph respond to her? Why?
- Why did the prison warden trust Joseph and put him in charge of other prisoners? What did this position give him the opportunity to do?
- After first being sold into slavery and then falsely accused and imprisoned, how do you think Joseph felt about his dreams? Did God appear to be fulfilling his purposes for Joseph? How would you have responded if you were in Joseph's situation?
- What dreams did Pharaoh have? What happened to Joseph when he helped Pharaoh with his dreams?
- Why did Joseph's brothers go down to Egypt?
- After almost twenty years to think about what his brothers had done to him, how do you think Joseph felt when he saw them? If you had been in Joseph's position, would you have forgiven your brothers? Why or why not?
- How did Joseph's brothers feel when they first realized who he was? How did they show that they had changed over the years?
- Looking back, it's easy to see how God orchestrated the course of Joseph's life to put him in exactly the right position, but that's hard to recognize when we are going through hard times. What do you think caused Joseph to understand that God, not his brothers, had really sent him to Egypt? Do you think God accomplishes His purposes in our hardships and trials too? In what ways does Joseph's story encourage us to trust God?

- What does this story teach us about the power of forgiveness?
- What does this story teach us about God's sovereignty over our lives?
- In what ways does this story show us God fulfilling His promises to Abraham, Isaac, and Jacob?

QUESTIONS FOR FAMILIES/CHILDREN

- What dreams did Joseph have?
- Why were Joseph's brothers so mad at him? What did they do to him?
- How do you think Joseph felt when his brothers sold him to slave traders? How do you feel when someone treats you unfairly? Is it easy to forgive that person? Why or why not?
- When the Bible says that God was with Joseph, does that mean Joseph never had any problems? What does it mean?
- What did Joseph do when someone tried to tempt him to do the wrong thing? What should we do when we are tempted?
- In what ways did God take care of Joseph? How did Joseph become a ruler in Egypt?
- What did Joseph do when he finally saw his brothers again after many years? Did he punish them or forgive them? Why?
- How did Joseph's position as a ruler help his family?
- In what ways did Joseph show that he trusted God? Do you think we can trust God the same way Joseph did?

MEMORY VERSE

You intended to harm me, but God intended it for good to accomplish what is now being done, the saving of many lives.

GENESIS 50:20

KEY APPLICATION

We must be strengthened by God's Word and Spirit to flee temptation, endure hardship in faith, and forgive others.

9

MOSES
A Momentous Mission

THEME

God calls Moses to deliver His enslaved people.

PASSAGE/REFERENCE

Exodus 3:1–4:18

BACKGROUND

Four hundred years went by and the people of Israel multiplied greatly in Egypt, but a king who did not know about Joseph enslaved the Israelites. Then he decided to limit their growth for a time by killing all male babies. But one newborn boy's parents saved him by floating him in a basket in the Nile. Pharaoh's daughter discovered him and raised him as her own—a Jewish boy in Egypt's royal house. But after he grew up, he took a stand for his people. He saw an Egyptian beating an Israelite and killed the Egyptian. He had to flee for his life and ended up in Midian, far away from Egypt.

PRE-STORY DIALOGUE

Moses may have thought he would spend the rest of his life in Midian, but God had other plans. The people had been crying out to Him because of their oppression, and God heard their pleas. Exodus 2:24 says that He remembered His covenant with Abraham, Isaac, and Jacob and had compassion on their descendants. In this session, we will hear how God planned to rescue His people from slavery. As you listen, try to put yourself in Moses' place and understand how he felt when God encountered him. What would you have said to God? How much faith would you have had about His plan? God's Word shows us a man with a lot of questions and a big task ahead of him.

TELL THE STORY

One day when Moses was tending his father-in-law's flocks near Mount Horeb (aka Mount Sinai), the angel of the Lord appeared to him in a burning bush. The bush was on fire, but it was not burning up. Moses was curious, so he went closer to see the bush. When he got near it, God spoke to him. He told Moses to take off his sandals because he was standing on holy ground. Then God identified Himself as the God of Abraham, Isaac, and Jacob, and Moses hid his face because he was afraid to look at God.

God said He had seen His people's misery in Egypt and was going to bring them to the Promised Land, a spacious land flowing with milk and honey. He was sending Moses to Pharaoh to bring the people out of Egypt.

Moses didn't understand. "Who am I, that I should go to Pharaoh and bring the Israelites out of Egypt?" he asked. But God assured Moses that He would be with him and that Israel would worship at that very mountain.

Moses asked what he should tell the Israelites when they asked who had sent him. God said, "I AM WHO I AM. This is what you are to say to the Israelites: 'I AM has sent me to you.'" He also said to tell them He was the God of their fathers Abraham, Isaac, and Jacob and that they should remember Him by that name for generation after generation. God told Moses to assemble the elders of Israel and go with them to Pharaoh, asking for permission to take a three-day journey into the desert to worship. But God also told him that Pharaoh would refuse, so He would do many powerful miracles to compel Pharaoh to let them go. He also promised that the Israelites would have favor among the Egyptian people and would leave with many gifts from them.

Moses wondered if the people would believe him, so God told him to throw his staff on the ground. It immediately turned into a snake, and Moses ran from it. Then God told him to pick it up by the tail, and when Moses did, it turned back into a staff. Then God told Moses to put his hand inside his cloak and take it out again, and when he did, his hand had turned leprous. Then Moses put it back in his cloak and took it out again, and the leprosy was gone. God said to show the people those miraculous signs, and if they still didn't believe, to take some water from the Nile and pour it on the ground. It would turn to blood.

Then Moses protested by saying he wasn't a good speaker, but God promised to help him and give him words to say. Still, Moses pleaded with God to send someone else. Now God was angry with Moses and insisted he go, promising to send Moses' brother, Aaron, with him to be his spokesman. God told Moses that Aaron was already on the way, and He promised to give both Moses and Aaron the right words to say. So Moses went to tell his father-in-law he was returning to Egypt, and his father-in-law blessed him and wished him well.

DISCUSSION QUESTIONS

- Where were the Israelites when Moses encountered God at the burning bush? What was life like for them? How did they express themselves to God?
- What does God's response show us about His concern for His

people? Do you think He feels the same way when we are in distress? Why or why not?

- What had God promised Abraham and Jacob about the land His people would live in? How well did the Israelites' current situation fit that promise?

- Why do you think God chose Moses? What did He ask Moses to do?

- How did Moses feel about being sent back to Egypt? How would you have felt? What fears would you have had about making demands of Pharaoh? Which would have occupied your thoughts more: the harshness of Pharaoh's probable reaction or the ability of God to protect you from it? Why?

- Has God ever called you to a big task? How have you responded? In what situations do we feel tension between fear and faith today?

- What did God tell Moses about His name? What do you think He meant?

- What did God predict about Pharaoh's response? How did He expect Moses to overcome the obstacles to this task?

- What did God do and say to reassure Moses? How did He show Moses His power? In what ways did He promise support and provision?

- After seeing God's power, why do you think Moses still wanted God to send someone else?

- What does this story tell us about how God accomplishes His purposes? What does it tell us about the servants He chooses?

- What does this story tell us about the need for us to obey God? What does it tell us about the need to believe God?

QUESTIONS FOR FAMILIES/CHILDREN

- What had happened to God's people that caused Him to feel compassion for them? What did God want to do for them?

- How did God appear to Moses? How did Moses feel when he knew he was in God's presence?
- What did God tell Moses to do? Why was Moses afraid to do that?
- How did Moses expect the people to respond to him? What did God say would happen?
- How did God show Moses His power?
- In what ways did Moses think he needed help? Why did he think he wasn't the right person for the job? What did God promise to do for him?
- Do you think God promises to help us like He promised to help Moses? How does He help us?

MEMORY VERSE

God said to Moses, "I am who I am. This is what you are to say to the Israelites: 'I am has sent me to you.'"

Exodus 3:14

KEY APPLICATION

God calls each of us to serve Him in specific, life-giving ways.

10

PASSOVER
A Dramatic Deliverance

THEME

God teaches that blood sacrifice is necessary for salvation.

PASSAGE/REFERENCE

Exodus 12:1-36

BACKGROUND

Pharaoh responded to Moses just as God said he would, and it took a series of plagues to convince Pharaoh to let the people of Israel leave. Even after experiencing nine serious plagues and making several broken promises, Pharaoh still refused to release his slaves. So a tenth plague was necessary as God's decisive judgment against Egypt. It would result in death for every firstborn male in the land and finally convince Pharaoh to heed Moses' words.

PRE-STORY DIALOGUE

God often speaks to us in pictures in His Word. We've already seen how the story of Abraham and Isaac was a picture of God sacrificing His own Son on a hill in Jerusalem, for example. In this story, we'll see another picture—a dramatic example of God's deliverance. As you listen, think about the symbolism in the Passover meal. Also notice the sacrifices involved and the great cost of this deliverance.

TELL THE STORY

God told Moses and Aaron to tell each family to take a lamb for its own household—or, if it was a small family, to share with another household—and to slaughter it on the fourteenth day of the month. Each lamb was to be one year old and without any defects. The Israelites were to paint the blood of the lamb on their doorposts and then eat the meat along with bitter herbs and unleavened bread. They were to eat with their robes tucked into their belts, their sandals on, and their staffs in hand—in other words, ready to leave.

God said He would pass through the country, and every firstborn son and male animal of every household in Egypt would die that night. But the blood on the doorframes would be a sign. Wherever God saw the blood, He would pass over that household, and no one there would die.

Then God told Israel to commemorate that day for all generations to come—"a lasting ordinance." It would be the Passover festival. For seven days each year, they would celebrate the Feast of Unleavened Bread, during which they would eat nothing with any yeast in it.

So Moses went and told the elders of Israel all that God had said. He sent them out to select a Passover lamb for each family and described how they were to dip a branch of hyssop in the blood and spread it on the doorposts. He told them God would keep them from the plague if they did this. Then he explained how they were to keep this Passover ceremony from now on, and when their children asked what the ceremony meant, they were to say, "It is the Passover sacrifice to the LORD, who passed over the houses of the Israelites in Egypt and spared our homes when he struck down the Egyptians." So Israel worshipped God for this and then went and did what He had said.

At midnight, God went through all the households of Egypt and struck down every firstborn male, from Pharaoh's household to the prisoners' households—even the firstborn animals of those households. Every house in Egypt had someone who died, and there was weeping and wailing throughout the country.

This was the last straw for Pharaoh. He finally told Moses to go and take all of Israel with him. And he asked Moses to bless him. The rest of the Egyptians also asked Israel to hurry and leave because they were afraid of anyone else dying. They even gave Israel whatever they asked for, so God's people left with plenty of gifts and treasures, just as God had said.

DISCUSSION QUESTIONS

- What had God done before the tenth plague to convince Pharaoh to let Israel go? Why do you think Pharaoh had resisted for so long? Why do you think the last plague had to be so harsh?
- What did God tell the Israelites to do to protect themselves from the last plague? Why do you think He gave them such strange instructions?
- What did God say He would look for to determine which households were under the plague and which ones weren't? Why do you think He chose this sign?
- In what ways did the Israelites have to demonstrate faith in order to be saved from the plague?
- How long was Israel supposed to remember and celebrate this event? Why do you think it was important for them to remember it in future generations? Why is it important for us to remember the things God does for us?
- What kind of deliverance did Israel experience? Was it physical or spiritual—or both? What long-term condition were they delivered from? What aspect of the plague were they delivered from?

- What are some spiritual parallels represented by this deliverance? What do we need to be delivered from today? How does the Passover apply to us? What does God pass over in our lives when we put our faith in Jesus and His sacrificial blood?

QUESTIONS FOR FAMILIES/CHILDREN

- Why do you think Pharaoh was so stubborn about letting Israel go? How did God finally convince him?
- How did God tell the Israelites to protect themselves from the last plague?
- Do you think the Israelites were afraid when God showed His power? How would you have felt on that night when so many people died? What would you have done to get ready to leave?
- What did God want the Israelites to do to remember how He delivered them? Why was it important for them to remember His works? Why is it important for us to remember what He has done for us?
- In what ways is the Passover lamb like Jesus? How does Jesus rescue us from slavery and from death?

MEMORY VERSE

The blood will be a sign for you on the houses where you are; and when I see the blood, I will pass over you.

EXODUS 12:13

KEY APPLICATION

Only the blood of Jesus Christ provides for our salvation.

11

RED SEA

Escape Through the Waters

THEME

God delivers His people from bondage.

PASSAGE/REFERENCE

Exodus 14

BACKGROUND

It had been a traumatic deliverance in the middle of the night. All of Israel left their homes in Egypt suddenly and went into the desert as God led them—with a cloud and fire going before them. What were they feeling? Awe at God's power? Fear of the repercussions? Anxiety about the unknown path in front of them? A mixture of all of the above? Any of those feelings would be understandable, and every human being can relate to them—especially in times of transition between the old and the new.

PRE-STORY DIALOGUE

God overcame the enemy of His people, but that didn't mean the enemy quit trying to enslave them or harass them. As you listen to the story in this session, think about how it illustrates what happens in our lives when God delivers us—what it's like to leave an old life behind and enter into a new life. Notice also how God led His people and how He was watching out for them.

TELL THE STORY

The Lord told Israel to camp by the edge of the Red Sea. He knew Pharaoh would think the Israelites were confused and just wandering around the desert, and He knew Pharaoh would pursue them. But He wanted to gain more glory and show Himself to the Egyptians, so He led them to a place that looked like they were hemmed in.

Soon Pharaoh regretted letting the Israelites go and losing all those laborers, so he decided to pursue them. He gathered his army—chariots, horses, horsemen, and troops—and set out after them. And he came upon them where they were camping by the edge of the sea.

When the Israelites saw the Egyptians marching toward them, they were terrified and cried out to God. They complained to Moses because it looked like they had been led out into the desert to die. They even said it would have been better to remain in Egypt than to have come out to the desert to be killed.

Moses told them not to worry. He assured them that God would fight for them and that they would never see these Egyptians again. In fact, all they had to do was stand firm and watch the deliverance God would provide for them.

God then instructed Moses to stretch out his staff over the sea to divide the waters and tell the Israelites to move forward. He said the Israelites would go through on dry ground and the Egyptian army would follow them. Then the angel of God and the cloud that had been leading Israel went to stand between them and the Egyptians. All night long, the cloud kept them separate. Moses stretched out his hand over the waters, and God drove the waters back with a wind throughout the night. The waters were divided, and the Israelites went through on dry ground with a wall of water on each side of them.

The Egyptians followed the Israelites into the sea, but God confused their army and caused the wheels of their chariots to come off. The Egyptians wanted to flee because they could tell God was fighting for Israel. After the Israelites had crossed to the other side and the Egyptians were in the middle of the sea, God told Moses to stretch his hand over the sea again. So Moses did, and at daybreak the water went back into its place. The Egyptians were swallowed up by the sea, and the entire army was destroyed. When the Israelites saw God's great power, they feared God and trusted Him, and they also trusted Moses.

DISCUSSION QUESTIONS

- Where did God lead the Israelites to camp? How do you think they felt about being led to such a vulnerable place?
- Why did God want to put His people in a vulnerable position? What did He say Pharaoh would do? What did He say He would do in response to Pharaoh's actions?
- How did the Israelites feel when they saw the Egyptian army coming toward them? Did they feel confident in God's power? Did they feel betrayed? Who did they blame for their predicament?
- What did Moses tell them they would have to do to be rescued?
- What did God do to protect Israel from Pharaoh and his army? What impossibilities did He overcome?
- How did the Israelites react to their deliverance?
- What do you think this story illustrates about our transition between an old life without Christ and a new life in Him? What past enemies do you have? What do we need to do to be rescued from our past enemies?
- What does this story teach us about the ways God leads us?
- How does this story make you feel about God's ability to handle your problems?

QUESTIONS FOR FAMILIES/CHILDREN

- What happened to the Israelites after they left Egypt? Where did they end up camping?
- How did Pharaoh feel about letting Israel go? What did he do to try to get them back?
- How did the Israelites feel when they saw Egypt's army coming after them? How would you have felt if you were stuck by a sea and an army was coming to get you? What would you say to God?
- How did God answer the Israelites? What did He tell them to do? How did He show that He was protecting them?
- Do you think God will protect us in the same way when we're in trouble? Why or why not?
- What did the Israelites think about God when they saw His power and protection? Do you think He wants us to trust Him in the same way?

MEMORY VERSES

Do not be afraid. Stand firm and you will see the deliverance the LORD will bring you today. . . . The LORD will fight for you; you need only to be still.

EXODUS 14:13-14

KEY APPLICATION

We must look to God to deliver us from whatever bondage we are in.

12

TEN COMMANDMENTS
The Making of a Covenant

THEME

God gives His timeless laws.

PASSAGE/REFERENCE

Exodus 19:1–20:21

BACKGROUND

There was a lot of celebrating—dancing and singing—on the safe side of the Red Sea, but the Israelites soon encountered the hardships of the desert. They complained to Moses about bitter water and lack of food, even suggesting that it would have been better to remain in Egypt as slaves and eat decent food. But God, who was very angry about their complaining, miraculously provided water from a rock and manna (like bread) from heaven. They were also attacked by Amalekites, but God gave them a great victory. Life in the wilderness was tough, but God was preparing His people for a special covenant with Him.

PRE-STORY DIALOGUE

When God first sent Moses to Egypt, do you remember what He told Moses to tell Pharaoh as the reason for delivering His people? It was so they could worship Him. He wanted a separate people for Himself—a people with whom He could develop a special relationship of love and commitment. This is His priority for us. In today's session, we will hear about the covenant God made with Israel. A covenant is an agreement that binds two parties together in a relationship. See if you can identify the terms of this covenant as you listen to this story from God's Word.

TELL THE STORY

In the third month after the Israelites had left Egypt, they came to the Desert of Sinai and camped at the foot of the mountain—the same mountain where Moses had seen the burning bush. Moses went up on the mountain, and God gave him a word for Israel: "If you obey me fully and keep my covenant, then out of all nations you will be my treasured possession." So Moses told the elders and the people, and they said they would do whatever God instructed.

God told Moses that He would come to him in a dense cloud and speak in a way that the people would hear and that would cause them to trust Moses. He told Moses to tell the people to get ready: In three days He would come down to the mountain and speak. They were to wash their clothes and stay away from the mountain. So the people did as Moses said.

On the third day, there was thunder and lightning, and a thick cloud descended on the mountain. Then there was a loud blast of a ram's horn. Everyone in the camp trembled, and Moses led them to the foot of the mountain. The mountain was covered in smoke because the Lord came down on it like fire, and the whole mountain shook violently. The sound of the horn grew louder and louder, and then Moses spoke and God answered him. God told Moses to tell the people not to come up on the mountain or they would die. But He told Moses to bring Aaron with him.

[Note: The following paragraph is a summary. The storyteller may want to read 20:1-17 word for word so the listeners can hear the Ten Commandments as Scripture presents them.] Then God said, "I am the LORD your God, who brought you out of Egypt, out of the land of slavery." He told them to have no other gods, to not make any idols because He is a jealous God, to not misuse His name; to keep the Sabbath day holy (separate and sacred), to honor their fathers and mothers, to not murder, to not commit adultery, to not steal, to not give a false testimony against anyone, and to not covet.

When the people saw the thunder, lightning, and smoke and heard the trumpet, they shook with fear. They kept their distance and asked Moses to speak to God for them. They felt that if they heard God's voice directly, they would die. Moses told them that God had allowed them to hear His voice so their awe of Him would keep them from sinning. So the people remained at a distance while Moses approached the thick darkness where God was.

DISCUSSION QUESTIONS

- What did God promise the Israelites if they would keep His covenant? How would you respond if God offered you a covenant that would make you a treasured possession? How does Jesus make this offer a reality for all of us?
- Why did God want His voice to be heard by the Israelites instead of being heard only by Moses?
- What did the people have to do to prepare for an encounter with God? How did they react when they saw and heard the signs of His presence?
- Who does God want us to worship? How does He feel about our worshipping anything or anyone else?
- What do people allow to take the place of God in their hearts?

What tends to take His place in your heart?

- How are we supposed to use God's name? In what ways can we show respect to His name?
- Why does God want us to rest every seventh day? Do you do that? Why or why not?
- What does God say about how we treat our parents? What does it mean to honor your father and mother?
- What does God say about murder? In what ways can we "kill" others with our attitudes or words?
- Why does God tell us not to commit adultery? In what ways can we commit adultery in our minds and hearts?
- What does it mean to covet? How can we be content with what we have? Is it always wrong to want something more? Why or why not?
- Which of these laws address our relationship with God? Which address our relationships with other people?
- What do these laws show us about God's character? What do they show us about His desire for us?
- Do these laws help you live in a way that's consistent with God's character? Why or why not?

QUESTIONS FOR FAMILIES/CHILDREN

- What did God promise the Israelites if they would keep His covenant?
- What sights and sounds did the Israelites experience when God came down to the mountain?
- What was the first commandment God gave the Israelites? Why do you think this one was first?
- What are some ways we can express our worship to God?
- What other kinds of commandments does God want His people to follow?

- Why do you think God gives commandments to His people? How do those instructions help us?

MEMORY VERSES

I am the LORD your God, who brought you out of Egypt, out of the land of slavery. You shall have no other gods before me . . . for I, the LORD your God, am a jealous God.

EXODUS 20:2-3,5

KEY APPLICATION

We do not live on bread alone but on every word that comes from God.

13

TWELVE SPIES

Faith Versus Unbelief

THEME

God disciplines His faithless people by causing them to wander.

PASSAGE/REFERENCE

Numbers 13:1-3,25-33; 14:1-38

BACKGROUND

At Mount Sinai, God had given Israel not only the Ten Commandments but also many other laws related to feasts and offerings, ethics, health, diet, and priestly duties. He also gave them detailed instructions for a tabernacle—a tent of worship—that they would carry with them and set up wherever they camped. In this tabernacle, which also housed the ark of the covenant and other deeply symbolic items, God would meet with them. Then the Israelites journeyed farther into the wilderness on their way to the Promised Land.

PRE-STORY DIALOGUE

How strong would your faith be if you had seen God's supernatural acts in the plagues in Egypt, the parting of the Red Sea, the provision of manna and water in the desert, and the thunderous drama of God's voice at Mount Sinai? Most people think their faith would never fail after witnessing such miracles. But the Israelites found life difficult in the wilderness, continuing to complain about their hardships and even attempting mutiny against Moses. Then, in this session's story, God sent some of their leaders on a mission. As you listen, put yourself in their place and think about how you would have reacted to what you saw.

TELL THE STORY

God told Moses to send twelve men — one from each tribe of Israel — into Canaan to scout out the Promised Land, so Moses chose some of Israel's best leaders and sent them out. After forty days, they returned and reported back to the people, even bringing some of the bounty of the land. They said the land was indeed flowing with milk and honey and the fruit was large and plentiful. But they also described how powerful the people were and how fortified their cities were.

Caleb, one of the twelve spies, said, "We should go up and take possession of the land, for we can certainly do it." But others said, "We can't attack those people; they are stronger than we are. . . . We seemed like grasshoppers in our own eyes, and we looked the same to them." They gave a very negative report to the people.

Then the people wept and began grumbling against Moses, saying it would have been better to die in Egypt or even in the wilderness than to go into battle and be defeated. Some of them even wanted to choose a leader to take them back to Egypt. Moses and Aaron fell facedown in front of the assembly, and Joshua and Caleb, the only two spies to bring back a good report, argued that God would lead them into the Promised Land. "Do not rebel against the LORD," they said. "And do not be afraid of the people of the land, because we will swallow them up. Their protection is gone, but the LORD is with us.

Do not be afraid of them." Still, the people talked about stoning them for suggesting such a thing.

Then the glory of the Lord came to the tent of meeting, or tabernacle, and spoke to Moses: "How long will these people treat me with contempt?" He asked. "How long will they refuse to believe in me, in spite of all the miraculous signs I have performed among them?" And God offered to send a plague to destroy them and make a great nation out of Moses.

But Moses argued that the Egyptians already knew how God had chosen, delivered, and led Israel, and the people of Canaan already knew that too. How would it look to all of them if God wiped out the people He had promised to lead into the Promised Land? It would appear that God wasn't able to keep His promises. Moses reminded God what He had said about Himself: that He is "slow to anger, abounding in love and forgiving sin and rebellion." He pleaded with God to forgive the Israelites.

God forgave them, just as Moses asked, but He said that no one in that generation would get to the Promised Land. "No one who has treated me with contempt will ever see it," He declared. The exceptions would be Joshua and Caleb because they had shown great faith by believing that God would lead Israel into the land and conquer their enemies.

So God told Moses to say to the Israelites that things would be just as they expected. They would all die in the wilderness. For forty years they would wander because of their unfaithfulness, and the people would not enter the land until the current generation died out and their children were adults. Only Joshua and Caleb would live long enough to enter the land.

Then God sent a plague, and it took the lives of the ten spies who had brought back a bad report from Canaan. They died because they were responsible for causing the whole community to grumble, complain, and lose faith.

DISCUSSION QUESTIONS

- What did God want the twelve spies to do? Were they supposed to explore the land to gain helpful information or assess whether taking the land was possible?

- What was the land like? How did the spies describe the people? How did they describe the quality of the land?

- What did ten of the spies recommend? Which ones disagreed with the majority?

- Why did Joshua and Caleb believe the land could be taken? What were they basing their belief on?

- How did the assembly of Israelites respond to the conflicting reports? What did they think would happen if they went forward? What did they want to do to Joshua and Caleb? What did they propose as an alternative to the Promised Land?

- What did God think of their unbelief? Why do you think He was so angry with them? What did God suggest He should do with the Israelites?

- What does God think about complaining? What does complaining reveal about our hearts and our beliefs about God?

- How did Moses respond to God's desire to make a great nation from him? Why did he want God to forgive the Israelites?

- Did God forgive the Israelites? What consequences would they face for their lack of faith?

- What kinds of "wilderness" have you faced in your life? Have you ever grumbled or complained during those times? What attitude does God want you to have toward His promises?

- What does this story teach us about the importance of believing God?

QUESTIONS FOR FAMILIES/CHILDREN

- How many spies went into the Promised Land? How many came back with a good report?
- What did ten of the spies say about the land and its people? Why do you think they were so frightened by what they saw?
- Which spies pleased God: the ten with a negative report or the two who had a lot of faith? Why did God get angry with some of the spies?
- What did God think of the people's complaining? Why?
- What did God want to do to the people who disbelieved His promise? Why did He forgive them? What consequence would the people face for rejecting God's promise?
- What are some of the promises God gives us? What does God want us to do when He gives us a promise?

MEMORY VERSES

If the LORD is pleased with us, he will lead us into that land, a land flowing with milk and honey, and will give it to us. Only do not rebel against the LORD. And do not be afraid of the people of the land, because . . . the LORD is with us.

NUMBERS 14:8-9

KEY APPLICATION

God disciplines us when we choose to disbelieve Him.

14

JOSHUA
Into the Promise

THEME

God uses Joshua to conquer the Promised Land.

PASSAGE/REFERENCE

Joshua 1:1-9; 2:1-24; 6:1-27

BACKGROUND

Moses and an entire generation of Israelites died during the forty years in the wilderness, and Joshua became the leader. As the people neared the Promised Land, God began to prepare Joshua for the big task ahead of him. The time for the fulfillment of God's promise had come.

PRE-STORY DIALOGUE

How do you feel when, either literally or figuratively, you have to venture into unknown territory? God often leads us in ways we have never been before. And sometimes His calling to us is overwhelming. We need to be told to be strong and courageous, and we need frequent reminders that He is always with us. Joshua needed such encouragement. As you listen to this story, think of how you would approach a huge mission in unknown territory. What fears would you have? What strategies would you try to develop? In what ways would you need to put forth your own effort, and in what ways would you need to depend on God? These are the questions Joshua and the people of Israel faced.

TELL THE STORY

After Moses died, God told Joshua and the Israelites to get ready to cross the Jordan River and enter the Promised Land. "I will give you every place where you set your foot, as I promised Moses," He said to Joshua. God urged Joshua again and again to be strong and courageous. He told Joshua to remind the people to walk in His ways and to remember that He would always be with them.

Joshua sent two spies into the Promised Land to investigate, and especially to scout out Jericho, the first city the people would encounter. The two spies stayed at the home of a prostitute named Rahab. When the king of Jericho found out, he told Rahab to turn the spies over to him. But she told him the men had come and gone, and she didn't know who they were. She had actually hidden them on her rooftop, but she told the king to send men out of the city to pursue them.

Then she went up on the roof and told the spies that the people of Jericho had heard about the Red Sea and how God had taken care of the Israelites in the wilderness. She said she knew God was with them, and she wanted them to promise to keep her and her family safe when the people entered the land. The spies swore they would deal faithfully with her, but only if she hung a scarlet cord from her window so the Israelites would know which household to protect. Then Rahab let them down through her window—her house was part of the city wall—and told them to go hide in the hills for three days until the king's men had returned. So after three days of hiding, they went back across the river and told Joshua everything that had happened. "The LORD has surely given the whole land into our hands," they said. "All the people are melting in fear because of us."

Jericho was shut up tight because everyone knew the Israelites were coming. No one could come in, and no one could leave. And the Lord told Joshua that He had already secured victory over Jericho. He instructed Joshua to have the armed men march around the city once a day for six days and seven priests with ram's horns walk in front of the ark of the covenant. Then on the seventh day they were to march around the city seven times. God told Joshua to have the priests blow a long blast on their trumpets and then have all the people shout loudly; the walls of Jericho would fall down, and they would be able to go straight in.

So that's what they did. The seven priests went in front of the ark, blowing their trumpets the whole way. The armed guard marched ahead of the priests, and the rear guard followed the ark. Joshua told the people to be quiet until he gave word for them to shout. So for six days, they all marched around the city with the trumpets blowing, and each night they returned to camp. Then on the seventh day, they marched around the city seven times. Finally, when the priests sounded a long trumpet blast, Joshua commanded everyone to shout. He commanded everyone to devote all the spoils of victory to the Lord—to keep nothing for themselves—and to spare no one except Rahab and her household. So everyone shouted, the wall collapsed, and the men charged the city and took it over. They destroyed every living thing in the city, but they spared Rahab and her parents and siblings. They burned the city and put all the valuables into the Lord's treasury, and Joshua pronounced a curse so that no one would rebuild the city. God showed that He was with Joshua, and his fame spread throughout the land.

DISCUSSION QUESTIONS

- Why did Joshua send spies into the land? How were the spies treated in Jericho?
- Who was Rahab? How is she described? Why did she protect

the spies? What did she ask in exchange for her help?

- What does Rahab's involvement tell us about the kind of people God chooses to use? Does He invite only sinless people to be a part of His plan? What does Rahab's story tell us about His ways?
- What kind of report did the spies give Joshua? How did their report compare with the report of the spies forty years earlier?
- What strategy did God give Joshua for taking Jericho? Why do you think He chose such an unusual strategy? In what ways did this approach demonstrate His power?
- If you were among the Israelites, what would you have thought of God's strategy for taking Jericho? How much faith would you have needed to follow this plan?
- What did God want the Israelites to do after they entered Jericho? What were they allowed to keep? Who were they allowed to protect?
- Why do you think the first city Israel encountered was required to be devoted to the Lord?
- What "walls" stand between you and the promises God has given you? What does the story teach us about God's willingness and ability to overcome insurmountable difficulties?
- In what ways is the story of Joshua an example for you to follow? In what ways does it encourage you?

QUESTIONS FOR FAMILIES/CHILDREN

- Why do you think Joshua needed to be told to be strong and courageous? What fears might he have had before entering the Promised Land?
- Who helped the spies who were scouting out Jericho for the Israelites? What did the spies promise her in exchange for her help?
- What did the spies say about the city when they reported back

to Joshua? Did they think God was going to help them win their battles? Why or why not?

- What did God tell the Israelites to do in order to conquer Jericho? Why do you think He told them that? How did this plan show God's power?
- What happened to Jericho's walls when the people obeyed God?
- Do you think God has a good strategy for our problems? How does He help us fight our battles?

MEMORY VERSE

Be strong and courageous. Do not be terrified; do not be discouraged, for the LORD your God will be with you wherever you go.

JOSHUA 1:9

KEY APPLICATION

God wants to use us to boldly accomplish His purposes.

15

GIDEON

Oppression, Fear, and a "Mighty Warrior"

THEME

God uses Gideon in spite of his weak faith.

PASSAGE/REFERENCE

Judges 6–7

BACKGROUND

Joshua led the Israelites into the Promised Land, and the twelve tribes overcame most of their enemies. But the land wasn't completely taken by Israel; pockets of Canaanites remained. And they or nearby nations often rose up in power and dominated Israel. In fact, the book of Judges describes a repeated cycle in which Israel disobeyed God (usually through idolatry), was subdued by an enemy, cried out for deliverance, was freed by a God-appointed deliverer, lived in peace, and then disobeyed and began the cycle all over again. For three hundred years this cycle continued; Israel lived in frequent rebellion and needed frequent deliverers (or judges) to free them and turn them back to God.

PRE-STORY DIALOGUE

God told Joshua to be strong and courageous. Today we will hear about a leader of Israel who wasn't very strong or courageous, at least when the story begins. But would his fears and insecurities limit God? Do ours? Listen to how God called and strengthened Gideon and used him to do great things in spite of his weaknesses. And think about how God might use you to do great things too.

TELL THE STORY

The Israelites did bad things in God's eyes, so He let the Midianites rule over them. The Midianites and other eastern peoples were so oppressive that the Israelites had to hide in mountains and caves. Whenever Israel planted crops, the oppressors would ruin them and ravage the land. So Israel cried out to God for help.

God sent a prophet to remind the Israelites how He had saved them from Egypt and to explain why they were being oppressed. Then an angel of God came to Gideon as he was secretly threshing wheat in a winepress to keep it from the Midianites. The angel said, "The LORD is with you, mighty warrior." Gideon asked why the people had been abandoned by God—why the miracles of old didn't happen anymore. The angel told him to use what strength he had to deliver Israel. Gideon asked how he could do that: After all, he was from the weakest clan and was the weakest in his family. "I will be with you," the angel said, "and you will strike down all the Midianites together."

Gideon wanted to know if this was really God speaking to him, so he asked if he could go get an offering and bring it back. Told yes, Gideon brought an offering of meat and bread. The Lord touched it with His staff, and fire flared up. Gideon realized it was the Lord, so he built an altar and named the place "The LORD is Peace."

That same night, God told Gideon to tear down his father's altar to Baal and build a true altar to the Lord in its place; he was to sacrifice a bull on it. Gideon took ten servants and did as the Lord said, but he did it at night because he was afraid of his father and the men of the town. When the men woke up the next morning and discovered what had happened, they found out Gideon was responsible. They went to Gideon's father and demanded that Gideon be put to death. But his father refused and told them that if Baal was a real god, he could contend for himself. So the people started calling Gideon "Jerub-Baal," which means "Let Baal contend."

Soon afterward, the Midianites crossed the Jordan to raid Israel. God's Spirit came upon Gideon, and Gideon blew a trumpet as a call to arms. Gideon still wanted to know if God was really going to save Israel through him, so he asked for a sign. He put fleece on the ground and told God that if dew was on the fleece and not on the ground around it, he would know God was with him. When Gideon got up the next morning, that's what he found: The ground was dry but the fleece was wet enough for him to squeeze a bowlful of water out of it. Then to make sure, he asked for the opposite sign: dry fleece and wet ground. The next morning, that's exactly what had happened.

So Gideon went out with his men to attack Midian. As they camped near the Midianites, God told Gideon he had too many people with him; the Israelites might think they won with their own strength if they defeated Midian with so many people. So God told Gideon to tell everyone who was afraid to leave; when Gideon did so, 22,000 men left and 10,000 remained. But the Lord said that was still too many, so He told Gideon to take all of the men down to the water and separate those who got down on their knees to drink from those who lifted it to their mouths with their hands and lapped it up with their tongues. Only 300 lifted the water with their hands, so God told Gideon to keep those and send the rest home. Gideon took up his position with only 300 men.

That night, God told Gideon to go down to the Midianite camp—and if he was afraid, to take his armor bearer with him. God promised Gideon that he would be encouraged by what he heard. So

Gideon went down to the camp of the Midianites and their many allies at night. Gideon and his armor bearer arrived just in time to hear one Midianite telling another about his dream. In the dream, a loaf of barley rolled down into the valley and overturned a Midianite tent. They realized this was a sign that the Midianites had been given into Israel's hands. Gideon was encouraged and thanked God. He went back to his camp and told his 300 men to get up because God was going to give them the victory.

Gideon divided his men into three groups and gave each man a trumpet and an empty jar with a torch inside. The three groups gathered around the edges of the Midianite camp, and when Gideon gave the signal, they all blew their trumpets, smashed their jars, held their torches up, and shouted, "A sword for the LORD and for Gideon!"

The Midianites thought they were surrounded, many began to run, and some started fighting against each other with their swords. As their army fled, many other men from Israel pursued them and cut them off from escaping. They captured and killed the two Midianite leaders and won a great victory over their oppressors.

DISCUSSION QUESTIONS

- Why did the Israelites cry out to God for help? According to God, why were they in the situation they were in?
- Do you think God rescues us when we're responsible for our own messes? Why or why not?
- Where was Gideon when God spoke to him? Why was he there?
- How did God address Gideon? Did that seem like an accurate description? Why or why not? Why do you think God called him that?
- What questions did Gideon ask God? Did God give him an answer? What did God tell Gideon to do?

- What did Gideon think about his ability to fulfill the mission God gave him?
- What did Gideon do to make sure he had been talking to God? How did God respond?
- What was Gideon's first big assignment? How did he feel about doing it? What was the result of his actions?
- Why did Gideon ask for a sign when it was time to go fight against Midian? How certain was Gideon about God's promise? How did God reassure Gideon?
- Why did God tell Gideon he had too many men to fight against Midian? What did He tell Gideon to do to fix the problem? Why was it important for God to be seen as Israel's strength?
- How did God encourage Gideon before the battle? Why do you think He needed to?
- What strategy did Gideon use to defeat the Midianites? Why did it work? How decisive was the victory?
- How do you think God feels about our insecurities and fears? In what ways does He encourage us today?
- Do you think God gives us assignments that are beyond our ability to carry out in our own strength? Has He given you one? How do you respond when He does that?
- In what ways does God help us overcome our fears, fight our battles, and accomplish His purposes?

QUESTIONS FOR FAMILIES/CHILDREN

- Why were the Israelites in trouble? What did God do when they prayed for His help?
- Where was Gideon when God spoke to him? Why was he hiding?
- Why do you think God called Gideon "a mighty warrior" even though he had never fought any battles and didn't seem very

brave? What did Gideon think about himself?

- What big mission did God give Gideon? Did Gideon think he could do it? Why or why not?
- What was Gideon's first assignment? Why was it important for Gideon to build an altar to the true God in place of the altar to a false god? How did the men of the town feel about Gideon's actions?
- What sign did Gideon ask for to make sure God had sent him to fight the Midianites? How did God answer?
- What did God tell Gideon about how many men he had? What did Gideon do about it? How many warriors went to battle with Gideon?
- How did God encourage Gideon before the battle? How does God encourage us when we're afraid?
- What was Gideon's strategy when he went to battle? What happened when the Midianites saw what the Israelites did?
- What does this story show us about the ways God helps us?

MEMORY VERSES

The LORD is with you, mighty warrior. . . . Go in the strength you have and save Israel out of Midian's hand. Am I not sending you?

JUDGES 6:12,14

KEY APPLICATION

If we make ourselves available to God, He will use us in spite of weakness in our faith.

16

RUTH
Restored and Redeemed

THEME

God blesses faithful Ruth with love and privilege.

PASSAGE/REFERENCE

Ruth
Focus: Ruth 1:1–2:12; 3:1-13; 4:1-6,13-17

BACKGROUND

With a few notable exceptions, the period of the judges was not a time known for great faithfulness in Israel. The spiritual climate of the time is summed up in Judges 17:6 and 21:25: "Everyone did what was right in his own eyes" (NKJV). But the story of Ruth gives us a snapshot of some people who did what was right in God's eyes—and, in the process, painted a memorable picture of redemption.

It's important to know a couple of cultural insights as the story begins. First, it was extremely important for each family's land and possessions—their piece of the Promised Land—to remain in the family, and for each family to have descendants to inherit the land. When married men died without children, it was the responsibility of a relative to father children through his widow. Naomi had no descendants, and her prospects seemed almost nonexistent. It's also important to know that Naomi's family was in Moab because her husband had left the Promised Land during a famine. This would have been seen as unfaithfulness in the eyes of many people — and the death of Naomi's husband and sons may have been seen as God's judgment on them. But judgment was not the end of this story. In fact, the hardships of the first chapter were only the beginning because God can always bring beauty out of ashes and turn trials into blessings.

PRE-STORY DIALOGUE

Have you ever felt abandoned by God? Naomi did, and she was very bitter about it. Life is filled with trials, and sometimes those trials cause us to despair. But the Bible never tells us to give up or lose hope. In fact, it teaches us just the opposite: that God can bring good out of the worst situations. As you listen to this story, think about the difficult circumstances you've experienced. Where is God in our time of need? What promises does God give us about our future? Consider how these questions apply to Naomi and Ruth — and to you.

TELL THE STORY

During a famine in the time of the judges, a man from Bethlehem took his family to live in Moab. The man died, and his widow, Naomi, was left with the two sons, who married Moabite women. Then both of the sons died. Naomi was alone in Moab with her two daughters-in-law, Orpah and Ruth.

When Naomi heard that the famine had ended, she and her daughters-in-law set out to return home to Judah. But on the way back, she urged each of them to go back to her mother's home to find a husband among her own people. They both wanted to go with Naomi, but she finally convinced Orpah to return to Moab. Ruth, however, insisted on staying with Naomi. "Where you go I will go, and where you stay I will stay," she said. "Your people will be my people and your God my God."

When they arrived in Bethlehem, people seemed pleasantly surprised to see Naomi. But Naomi, whose name means "pleasant," told them not to call her that anymore. Instead, they should call her Mara, which means "bitter," because God had made her life very bitter. She felt that He had treated her harshly.

Naomi and Ruth arrived in Bethlehem just as the barley harvest was beginning. One day Ruth went out into the fields to gather any leftover grain dropped by the harvesters. As it turns out, she ended up in a field owned by Boaz, a relative of Naomi's late husband. When Boaz saw her, he asked the foreman of his harvesters who she was, and the foreman told him that she was the Moabite who had come back with Naomi and that she had been working very hard. So Boaz went and told Ruth that she could continue to work in his fields, that she would be safe there, and that she could drink all she needed from his water. When she asked why he showed her so much favor, he said he had heard how loyal she had been to Naomi. Boaz blessed her and hoped the Lord would richly reward her.

After some time, Naomi came up with a plan for getting a husband for Ruth. Because Boaz was a kinsman and had treated Ruth well, Naomi suggested that Ruth wash, put on her best clothes and some perfume, and go down to the threshing floor, where Boaz would be working. Naomi told her to wait until Boaz had finished eating and drinking, and then to go over to where he was lying, uncover his feet, and lie down. Ruth agreed to do exactly that. She approached Boaz quietly during the night, uncovered his feet, and lay down. In the middle of the night, Boaz was startled to discover a woman lying there and asked who she was. She answered and asked him to spread his garment over her—a suggestion that he be the kinsman-redeemer who would marry her. He blessed her, commended her for not going after a younger man, and said he would redeem and marry her. But there was one closer relative who would have the right to redeem her first, if he wanted to. Boaz had to give him a chance. But if the man didn't, Boaz would gladly redeem her.

So Boaz went to the town gate and waited for the man to come. When they finally met, Boaz explained the situation to him in front of the town's elders and offered him the land once owned by Naomi's husband. The kinsman said he would redeem it, but then Boaz mentioned that the Moabite widow would be part of the deal. When he heard that, the man turned it down and said Boaz could redeem the land and the widow.

Boaz and Ruth got married, and eventually they had a son. The women of the town praised God for how He had blessed Naomi by renewing her life in her old age. They said Ruth had been better to her than seven sons. And the son of Boaz and Ruth was named Obed, who would one day be the grandfather of King David.

DISCUSSION QUESTIONS

- Why was Naomi bitter? What was her family situation?
- Why did Naomi decide to return to Bethlehem? Who went with her?
- Why did it make more sense for Ruth and Orpah to return to Moab? Why did Ruth choose to stay with Naomi?
- Whose field did Ruth end up in? How did Boaz treat Ruth? How did Ruth respond to him?
- Why was it important to Naomi for Ruth to find a husband? What plan did Naomi come up with?
- In what ways did Ruth demonstrate faith by following Naomi's plan? What risks did she take? What might have happened if Boaz did not respond favorably? What may have been the consequences if her suggestive act was misunderstood?
- How did Boaz respond to Ruth when she went to him on the threshing floor? Why did he commend her? What did he say he would do?

- Why do you think Boaz didn't mention Ruth to the other kinsman when he first explained the situation? What happened when Boaz did mention Ruth?
- In what ways did Ruth's marriage benefit Naomi? How did Naomi see her life after Boaz and Ruth had a child? What famous descendent came from Boaz and Ruth's marriage?
- What does this story teach us about God's compassion for widows and others in need?
- Has any situation in life made you feel bitter or hopeless? What does this story teach us about God's ability to redeem tragic situations? How might He redeem your tragedies?

QUESTIONS FOR FAMILIES/CHILDREN

- Why was Naomi so sad? What had happened to make her feel hopeless?
- How did Ruth show that she loved Naomi?
- How did God take care of Ruth and Naomi? What did Boaz do to help them? What kind of worker was Ruth? How did Boaz treat her?
- Why did Naomi want Boaz and Ruth to get married?
- What did Ruth do to let Boaz know she wanted him to marry her? What did Boaz think about the idea?
- Did Naomi still feel sad at the end of the story? Why or why not?
- What did God do in this story to make a bad situation good?
- What does this story teach us about how God takes care of His people? What does it teach us about the ways we can show His love and take care of each other?
- In what ways is the story of Ruth and Boaz a picture of what Jesus does for us?

MEMORY VERSE

Where you go I will go, and where you stay I will stay. Your people will be my people and your God my God.

RUTH 1:16

KEY APPLICATION

God will bless our faithfulness with love and opportunity.

17

SAUL

A King's Compromise

THEME

God rejects King Saul because of his disobedient heart.

PASSAGE/REFERENCE

1 Samuel 15

BACKGROUND

The Israelites cried out for a king, so God gave them one—a man named Saul. By the time of this session's story, Saul had already led Israel successfully into battle. But he had also demonstrated a tendency to be impatient and make rash decisions. His lack of attention to God's instructions would have dire consequences when he fought the Amalekites, descendants of one of Israel's first enemies when they left Egypt. Centuries earlier, the Amalekites had attacked Israel in the wilderness after they had crossed the Red Sea, and only an exhausting battle led by Joshua defeated them. Afterward, Moses prophesied that the Lord would be at war against the Amalekites for generation after generation.

PRE-STORY DIALOGUE

How important is it to obey God? A lot of people approach His instructions as good advice, not vital information. But God doesn't give us suggestions; He gives us commands. And those who don't follow them inevitably regret their decisions. As you listen to today's story, ask yourself what you would have done in Saul's situation. What should we do when plans haven't unfolded on time? Should we wait for God or move forward in faith? When is moving forward *faith*, and when is it *presumption*? How can we know the difference?

TELL THE STORY

Samuel, God's prophet for the nation during Saul's reign, gave the king a message from God. He told Saul that God wanted to punish the Amalekites for attacking Israel long ago in the wilderness. He commanded Saul to attack the Amalekites and destroy them completely — their men, women, children, and livestock. So Saul gathered more than 200,000 soldiers and went to the city of Amalek to ambush it. He told the Kenites to leave so they wouldn't be destroyed in the battle, and he attacked.

Saul and his soldiers killed the Amalekites, but they took Agag the king alive. They also spared the best of the sheep and cattle. They didn't destroy Amalek completely—just the things that were less valuable.

Then God spoke to Samuel and told him He regretted making Saul king. "He has turned away from me and has not carried out my instructions," God said. This troubled Samuel deeply, and he cried out to God all night. He went to meet Saul the next morning, only to find that Saul had set up a monument in his own honor and left the area.

When Samuel finally caught up with him, Saul said, "The LORD bless you! I have carried out the LORD's instructions." So Samuel asked why he heard the sounds of cattle and sheep. Saul answered that the soldiers had brought the best of the Amalekites' animals to sacrifice to God. "But we totally destroyed the rest," Saul said.

Samuel interrupted him and told Saul what God had said: that Saul had not completely obeyed. Saul protested. "I went on the mission the LORD assigned me," he said. He assured the prophet that he had completely destroyed the Amalekites (except for King Agag, whom he had captured and brought with him). Again, Saul told Samuel that the soldiers had taken the best of what was devoted to God in order to sacrifice it.

Samuel answered with very stern words: "To obey is better than sacrifice. . . . Because you have rejected the word of the LORD, he has rejected you as king."

Then Saul confessed that he had sinned. He had been afraid of the people and gave in to them. He asked Samuel to forgive his sin and to return with him so he could worship God, but Samuel refused. When Samuel turned to leave, Saul grabbed the corner of his robe and tore it. Samuel said that was how God had torn the kingdom from him. God was going to give the kingdom to someone else, and He wasn't going to change His mind.

Again, Saul pleaded for Samuel to come with him and honor him before the elders of Israel. He confessed his sin but asked Samuel to come so he could worship God. So Samuel went and Saul worshipped.

Samuel then called for Agag to be brought to him. Agag was confident; he thought if he was going to be killed, it would have happened already. But Samuel rebuked Agag for all the people he had killed and put him to death on the spot. Then Samuel left, and Saul returned to his home. Samuel never went to see Saul again, though he grieved for him. And God was sorry He had ever made Saul king over Israel.

DISCUSSION QUESTIONS

- What message did God tell Samuel to give Saul? Why did God want to do this? How did Saul first respond to his assignment?
- Did Saul follow God's instructions? What did he do well? What did he not do well?
- How did God feel about Saul's response? How did Samuel feel about what God said about Saul?
- What did Saul say when Samuel confronted him? Why did he think he had done what God had required? What reasons did he give for not completely obeying?
- What did Samuel say about sacrifices? How much does God value our obedience?
- What consequences did Saul's disobedience have?
- How did Samuel finish Saul's unfinished task?
- In what ways do you think we compromise God's instructions today?
- Has God wanted you to do something that you were tempted to do only halfheartedly? How did you respond? In what areas of life do you think you've only partially obeyed? What do you think God would have you do about that now?
- What opportunities do we miss when we disobey God? In what ways does God bless those who fully obey?

QUESTIONS FOR FAMILIES/CHILDREN

- What did God tell Saul to do?
- Did Saul obey halfway or all the way? What did God say about Saul's obedience? What did Saul say about it?
- Have you ever obeyed halfway and then given excuses about why you didn't completely obey? How do you think God felt about that?
- What did God decide to do in response to Saul's disobedience?

Why do you think it was important to God to have a king who would obey Him?

- What does this story teach us about listening carefully to what God tells us? What does it teach us about being careless with God's instructions?
- How do you think God will treat us if we have obedient hearts?

MEMORY VERSE

Does the LORD delight in burnt offerings and sacrifices as much as in obeying the voice of the LORD? To obey is better than sacrifice, and to heed is better than the fat of rams.

1 SAMUEL 15:22

KEY APPLICATION

God will set us aside from service if we live disobediently.

18

DAVID

Wholehearted Love and Faith

THEME

God seeks those who love Him.

PASSAGE/REFERENCE

2 Samuel 6:12–7:29

BACKGROUND

God had twice expressed regret about making Saul king and made it clear that another king was coming—a "man after his own heart" (1 Samuel 13:14). During the course of his life, David would demonstrate great faith and defeat a giant, flee for his life for years, gather a group of mighty men around him, show respect for God's people and purposes, unite Israel's tribes under his reign, worship wildly, write many psalms and prayers, and conquer many enemies. He would also demonstrate his human nature in some serious sins and character flaws. But his heart always turned back toward God. He became an example of what it means to love God wholeheartedly and how that love affects every area of life. As this story begins, the ark of God—the sign of His presence—is far from Jerusalem, but David wanted it in the city for people to honor God there. He had tried to bring it before, but someone died by casually touching this holy ark and the move was abandoned. Now, after some time, David was ready to try again.

PRE-STORY DIALOGUE

Do you know your ultimate purpose in life—the reason you were created? Not many people do. Some think it's to accomplish a certain goal or mission. Others believe it's to develop godly character or be a good example. And while all of those are important, even in God's eyes, there's a higher purpose: to love Him. We know this because Jesus said the commandment to love God with all our heart, soul, and strength was the greatest commandment ever given. That means it's God's highest priority for us. As you listen to this story, notice how David embodied this purpose. Then ask yourself if this is what you seek as your highest priority. In what ways do you love God? How do you show Him? How can you cultivate a deeper passion for Him?

TELL THE STORY

David heard that the household of Obed-Edom, where the ark was being stored, had been blessed by God's presence. So David decided to bring the ark to Jerusalem. He and many priests and helpers went down to get it, and they made sacrifices along the way in devotion to God and in respect for this holy sign of His presence they were carrying. David was wearing an ephod, a priest's garment, and he danced wildly in celebration. He and many Israelites brought the ark into Jerusalem with loud shouts and trumpets blaring.

As the ark entered Jerusalem, David's wife, Michal (a daughter of Saul), watched it all from a window. She saw David leaping and dancing and despised him for it. David and his men brought the ark to a special tent that had been pitched for it, and they made lots of ceremonial sacrifices and offerings to bless the ark and the people and to honor God. Everybody there got a loaf of bread and cakes of dates and raisins.

When David arrived home, Michal was angry. She rebuked him sarcastically for taking off his robes in front of all the servant girls as a commoner would. But David reminded her that God had chosen him—in place of her father, Saul—to rule Israel. He insisted that he would celebrate like that in front of God. In fact, he would become even more undignified in his worship and humiliate himself even more if he needed to. And Michal never bore a child after this.

Later, David told Nathan the prophet that it didn't seem right to live in a palace while the ark of God was in a tent. Nathan told him to do whatever he wanted to do about it; God was with David. But that night, God gave Nathan a different message for David: "Are you the one to build me a house?" God reminded Nathan that He had never lived in a house before; He had always moved from place to place with Israel in the past, and He had never ordered otherwise. God told Nathan to tell David that He would make his name great and give him rest from all his enemies. The Lord would establish a house for David, and one of his sons would become king and build a temple for God. David's house and kingdom and throne would be everlasting. So Nathan went to David and gave him this message.

David went into God's presence and prayed, "Who am I, O Sovereign LORD, and what is my family, that you have brought me this far?" David worshipped and gave thanks for God's goodness to him—and for making His plans known to him. He praised God for making Israel a nation, for redeeming people to Himself, and for doing great and awesome works to deliver and establish His people. Then he asked God to keep His promise forever so that God's name would be great forever. He knew God's words were trustworthy and that God promises good things. He was zealous for God's reputation to be established through his own life, his household, and his kingdom.

DISCUSSION QUESTIONS

- What did the ark represent to David and to Israel? What was special about it? Why did David want it in Jerusalem?
- What attitude did David have when he brought the ark into Jerusalem? Why was there such a big celebration? What did David do to celebrate?
- What did David's wife rebuke him for doing? How did David respond to this? What happened to Michal after she criticized David's worship?
- What did God think about David's dancing? What kind of worship do you think He wants from us?
- What bothered David about living in a palace? Where was God's ark during this time? Why did this seem like a problem?
- What did Nathan tell David to do? What message did God give Nathan to tell David?
- Did God ever instruct anyone to build a temple for Him? Whose idea was it? Why do you think David was so zealous about having a temple in Jerusalem? What would the temple represent?
- Did God grant David's request? Who would build the temple? What did God promise to do for David's house—his descendants and his throne?
- How did David respond to God's words through Nathan? What did he thank God for? What did he praise God for doing? What did he ask God to do? Whose reputation was David concerned for?
- How certain was David that God's words were trustworthy? What evidence of faith can you see in David's prayer?
- David was called "a man after [God's] own heart" earlier in 1 Samuel and also later in Acts. How does this story demonstrate David's love for God? How well do you think David fulfilled the greatest commandment?

- What qualifies someone to be called a person after God's heart? In what ways can we seek His heart?
- Why do you think the commandment to love God with all our heart, soul, and strength is God's highest priority for us? Do you think we can be fulfilled without doing this? Why or why not?

QUESTIONS FOR FAMILIES/CHILDREN

- What did David want to bring to Jerusalem? Why? Whose presence was in the ark?
- How did David feel about bringing the ark into the city? How did he show his feelings?
- Was it good for David to worship God this way? Who disagreed? What did David say about that? What kind of worship do you think God wants from us?
- What did David want to do for God? Why?
- Did God command David to build a temple? Whose idea was it?
- What did God promise to do for David's household and his descendants?
- How did David pray after he heard God's plans for him? Was he glad and thankful or sad and disappointed?
- What did David thank and praise God for? What did he ask God to do next?
- How important is it to love God? How did David show that he loved God in this story? How can we show that we love God?

MEMORY VERSES

How great you are, O Sovereign Lord! There is no one like you, and there is no God but you, as we have heard with our own ears.

2 Samuel 7:22

And now, LORD God, keep forever the promise you have made concerning your servant and his house. Do as you promised, so that your name will be great forever.

2 SAMUEL 7:25-26

KEY APPLICATION

Our ultimate purpose is to love God with a whole heart.

19

SOLOMON

A Dwelling Place for God

THEME

King Solomon builds a temple for God.

PASSAGE/REFERENCE

2 Chronicles 3–7
Focus: 2 Chronicles 3:1-2; 5:1–7:22

BACKGROUND

Solomon, one of David's sons, succeeded him as king, and he started out well. He asked for great wisdom, and God blessed him with that and much more. Solomon would become famous for his wise judgments, write many proverbs, and rule over an expanded and prosperous land. He would also violate several of God's commands and end up disobedient and depressed. He did not have the whole heart his father had. But at the peak of Solomon's power, God used him to fulfill a promise once given to his father, David. Solomon built the temple that David longed to see.

PRE-STORY DIALOGUE

Where does God dwell? The Bible tells us He is everywhere, but it also tells us that His presence filled the tabernacle Israel built in the wilderness. The story in today's session will tell us that He came to dwell in a temple built by Solomon. And the New Testament will tell us He came to dwell in those who believe in Jesus. Where do you envision God when you pray to Him? Where is He when you need encouragement? What would it be like to sense His presence in tangible ways? Listen to how He showed Himself in the house that Solomon built for Him.

TELL THE STORY

Solomon began to build the temple on Mount Moriah in Jerusalem, right where God had appeared to his father, David. He started building in the fourth year of his reign.

When he had finished building, he brought all the valuable worship items that his father had dedicated for the temple and put them in the treasuries. Then Solomon called all of Israel's elders to Jerusalem to bring the ark of the covenant into the temple. When they arrived, the Levites (priests) brought up the ark and furnishings from the tabernacle, with many sacrifices being made along the way. They took the ark into the inner sanctuary of the temple, the Most Holy Place, and placed it under wings of the sculptured cherubim (angels). The two tablets from Mount Sinai with God's commandments written on them were in the ark.

Then the priests withdrew from the Holy Place. Those who were musicians stood on the east side of the altar playing cymbals and stringed instruments. They were joined by 120 priests playing trumpets and singers giving praise and thanks to God. "He is good; his love endures forever," they sang.

The temple was filled with a cloud of God's glory, so much so that the priests couldn't continue performing their functions. Solomon said,

"I have built a magnificent temple for you, a place for you to dwell forever." Then he turned around and blessed the people. He praised God for fulfilling what He had promised to David: a temple in Jerusalem and a lasting dynasty. He recalled how David had it in his heart to build the temple and how God told him one of his sons would do it. "The LORD has kept the promise he made," Solomon said. "I have succeeded David my father and now I sit on the throne of Israel, just as the LORD promised, and I have built the temple for the Name of the LORD, the God of Israel."

Solomon stood before the altar in front of the whole assembly and spread out his hands. Then he knelt down on the platform and lifted his hands to heaven and prayed. He praised God for keeping His covenant of love and fulfilling His promise to David. He asked God to keep His promise for David's dynasty to always have a man on the throne. He acknowledged that even the highest heavens couldn't contain God, much less the new temple. But he asked that God's eyes would be on the temple, that He would put His Name there, and that He would hear the prayers of His people there.

Solomon asked God to forgive His people when they sinned, to restore them after they had been defeated by an enemy, and always to bring them back to the land He had given them. He prayed that when God judged them with a drought or famine or plague, He would hear their prayers of repentance and forgive them—and that He would teach them the right way to live. He asked God to deal with each person's heart and to help each one walk in His ways. He even prayed for foreigners who would come from a great distance—that God would hear their prayers and that all the peoples of the earth would learn about Him and worship Him. Solomon prayed for God's help in battles against enemies, for restoration when they would one day be held captive in a foreign land, and for forgiveness when they confessed their sins. Then he asked God to come to His resting place, clothe the priests with salvation, and let His people rejoice in His goodness.

When Solomon finished praying, fire came down from heaven and burned the sacrifices, and God's glory filled the temple. Now the priests couldn't even enter the temple because of God's glory. When everyone saw the fire and the glory, they knelt down and put their faces to the ground. They worshipped God and thanked Him. Then the king and the people offered many more sacrifices—thousands of them—and dedicated the temple to God. The priests took their positions, including the musicians and trumpet blowers. All of Israel was standing.

Solomon consecrated the courtyard and offered burnt offerings there. And the festival continued for about three weeks before Solomon sent people back to their homes. They left feeling joyful for all that the Lord had done for David, Solomon, and Israel.

Later, God appeared to him at night and said He had heard Solomon's prayers and chosen the temple as a place for sacrifices. He assured Solomon that He would hear the prayers of His people and forgive them when they confessed their sins and repented. "My eyes and my heart will always be there," He said.

Then God told Solomon that if he walked in God's ways and observed His laws, God would establish his throne just as He had with David. But He also warned that if Solomon turned away, forsook God's laws, and went after other gods, then Israel would be uprooted from the land, the temple would be rejected, and other nations would know that Israel had been forsaken because they had forsaken the God who brought them out of Egypt.

DISCUSSION QUESTIONS

- Where did Solomon build the temple? Can you remember another story in which Mount Moriah was mentioned? What happened there?
- What did Solomon do when the construction of the temple was finished? What did the priests bring into the Most Holy Place of the temple?

- What did the musicians sing about at the temple dedication? What did God do when they finished singing? Do you think there's a connection between their praises and God's response? If so, what?
- What did Solomon say in his prayer about his father? In what ways did God show His faithfulness to David? What did Solomon say about God keeping His promises?
- According to Solomon, what was the purpose of the temple? Did he think God could be contained in a temple? Why or why not? In what ways and for what purposes did he expect God to dwell in the temple?
- What kinds of requests did Solomon pray for the people of Israel? What did he ask God to do for them?
- What did Solomon say about foreigners in his prayer? In what ways does his prayer reflect the original mission God gave to Adam and Eve?
- How did God respond to Solomon's prayer? How did He show Himself? What did the people do when they saw and felt God's presence?
- How long did the people celebrate at the dedication of the temple? How did they feel when it was over?
- What did God say to Solomon later? How did God encourage him? What warnings did He give?
- In light of the fact that Solomon would later disobey God and even worship at pagan altars, why do you think God allowed him to be the one to build the temple? What does this say about God's willingness to use imperfect people?
- What does this story teach us about God's desire to be with His people? What can we do to sense His presence more in our lives? How do you think He would respond if you asked for a greater sense of His presence?

QUESTIONS FOR FAMILIES/CHILDREN

- What did Solomon build for God? What was the purpose of this building?
- What did Solomon do when the building was finished? What did the priests bring into it? What did the musicians sing?
- What did God do when He saw the sacrifices and heard the praises and prayers of His people? In what ways did He show Himself?
- How big is God? Where is He? Do you think He can live only in a temple? Did Solomon know that God is everywhere? In what ways did Solomon want God to specifically show His presence in the temple?
- What did Solomon pray for the people of Israel? What did he pray for the people of other countries?
- What did God do after Solomon's prayers? Do you think He enjoys being with His people? Why or why not?
- Do you want to spend time with God and have Him spend time with you? How do you think He would respond if you asked Him to?

MEMORY VERSE

If my people, who are called by my name, will humble themselves and pray and seek my face and turn from their wicked ways, then will I hear from heaven and will forgive their sin and will heal their land.

2 CHRONICLES 7:14

KEY APPLICATION

God wants to be with His people and will show Himself to those who seek Him.

20

JOB

Pain, Prayers, and Patience

THEME

God allows Satan to afflict Job but rewards Job in the end.

PASSAGE/REFERENCE

Job 1–2; 38:1-41; 40:1-5; 42:1-17

BACKGROUND

No one really knows when the book of Job was written or where Job fits in the history of God's people. The book itself doesn't tell us. Some say it's the earliest book of the Bible, while others argue that it refers to names and places that developed much later in history. Perhaps it's best that we don't know when and where Job lived because the themes are timeless. All we need to know is that Job was a human being who lived in a fallen world, just as we do. And his story applies to everyone who has experienced hardship and pain.

PRE-STORY DIALOGUE

"Where was God when that happened?" "Why is this happening to me?" "Why aren't my prayers being answered?" Can you relate to any of these questions? These are the kinds of questions we ask when we suffer. When we go through dark times, few things seem to make sense. Even the one we normally turn to for help—God Himself—seems far away. Try to imagine how Job must have felt as you listen to this story. That may not be hard for some of us because pain is a part of all of our lives, but Job's was extreme—and we can be encouraged that God's purposes apply even to the worst of our trials.

TELL THE STORY

In the land of Uz, there was a righteous man who served God faithfully. He was very blessed; he had ten children, thousands of animals for livestock, and a great reputation. Whenever his children had a feast, Job would make sacrifices to God in case any of them had sinned. That's the kind of devotion he had.

One day, the angels and Satan came into God's presence. God asked Satan where he had come from; Satan answered that he had been roaming the earth. God asked if he had noticed how righteous Job was. "Does Job fear God for nothing?" Satan answered. He suggested that Job was righteous only because God had blessed him so much and nothing was really wrong in his life. But, Satan argued, if God caused Job to lose some things and experience hardship, he would end up cursing God. So God gave Satan permission to wreak havoc in Job's life but not to hurt Job himself. Then Satan left God's presence.

Soon after that, Job received urgent news from several messengers. Each one came as the previous one was still speaking. One told him how all of his oxen and donkeys were carried off by raiding Sabeans and some of his servants were killed. Another described how fire fell from heaven and killed all of Job's sheep and more of his servants. Then another came and told how the Chaldeans had come and taken all of his camels and killed his servants. And finally, one reported that all of Job's children had been feasting together when a violent wind destroyed their house, and the roof fell and killed them all.

As soon as Job heard this, he tore his robe and shaved his head—signs of extreme grief. He fell to the ground and worshipped God, saying,

> Naked I came from my mother's womb,
>   and naked I will depart.
> The LORD gave and the LORD has taken away;
>   may the name of the LORD be praised.

And he never accused God of wrongdoing.

The angels came back into God's presence, and Satan came with them. As before, God asked him where he had come from. Again, Satan answered that he had been going back and forth, roaming the earth. God asked him about Job. "He still maintains his integrity," God said, "though you incited me against him to ruin him without any reason." But Satan didn't give up. He still believed Job would curse God if he suffered in his own body. So God gave Satan permission to strike Job with all kinds of diseases as long as Satan didn't take his life.

Satan afflicted Job with sores all over his body, from head to toe. Job tried to scrape his skin with broken pottery and sat among the ashes. His wife wondered why he was maintaining his integrity. "Curse God and die!" she told him. But he argued that it didn't make sense to accept good from God without also accepting trouble. And he still didn't sin in anything he said.

Three of Job's friends heard about all of his troubles and came to visit him and comfort him. But when they saw him, they wept. They could hardly recognize him. They sat with him for seven days without saying anything because his suffering was so great.

Finally, Job's friends started talking. They kept insisting that Job must have sinned; otherwise God wouldn't be allowing him to suffer so much. They believed God always blessed obedience with good circumstances and punished sin with evil circumstances—without exception. Therefore, Job must have sinned to be experiencing such punishment.

But Job maintained his innocence and righteousness throughout the discussions. He did question God once, but he never accused God of injustice. Toward the end, a fourth friend, who was much younger than the other three, offered his point of view: Though Job was a righteous man, human beings don't have the authority to present a case before God and prove their innocence, as Job said he wished he could do. He pointed out that Job was not perfect, and Job didn't argue with him about that.

Finally, God spoke to Job out of a storm. "Who is this that darkens my counsel with words without knowledge?" He asked. "Brace yourself like a man; I will question you, and you shall answer me." Then God described the vastness and majesty of the universe He created and how no human being was there at the foundation of the world. All of God's words showed how limited the human perspective is and how much higher God's wisdom is. Then God challenged Job: "Let him who accuses God answer him!"

Job answered with words about his own unworthiness. He said he was speechless and had no more answers to offer. After God described more of His wisdom and power, Job admitted, "Surely I spoke of things I did not understand, things too wonderful for me to know." Then he humbly repented for all the things he had said.

Next God turned to Job's three friends—but not the fourth who spoke later—and told them He was angry at them for misrepresenting Him. He defended Job for speaking the truth about God. He told the three friends to repent and offer sacrifices; Job would pray for their forgiveness, and God would accept his prayer. Again, He told them they had spoken things about God that weren't right, but Job had spoken correctly.

After Job prayed for his friends, God made him prosperous again. In fact, God blessed him with double what he had had before—twice the number of all his possessions and animals, and ten children as he had before. He lived long enough to see his grandchildren and died at an old age.

DISCUSSION QUESTIONS

- How is Job described at the beginning of his story? What kind of person was he?
- When the angels and Satan came before God, who brought Job's name up first? Why?
- Why did Satan think Job's devotion to God wasn't legitimate? What did he suggest doing in order to prove his point? Why do you think God let him?
- In what ways had God protected Job? In what ways did He limit Satan? What does this tell us about the ways God cares for us in a dangerous world? Who is more powerful in this story: God or Satan?
- What happened to Job after Satan's first conversation with God? How did Job respond?
- What did Satan say the second time he talked with God? Why wasn't he convinced about Job's devotion and integrity? What did God allow him to do next?
- How did Job respond to the next round of adversity? What did his wife suggest that he do?
- How would you have felt if you were in Job's situation? What would you think about God? How strong would your faith be? What would you have done if you experienced that kind of pain in so many different ways and in so short a time?
- What did Job's friends think about how God deals with people? In what ways were they right? In what ways were they wrong?
- What do the words and actions of Job's friends teach us about how to show compassion (or how *not* to show compassion) when someone we know is hurting?
- What did God say when He finally spoke? Did He give Job a clear explanation of why he suffered? Why or why not?
- Does God always give us a clear explanation when we suffer?

Why or why not? Why do you think He allows good people to experience extreme pain? What attitude does He want us to have toward Him when we suffer?

- What are we tempted to believe about God when we go through difficult trials? What happens to our perspective in a trial? What can we do to maintain the right perspective?
- How did God vindicate Job in front of his friends?
- How did Job's story end? Did God leave him in his pain? How did God show His favor to Job? What implications does this have for us? What promises does God give us about the end of our story?

QUESTIONS FOR FAMILIES/CHILDREN

- Do you think people who suffer are being punished by God? Why or why not?
- Could Satan do anything he wanted to Job? Who decided what Satan was allowed to do?
- How would you have felt if most of the people you loved died, all your possessions were taken, and you got very sick all at once? How do you think Job felt?
- How do you think Job was able to keep believing in God's goodness?
- What kind of questions would you ask God if you had as much trouble as Job did? Do you think God understands our feelings when we ask hard questions?
- Why were Job's friends not such good friends after all? What did God tell them about how they treated Job?
- Did God ever explain why Job suffered so much? Do you think He always explains things to us? Why or why not?
- How did God bless Job in the end? What promises does God give us when we go through hard times?

MEMORY VERSES

Naked I came from my mother's womb, and naked I will depart. The
LORD gave and the LORD has taken away; may the name of the LORD
be praised.

JOB 1:21

trust
Though he slay me, yet will I ~~hope~~ in him.

JOB 13:15

I know that my Redeemer lives, and that in the end he will stand upon
the earth. *For I know that my redeemer liveth, and that he
shall stand at the latter day upon the earth.* JOB 19:25

KEY APPLICATION

God will not allow Satan to touch us beyond His grace.

*Job 1:21 - And said, Naked came I out of my mothers
womb, and naked shall I return thither: the Lord
gave, and the Lord hath taken away; blessed be
the name of the Lord.*

21

ELIJAH
A Spiritual Showdown

THEME

God sends fire from heaven to defeat the prophets of Baal.

PASSAGE/REFERENCE

1 Kings 18

BACKGROUND

Israel's kings had completely turned away from God. The people of Israel worshipped many different gods, sometimes in addition to the true God. The nation's spiritual slide seemed to have begun with Solomon's failures toward the end of his reign, and his successors became more and more unfaithful. Now, several generations later, a wicked king named Ahab and his wicked queen, Jezebel, worshipped Baal as the nation's god. And, as the law had long ago warned, God sent a drought to discipline His people. A prophet named Elijah first declared that drought, and it had gone on for three years. As our story begins, God has the attention of His people because of the hard times He has allowed.

PRE-STORY DIALOGUE

Do you remember what the first two of the Ten Commandments were? They were about worship—and specifically about worshipping no other god but the true God. This fits right in line with what Jesus said was the greatest commandment in Scripture: to love God with all your heart, soul, strength, and mind (see Luke 10:27). But human hearts are fickle, aren't they? As you listen to this story, think about the things that tempt you to turn your heart away from God. Notice also how much God wants the love and worship of His people—and how much He wants your love and worship, too.

TELL THE STORY

In the third year of the drought, God told Elijah to go present himself to King Ahab, and then He would send rain on the land. The famine was severe, and Ahab had sent Obadiah out to search for some grass to feed the animals so they wouldn't have to kill them. (Obadiah was a good prophet who loved God, but he had to serve in Ahab's palace. He had once hidden one hundred prophets in caves so Queen Jezebel wouldn't find and kill them.) As Obadiah was walking along on his search for grass, Elijah met him.

Obadiah recognized Elijah and bowed down. Elijah told him to inform Ahab that he was coming. This scared Obadiah because he knew Elijah's reputation for being hard to find. (Ahab had searched for Elijah for years, but Elijah had always eluded him.) Obadiah was afraid that if he went and told Ahab about Elijah and then Ahab found Elijah gone again, Obadiah would be killed. But Elijah promised that he would meet with Ahab that very day.

When Ahab came out to see Elijah, each accused the other of causing trouble for Israel. Elijah accused Ahab of abandoning God's commands and following false gods. Then he challenged Ahab to gather people from all over Israel to Mount Carmel and bring the 450 prophets of Baal and 400 priestesses of Asherah who served Ahab and Jezebel. So Ahab did that, and Elijah stood before the people of Israel and said, "How long will you waver between two opinions? If the LORD is God, follow him; but if Baal is God, follow him." But the people said nothing.

Elijah pointed out that he was the only one of God's prophets there, but 450 prophets of Baal had come. Then he issued a challenge. Each side would prepare a bull for sacrifice but not light the fire and then call on their god. "The god who answers by fire—he is God," Elijah said. And the people agreed.

Elijah let the priests of Baal go first. They put their bull on the altar and started calling on the name of Baal. From morning to noon they begged Baal to answer, but no response came. They danced around the altar, and at noon Elijah began taunting them. He told them to shout louder—perhaps Baal was busy or traveling or deep in thought. So the prophets of Baal shouted even louder and cut themselves with swords and spears so their blood would flow, which was a custom to show their devotion. They did this until evening, prophesying frantically to get Baal to pay attention, but no one answered.

Finally, Elijah told the people to gather around him. He repaired the altar of the Lord that was once there but now was in ruins. He took twelve stones—one for each tribe of Israel—and rebuilt the altar, dug a trench around it, arranged wood, and prepared the bull, and then he told the people to fill four large jars with water and pour it on the offering and the wood. He had them do this three times—three sets of four jars, so twelve jars of water overall—and the water ran down around the altar and filled the trench. Then Elijah stepped forward and prayed to God: "Let it be known today that you are God in Israel and that I am your servant and have done all these things at your command. Answer me, O LORD, answer me, so these people will know that you, O LORD, are God, and that you are turning their hearts back again."

When Elijah finished praying, the fire of God fell on the sacrifice and burned everything up, even the water in the trench. The people fell down and kept crying out, "The LORD — he is God!" Elijah commanded them to seize the prophets of Baal and put them to death. Then he told Ahab to go home and eat and drink — rain was on its way.

After Ahab left, Elijah went to the top of the mountain, bent down, and put his face between his knees. He told his servant to go look out toward the sea, but his servant reported that he saw nothing. Elijah asked him seven times to go look, and finally by the seventh time, the servant saw a cloud as small as a man's hand rising up from the sea. So Elijah told his servant to run after Ahab and tell him to hurry home before the rain stopped him. Then the sky grew black with clouds, the wind rose, and it started raining heavily. The power of God came on Elijah, and he ran ahead of Ahab all the way to Jezreel.

DISCUSSION QUESTIONS

- Why was there a drought in Israel? What message was the drought meant to send to God's people? Who first declared the drought?
- Why did God tell Elijah to go see Ahab, the king who had been trying to find and kill him? What was God about to do?
- Why was Obadiah afraid to tell Ahab he had seen Elijah? What did Elijah say to reassure him?
- When Ahab encountered Elijah, what did the king accuse him of doing? What did Elijah accuse Ahab of doing?
- What challenge did Elijah issue? What risks did he take by issuing this challenge? What would have happened if God hadn't shown up?
- Have you ever had to put your faith on the line like Elijah did? If so, how confident were you that God would support you? What was the result?
- Have you ever backed away from a situation that would put your faith on the line and cause you to be embarrassed if God

didn't confirm it? If so, what do you think would happen if you had taken the risk?

- How long did Elijah give the prophets of Baal to call upon their god? What did they do to get Baal's attention? What response did they get?

- How long did Elijah pray before God answered? How did God answer?

- How did the people respond to God's power? What did they do to the prophets of Baal? How did Ahab respond?

- What did Elijah do next? Why do you think he had to pray for rain to come? Why did he send his servant out seven times before he saw any results? What does his persistence teach us about prayer?

- What does this story teach us about bold faith? How can we know when God will support us in crisis moments and when He won't? What kinds of risks do you think He might want us to take when we step out in faith?

- What does this story teach us about how much God desires our worship? In what ways does it encourage you to worship Him with greater passion and devotion?

QUESTIONS FOR FAMILIES/CHILDREN

- Why did God keep it from raining in Israel for so long? What did He want to teach His people?

- Why was Obadiah afraid of King Ahab? Why wasn't Elijah afraid of him?

- What did Elijah challenge Ahab to do at Mount Carmel? How many people were on Ahab's side? How many people were on Elijah's side?

- What do you think would have happened to Elijah if God had not set his altar on fire? Do you think Elijah was worried about that? Why or why not?

- What did the people do when God answered Elijah's prayer? Who did they decide to worship?
- Why did Elijah pray for rain after his victory? Why do you think it took seven times before rain came? What does that teach us about not giving up when we pray?
- What does this story teach us about faith? How does God respond when we believe in Him?
- What does this story teach us about worship? How much does God want us to worship Him? In what ways can we show our love for Him?

MEMORY VERSES

O LORD, God of Abraham, Isaac and Israel, let it be known today that you are God in Israel and that I am your servant and have done all these things at your command. Answer me, O LORD, answer me, so these people will know that you, O LORD, are God, and that you are turning their hearts back again.

1 KINGS 18:36-37

KEY APPLICATION

God can miraculously intervene in our spiritual battles.

22

JONAH
The Reluctant Prophet

THEME

God turns a runaway prophet back to his mission and shows compassion for those who do not know Him.

PASSAGE/REFERENCE

Jonah

BACKGROUND

Nineveh was the leading city of Assyria, Israel's most threatening enemy, well known for its violent war tactics. Jonah was a prophet who had already preached a message against Israel's oppression by its enemies (see 2 Kings 14:25); he would likely have been a strong supporter of judgment against Nineveh. But he would not have wanted to preach against Nineveh as a lone voice in hostile territory, nor to give the Ninevites an opportunity to repent.

PRE-STORY DIALOGUE

God invites us into His mission, but many people don't accept the invitation. Why? Maybe it seems too hard or they think they aren't qualified. And some people are too busy pursuing their own agenda in life to pay much attention to God's. But those who love Him and take His Word seriously soon realize the opportunity and joy of being part of His purposes. In this session, we see a prophet who wasn't quite ready for a particular invitation from God. Think about the following questions: What's the hardest thing you can imagine God asking you to do? Would you do it if you knew it was God who was asking? How concerned are you for people who do not know God, or perhaps do not even *want* to know Him?

TELL THE STORY

Jonah received an ominous assignment: Walk up and down the streets of a city in enemy territory and preach a message of God's judgment. Could any prophet survive such a mission? Jonah didn't want to find out. He fled—in the opposite direction from where God told him to go.

The prophet hastily boarded a ship heading west into the Mediterranean, and God sent a violent storm to threaten the ship. The other sailors were very afraid and all called on their own gods to help. They threw a lot of their cargo overboard to try to save the ship. But Jonah was asleep down in the bottom of the ship. The captain told him to get up and pray to his God because the ship was in danger. Then the sailors cast lots to find out who was responsible for making the gods so angry, and the answer pointed to Jonah.

They asked Jonah who he was, where he came from, and what he had done to cause so much trouble. (They already knew he was running from God because he had told them.) "What should we do to you to make the sea calm down for us?" they asked. Jonah answered, "Pick me up and throw me into the sea . . . and it will become calm. I know that it is my fault that this great storm has come upon you." They didn't want to do that, so they tried rowing back to land but it was futile. Finally they agreed to throw Jonah overboard and asked God to forgive them for taking his life. When they threw Jonah into the sea, the storm was immediately calmed. Jonah was swallowed by a great fish and lived in the fish's belly for three days and three nights.

As Jonah prayed while he was in the fish, he repented for disobeying God. When the fish spit Jonah up onto dry land, Jonah obeyed God and took His message to Nineveh: "Forty more days and Nineveh will be overturned." Surprisingly, the citizens of this foreign city repented and believed God. They declared a fast. Even the king repented and made the time of fasting and repentance an official decree. He told everyone to urgently pray to God. "Who knows?" he said. "God may yet relent and with compassion turn from his fierce anger so that we will not perish." Because of their repentance, God did not destroy them as Jonah had declared.

Jonah did not rejoice when Nineveh repented. In fact, he became very angry that God had mercy on one of Israel's worst enemies. He was so angry that he asked God to take his life. So God taught Jonah by giving him an object lesson: A vine grew up quickly to provide shade for the prophet, but soon it withered under the hot sun. Jonah's anger about losing the vine demonstrated that he could be more concerned for a plant than he was for a vast city full of people who had not known God. God's last words to the prophet in the book of Jonah declare His compassion over those who are lost: "Should I not be concerned about that great city?"

DISCUSSION QUESTIONS

- Why do you think Jonah was so offended by the mission God sent him on?
- How would you respond if God told you to go to an enemy city by yourself, stand in the public square, and preach His impending judgment?
- Have you ever felt like fleeing from God? Why? When is it hard for you to obey God? What are the consequences when we don't?

- Why do you think God was so concerned for Nineveh, a city that had oppressed His people?
- When Jonah rejected God's assignment, God gave him a second chance. How relentlessly do you think God pursues us when we reject His purposes? Do you think He ever gives up on us and gives our assignment to someone else? Why or why not?
- In what ways did Jonah change? In what ways did he not?
- Why do you think Jonah was angry when Nineveh repented?
- What does the book of Jonah teach us about God's compassion? What implications does this message have for our lives today?
- In what ways does God want us to share His heart? How does He teach us His thoughts and impart His vision to us?
- How does God see our enemies? How does He expect us to treat them? What modern-day enemies can you think of that God's people might be reluctant to love?
- Do you think God sends people on a mission to great cities today? If so, in what ways can we join Him in His mission?

QUESTIONS FOR FAMILIES/CHILDREN

- What did God tell Jonah to do? Why do you think God was concerned for people who had done a lot of bad things to His people?
- Why was it hard for Jonah to obey God? Why is it hard for us to obey God sometimes?
- How did God get Jonah to change his mind?
- Do you think Jonah was glad God gave him a second chance to obey? When have you needed God's forgiveness?
- How did the people of Nineveh respond when Jonah preached to them? What did God decide to do for them?
- Why did God's mercy make Jonah mad? Did God give up on

teaching Jonah then? Why not? What did God do to show Jonah His compassion?

- Why is it hard for us to love some of the people God loves? How should we show love to people we don't like?

MEMORY VERSE

Nineveh has more than a hundred and twenty thousand people who cannot tell their right hand from their left, and many cattle as well. Should I not be concerned about that great city?

Jonah 4:11

KEY APPLICATION

God gives us second chances in life and invites us to share His compassion for others.

23

ISAIAH

Visions of Things to Come

THEME

God predicts His coming Suffering Servant.

PASSAGE/REFERENCE

Isaiah 7:14; 9:2-7; 53:1-12

BACKGROUND

In about 740 BC, nearly a century after Elijah and a couple of decades after Jonah, a prophet named Isaiah had an encounter with God. He saw God on His throne in His temple, with angels declaring His holiness and glory. Deeply humbled, Isaiah received his calling to go to the nation and declare both judgment and hope. He would urge the people to repent, predict a downfall and a restoration, and look far into the future to see a coming Savior and an eternal kingdom.

PRE-STORY DIALOGUE

Do you ever wish you could know the future? Sometimes God gives us glimpses of what He is going to do. In today's session, we'll see some remarkable prophecies from a man who lived several hundred years before the Messiah would come, yet he predicted the Messiah in great detail. As you listen, see if you can recognize the child he foretells and the suffering servant he describes.

TELL THE STORY

Today we are looking at three prophecies from Isaiah, the first two about a birth. In the first, the prophet tells us that the Lord would give a sign: A virgin would conceive and give birth to a son, and He would be called Immanuel ("God with us").

The second prophecy says that a people walking in darkness have seen a great light. God has enlarged the nation and increased joy; the people rejoice as they do when they are harvesting or dividing plunder after a battle. Isaiah speaks of God shattering the yoke that burdens His people, delivering them from oppression. The garments of warfare will be burned up because the battle is over. Then he says,

> *For to us a child is born,*
> > *to us a son is given,*
> > *and the government will be on his shoulders.*
> *And he will be called*
> > *Wonderful Counselor, Mighty God,*
> > *Everlasting Father, Prince of Peace.*

And His righteous reign would always increase; He would rule forever on David's throne. God's own zeal would make sure of it.

The third prophecy pictures a death. It tells us about someone who would grow up like a tender shoot, a root out of dry ground — someone humble in appearance without any particular beauty or majesty: "He was despised and rejected by men, a man of sorrows, and familiar with suffering." People would hide their faces from Him and despise Him. But He would carry our sickness and sorrow. He would be pierced for our sins, and the punishment He bore would bring us peace and heal our wounds. All of us have gone our own way like wandering sheep, but the Lord would lay our sin on Him for Him to carry instead. He would be oppressed but would refrain from protesting: "He was led like a lamb to the slaughter, and as a sheep before her shearers is silent, so he did not open his mouth." He would be carried away, cut off from the land of the living, and put in a grave among the wicked and with the rich, even though He had done nothing wrong—no violence, no deceit. But it would be God's will to crush Him with suffering and make His life a guilt offering. Even so, God would prolong His days and He would prosper in God's will. After His suffering, He would see life and be satisfied. He would justify many and bear their sins. God therefore would give Him the rewards of greatness and the spoils of victors—because He gave up His life among sinners.

DISCUSSION QUESTIONS

- Who do these prophecies seem to be describing?
- How do the birth prophecies describe the Messiah? What characteristics does He have?
- What does "Immanuel" mean? In what ways is this name a comfort to us? At what times in your life would it be most encouraging to depend on the truth of this name?
- Of all the names listed for the child who would be born—Wonderful Counselor, Mighty God, Everlasting Father, Prince of Peace—which one is most meaningful to you? Why?
- How long does the Messiah's reign last? What does it mean that His reign will always increase? How is that possible? In what ways does that encourage you?
- How is the Messiah described in the prophecy of His death? What characteristics does He have? What does He experience?
- What are the benefits of the Suffering Servant's death for God's people? What did His death accomplish for our "sorrows" and "infirmities"?

- Why do you think the Messiah had to suffer? What does it mean that He was a "guilt offering"? Thinking back to the laws of Moses, do you remember what kind of sacrifice was required to cover sins? How did Jesus fit the description of this sacrifice?
- Why did we need this Servant to suffer? In what way does Isaiah compare us to sheep? In what way does he compare Jesus to a lamb?
- What rewards does the Suffering Servant receive at the end of this prophecy?
- Why is it significant that these prophecies were given hundreds of years before Jesus' birth?
- What do these prophecies tell us about God's plan to redeem humanity? What kind of preparation went into His plan?
- What do these prophecies teach us about God's sovereignty over the future? How do they encourage us personally about God's control of our future?

QUESTIONS FOR FAMILIES/CHILDREN

- In the prophecies that tell us a baby will be born, how is that child described? What names is He given? What's special about this baby?
- How long is the Messiah going to live and rule?
- According to Isaiah's prophecies, would Jesus be impressive to look at? Did He look like an ordinary man, or was it obvious He was God's Son?
- What did Jesus need to do for our sin? How are we like sheep? In what ways did He suffer for us?
- According to the prophecy, had Jesus done anything wrong? Why did He let people kill Him?
- How far into the future can God see? What do you think He

knows about your future? How well do you think He is planning for your future?

MEMORY VERSES

He was pierced for our transgressions, he was crushed for our iniquities; the punishment that brought us peace was upon him, and by his wounds we are healed. We all, like sheep, have gone astray, each of us has turned to his own way; and the LORD has laid on him the iniquity of us all.

ISAIAH 53:5-6

KEY APPLICATION

God has sent Jesus, His Suffering Servant, to die for us.

24

DANIEL
No Compromise

THEME

God is to be obeyed rather than man.

PASSAGE/REFERENCE

Daniel 1

BACKGROUND

God had sent many prophets to His people, but their hearts would not turn back to Him. Finally, He sent one of their enemies to overthrow them. Babylonians destroyed Jerusalem and carried off its people into captivity, but God did not stop speaking to His people. One of the prophets He raised up in Babylon was a young man named Daniel. Daniel and his friends were young Jews assigned to serve in King Nebuchadnezzar's court. Daniel would interpret many dreams and see many visions during his years in Babylon, but today's story focuses on his character and how God had prepared him for great purposes.

PRE-STORY DIALOGUE

We've seen how God takes His time in developing the character of those who serve Him. He spent years preparing Joseph, David, and many others for the responsibilities He had planned for them. Today we'll see the character of someone in a difficult position. Many of Judah's best and brightest young men had been taken to serve in Babylon's royal courts. Daniel remained faithful to God in spite of the pressures put on him to compromise. As you listen to the story, think about the ways you've been tempted to compromise with the world's way of doing things. What do you do in those situations? How do you resist the pressure? Here's how Daniel handled it.

TELL THE STORY

King Nebuchadnezzar of Babylon came to Jerusalem and besieged it, and God allowed the king of Judah to be captured and the valuable articles of the temple to be taken. Nebuchadnezzar carried Judah's treasures off to the temple of his god. He also ordered his chief court official to bring some Israelites from royal and noble families—young men who had strong physical and intellectual attributes. For three years, the official was to teach them the language and literature of Babylon and prepare them to serve in the king's palace. And he prepared a healthy diet of the king's finest foods for them.

The young men included Daniel and three of his friends: Hananiah, Mishael, and Azariah. But the official gave them Babylonian names. Daniel became Belteshazzar, and his friends became Shadrach, Meshach, and Abednego. (All of these names referred to Babylonian gods.)

Daniel didn't want to break the dietary laws God had given by eating Babylonian foods, so he asked permission not to defile himself. God had given the chief official a sympathetic attitude toward Daniel, but he was afraid of the king. The king had assigned the food, and if he saw Daniel and his friends looking unhealthy, he would take it out on the official. Daniel asked him to try an experiment for ten days: Give them only vegetables and water, compare their appearance to that of the men who ate the royal food, and then treat Daniel and his friends according to the results. The official agreed to try that. After ten days, Daniel and his friends looked healthier than any of their peers. So the official allowed them to continue eating only food that was allowed by Jewish law.

God gave knowledge and understanding in all areas of learning to these four men. Daniel in particular could understand visions and dreams. After the three years of preparation, the chief official presented them to the king, who talked with them and was very impressed. He found them to be unequaled in their wisdom and understanding, much better than all the magicians and sages in the entire kingdom.

DISCUSSION QUESTIONS

- Why were Daniel and his friends in King Nebuchadnezzar's court? What happened in their lives that caused them to end up in Babylon?
- What kind of names were Daniel and his friends given? In a culture in which names often defined identity, what impact do you think this might have had on them?
- What predicament did Daniel and his friends find themselves in when their diet was planned for them? Why was this a problem?
- Why was the official afraid? What kind of pressure do you think this situation created for Daniel and his friends? What kind of pressure did it create for the official?
- When we decide to do the right thing, is it convenient for us and everyone around us? Why or why not?
- What would you have done if you were in Daniel's situation?

- In what ways did Daniel show respect for the human authorities above him? In what ways did he show greater respect for God? How was he able to do both?
- How did Daniel convince the official to let them avoid eating unlawful food? What do you think they would have done if they appeared to be less healthy and strong after ten days?
- According to the Bible, where did Daniel and his friends get all their wisdom and understanding? Why do you think God gave them such favor?
- When have you been tempted to compromise the standards God has given you? What did you do in those situations? When you have compromised, how did it feel? When you have stood firm, how did it feel? In what ways have you sensed God encouraging, supporting, and/or forgiving you during those times?
- Are you aware when you go through tempting or trying times that God may be preparing you for a bigger assignment? Why or why not? How would that awareness help you in a moment of trial?
- In what ways do our character and integrity relate to our service for God? In what ways does God prepare and refine our character and integrity?

QUESTIONS FOR FAMILIES/CHILDREN

- Why were Daniel and his friends in Babylon? Did they want to be there?
- What kind of attitude did they have about their situation? Did they complain about it? How does the Bible describe their appearance and intelligence?
- What did the king's official want Daniel and his friends to do that would have broken God's laws? Why didn't they want to do it?

- Which was more important: for Daniel and his friends to obey the king or to obey God? Why? What might have happened if they disobeyed the king?
- Have you been tempted to do things God didn't want you to do? When? What kind of pressure did you feel from other people or yourself? How did you handle it?
- When you have done something you knew God didn't like, how did that feel? Do you think He will forgive us when we do the wrong thing if we ask Him to? When you have done what God wanted you to do, how did that feel? Do you think God has been pleased with your decision to obey Him?
- What does this story teach us about having good character and being faithful? Are these qualities important to God? In what ways does God bless and support those who have strong character?

MEMORY VERSES

Praise be to the name of God for ever and ever; wisdom and power are his. He changes times and seasons; he sets up kings and deposes them. He gives wisdom to the wise and knowledge to the discerning. He reveals deep and hidden things; he knows what lies in darkness, and light dwells with him.

DANIEL 2:20-22

KEY APPLICATION

When we get conflicting instructions, we must obey God rather than man.

25

ESTHER
Fear and Faith in a Crisis

THEME

God appoints Esther for her unique time.

PASSAGE/REFERENCE

Esther
Focus: Esther 3:1–7:10; 8:3-4,7-8,11-13; 9:1-4

BACKGROUND

Years after the Babylonians overthrew Jerusalem and took the Jews captive, the Persians overthrew Babylon, and a Persian king named Cyrus allowed the Jews to return to their land and rebuild Jerusalem. Many did, but many remained scattered throughout the empire. Our story in this session happens during the time of a later Persian king named Xerxes (also called Ahasuerus), who banished his queen when she didn't satisfy his whims at a feast. Xerxes searched among the women of his realm for a new queen, finally choosing Esther, a young Jewish woman who pleased him greatly. Her cousin Mordecai discovered and exposed a plot to kill the king, an act of loyalty that was written in the royal records. But the king's right-hand man—a descendant of the Amalekite king Agag, whose people King Saul long ago neglected to destroy—took offense at Mordecai the Jew, and an ancient ethnic rivalry would soon erupt again.

PRE-STORY DIALOGUE

What would you do in a make-or-break moment of crisis, a high-risk situation that required you to put your faith—and maybe your life—on the line? Most of us would like to think we would demonstrate bold, biblical faith at such moments. Many of us, however, would try to avoid being in such a difficult position. There are times in life when we know we should probably step forward in faith, but our instincts tell us to back away. In today's story, we'll hear about a young woman who was scared to death but stepped forward anyway. As you listen, think about what you would have done in Esther's position.

TELL THE STORY

King Xerxes honored Haman the Agagite by making him the king's right-hand man. By the king's command, all the royal officials at the king's gate had to kneel down in honor of Haman. But Mordecai the Jew wouldn't kneel down or honor him at all. The royal officials asked him why he disobeyed the king's command and tried to talk to him about it, but he wouldn't comply. They told Haman about it, and he was furious. He wanted to kill Mordecai, but that wasn't enough: He knew that Mordecai was a Jew, and this made him want to kill all Jews. So Haman cast a lot (a *pur*) to see when would be the best time to arrange that, and it fell on a date several months in the future.

Then Haman went to the king to tell him about the problem of these people who were scattered throughout the empire. Without naming Jews specifically, he told Xerxes that these people had different customs, didn't obey the king's laws, and shouldn't be tolerated. Haman suggested a decree to destroy them and offered to fund the project personally. So the king gave his signet ring to this enemy of the Jews and said, "Do with the people as you please." Haman wrote a decree in Xerxes' name, sealed it with the king's seal, and sent it all over the empire. The Jews—young and old, women and children—were scheduled to be destroyed and plundered in a single day. After sending out the decree, the king and Haman sat down to drink, but the capital city of Susa was bewildered.

When Mordecai heard about this, he grieved and cried out bitterly in the city streets, even up to the king's gate. All the Jews mourned with fasting, weeping, and wailing. Esther was told about Mordecai and the Jews grieving, so she sent one of her attendants to find out why. Mordecai gave the attendant a copy of the decree and told him to urge Esther to go beg the king for mercy. This idea frightened Esther; she sent the attendant back to tell Mordecai that no one could approach the king in his court without being summoned. The penalty for this was death, and the only exception was when the king extended his scepter to pardon the person who approached him. Esther hadn't been summoned by the king in over a month, so she wasn't sure she still had his favor.

Mordecai sent back an answer to Esther: "Do not think that because you are in the king's house you alone of all the Jews will escape. For if you remain silent at this time, relief and deliverance for the Jews will arise from another place, but you and your father's family will perish. And who knows but that you have come to royal position for such a time as this?" Then Esther sent a reply to Mordecai, asking him to gather all the Jews in the capital and fast for her—no food or drink for three days and nights. Then she would go in to the king, even though it was against the law. "And if I perish, I perish," she said. Mordecai went away and carried out her instructions.

Three days later, Esther went to the king's inner court. When the king saw her, he held out his scepter, welcoming her into his presence. "What is your request?" he asked her. "Even up to half the kingdom, it will be given you." Esther requested that the king and Haman come to a banquet she had prepared, and the king agreed. But at the banquet,

Esther didn't present her case yet; she asked for another banquet and promised she would speak freely then. In the meantime, Haman was boasting to his friends about how important he was and complaining about Mordecai. Haman's wife and friends suggested he build a gallows and ask the king to have Mordecai hanged on it. Haman thought that was a great idea, so he had the gallows built.

That night the king couldn't sleep, so he asked someone to read the chronicles of his reign to him. The records reminded Xerxes of when Mordecai foiled an assassination plot against him, so the king asked how Mordecai had been honored for his actions. His attendants told him that nothing had been done. Just then, Haman entered the court to ask Xerxes about hanging Mordecai on the gallows. The king asked his advice about the best way to honor someone. Haman thought the king was referring to *himself*, so he suggested some extravagant honors, including wearing royal robes and acting like the king for a day. Xerxes thought that sounded good, so he ordered Haman to go arrange the honors—for Mordecai! Haman had to dress Mordecai in royal robes and lead him through the streets on horseback, proclaiming, "This is what is done for the man the king delights to honor!" Afterward, Haman rushed home in grief and told his wife and friends. His wife told him that because Mordecai was a Jew, Haman would come to ruin by opposing him.

Haman went to the banquet with Esther and Xerxes, and the king again asked what Esther wanted. Finally she told him about the decree against her people and how her own life was in danger. Xerxes was outraged and asked who had proposed such a thing. Esther said, "The adversary and enemy is this vile Haman." Haman was terrified.

The king walked out in a rage, but Haman stayed behind to beg Esther for his life. As the king was coming back into the room, Haman was falling on the couch where Esther was reclining, and the king thought he was molesting her. So the king had Haman taken and hung on the very gallows he had built for Mordecai.

The king elevated Mordecai to Haman's former position and gave him the signet ring of authority. Then Esther went into the court and pleaded with the king to revoke the decree against the Jews. He said no royal decree could be revoked, but he told Mordecai to write another decree giving the Jews the right to defend themselves and do to their enemies what had been planned against them. The Jews were given permission to assemble and fight against any who attacked them.

Finally the day came for both decrees to be carried out. The enemies of the Jews had hoped to destroy them, but the tables were turned and the Jews got the upper hand. A lot of people, including governors and administrators in the provinces, helped the Jews. And Mordecai became more prominent and more powerful in the palace.

DISCUSSION QUESTIONS

- What did Mordecai do to enrage Haman? Why do you think Haman vented his anger on all Jews instead of just Mordecai?
- What did Haman propose as a solution to his problem? How did he convince the king that this was a good plan? Did Xerxes seem to know that his queen was a Jew? Why do you think he didn't ask Haman for any details about these people who had offended him?
- Why was Queen Esther afraid to go before the king and plead for her people? What did Mordecai say to convince her? What did she ask the Jews of Susa to do before she approached the king?
- What attitude did Esther have about preserving her own life? In what ways did she demonstrate faith?
- Do you think it's possible for us to be afraid and have faith at the same time? Why or why not?
- Why do you think Esther didn't present her petition to the king at the first banquet?
- What happened with Haman between the two banquets? With Mordecai? With the king?

- How did God show that He was protecting His people throughout this story? How did Haman's casting lots work in their favor? How did Esther's reluctance to share her request at the first banquet turn into an advantage? How did Xerxes' sleepless night help the case of the Jews?
- What does this story teach us about God's sovereignty over our lives?
- How confident are you about God's ability to handle your "enemies"—either literal or figurative ones? How confident are you in His ability to work out His timing in your life? How does the book of Esther encourage us when we lack faith in either of these areas?
- How can we recognize the God-appointed moments in our lives—those situations in which we might have been born "for such a time as this"? How does the story of Esther encourage you to take advantage of those moments?
- How much pressure do you feel to handle those moments perfectly? In what ways does the story of Esther relieve that pressure?

QUESTIONS FOR FAMILIES/CHILDREN

- Why did Haman get so angry at Mordecai and the Jews? What did he decide to do to punish Mordecai and his people?
- What happened when the Jews heard about Haman's plans? What did Mordecai do? What did he urge Esther to do?
- How did Esther feel about going in to see the king? Why was this such a big deal? What could have happened if the king didn't want her there?
- How do you think Esther overcame her fear? Do you think it took courage for her to do what she did even when she was afraid?

- Have you ever been afraid to do something you knew you should do? When? What did you decide to do about it?
- How did Haman's plan backfire on him? How did God show that He was protecting His people?
- What does this story teach us about the way God takes care of us? What does it teach us about being brave and standing up for what we believe in?

MEMORY VERSE

If you remain silent at this time, relief and deliverance for the Jews will arise from another place, but you and your father's family will perish. And who knows but that you have come to royal position for such a time as this?

ESTHER 4:14

KEY APPLICATION

Each of us is appointed by God to live faithfully in our time.

26

NEHEMIAH
Tenacious Faith

THEME

God uses Nehemiah to lead a rebuilding project for Jerusalem's wall.

PASSAGE/REFERENCE

Nehemiah 1:1–2:20; 4:1–6:19; 7:1-5; 8:1-12

BACKGROUND

Many of the Jews had returned to Jerusalem, but reestablishing the city—and, more importantly, the temple-based worship of God by His people—was a long-term process. About thirty years after Esther, Nehemiah returned to Jerusalem to join the priest Ezra in rebuilding the city. He found a city in shambles, a temple still in disrepair, and a wall partly standing among rubble with gaping holes in it. There was much work to be done, and Nehemiah was sent by God to lead the way.

PRE-STORY DIALOGUE

We've seen from the very beginning that God had a mission in the world. And we've also seen how He calls His people to participate in that mission. But most of us run into quite a few obstacles when we try to serve Him. We get distracted, intimidated, or overwhelmed by the size of the mission or by those who oppose it. In this session, we'll hear about a man who refused to back down from what God called him to do. As you listen, ask yourself: What distracts me from following God fully? What characteristics did Nehemiah have that would help me follow God more faithfully?

TELL THE STORY

When Nehemiah's brother and some other men came from Judah to Susa, a Persian capital, Nehemiah asked them about the Jews in Jerusalem. They told him about all the troubles the Jews faced—how Jerusalem's wall was destroyed and its gates burned. Nehemiah was troubled, and he wept and fasted and prayed for days.

Nehemiah called upon God. He confessed the sins of the Israelites and asked God to keep His promise to return exiles who repented of their sins. And Nehemiah, who was the cupbearer and an adviser to the king, asked God for favor in the king's sight.

Soon after, Nehemiah took wine to King Artaxerxes. He had not been sad in the king's presence before, so the king noticed and asked him why he looked discouraged. Nehemiah was afraid—grief in the king's presence wasn't considered appropriate—but told the king about the report from Jerusalem, the city of his fathers. "What is it you want?" the king asked. Nehemiah prayed to God and then answered, "If it pleases the king and if your servant has found favor in his sight, let him send me to the city in Judah where my fathers are buried so that I can rebuild it."

The king gave him permission and agreed to give Nehemiah letters of authorization so he would have safe travel and supplies for rebuilding. Because God's hand was on Nehemiah, the king even sent army officers and cavalry with him. But the Jews had enemies who disapproved of Nehemiah's mission—Sanballat and Tobiah, officials of territories near Jerusalem. They were very displeased.

When Nehemiah first arrived in Jerusalem, he didn't tell anybody why he was there. He surveyed the city and its walls and gates for three days. The Jews and priests and officials who would be doing the repair work didn't know why he was there. Then Nehemiah pointed out the disgraceful condition of the city and explained that the king had given him permission to come and rebuild, so they all began working together.

But when Sanballat and Tobiah and an Arab named Geshem heard about the work, they began mocking and ridiculing. They even accused Nehemiah and the Jews of rebelling against the king. Nehemiah answered, "The God of heaven will give us success. We his servants will start rebuilding, but as for you, you have no share in Jerusalem or any claim or historic right to it." But the opponents kept mocking "those feeble Jews" and said the walls were so fragile even a fox could break them down.

Nehemiah asked God to turn his enemies' insults back on their own heads. The people managed to rebuild the wall to half its height and kept working with all their hearts. This made Sanballat, Tobiah, the Arabs, the Ammonites, and some Philistines very angry, so they plotted to come fight against Jerusalem and stir up trouble. Nehemiah knew about the threat and posted a guard day and night.

But the people were beginning to lose heart. They were getting tired, a lot of rubble was in the way, and the threat of enemy attack discouraged them. So Nehemiah stationed people with spears and swords at all the exposed places of the wall. He encouraged them, "Don't be afraid of them. Remember the Lord, who is great and awesome, and fight for your brothers, your sons and your daughters, your wives and your homes." When the enemies heard that the Jews were aware of their plot and had taken measures against it, the people returned to their work. But from that day forward, half the men worked on the wall while the other half stood guard with weapons ready. Many worked with one hand and held a weapon in the other. And the trumpeter stayed with Nehemiah, ready to sound an alarm. Night and day they worked, always busy and always ready to defend themselves.

When the enemies heard that the wall was rebuilt and there were no more gaps in it, they sent a message to Nehemiah to meet in one of the villages of the plains. But Nehemiah knew they were scheming to harm him, so he sent messengers telling them that he couldn't leave such an important project. Four times they sent the same message, and four times Nehemiah sent the same answer. Then Sanballat sent a fifth message accusing Nehemiah of plotting to revolt against Persia and make himself king of Judah. He threatened to spread this rumor so that the king would hear it. But Nehemiah still refused to be swayed. He knew Sanballat was trying to frighten him and cause him to abandon the work. So he prayed for God to strengthen his hands.

One day, someone urged Nehemiah to shut himself inside the temple because of an assassination plot against him. But Nehemiah refused to run away. He realized this person was not sent by God but was a "prophet" hired by Sanballat and Tobiah. They had wanted to intimidate Nehemiah so he would commit a sin by hiding and give them an opportunity to discredit him.

Finally the wall was completed in only fifty-two days. When all the enemies and surrounding nations heard about this, they were afraid because they realized God had been helping the Jews rebuild. Many of the nobles of Judah who had agreements or had sworn oaths of loyalty to Tobiah tried to convince Nehemiah that Tobiah was good and would make a good ally. And Tobiah kept sending letters to Nehemiah to intimidate him.

After the wall was complete and the doors were in place, gatekeepers and priests were appointed. Nehemiah put his brother in charge of Jerusalem along with the commander of the citadel, who was a godly man. The city was large, but few people lived there because houses had not yet been rebuilt. Then God put it in Nehemiah's heart to assemble the nobles, officials, and commoners to register each family.

All the people assembled in the square. Ezra the scribe brought out the book of the law of Moses and read it aloud while all the people listened carefully. (Some Levites translated because not everyone who had returned from captivity could still understand Hebrew.) The people raised their hands and said, "Amen! Amen!" Then they bowed down and worshipped with their faces to the ground. As Ezra read and the Levites translated and taught, people began to weep. But Nehemiah and the leaders told them not to weep because "this day is sacred to the LORD." He told them to go and celebrate, "for the joy of the LORD is your strength." So the people celebrated with great joy because they understood the words that had been read to them.

DISCUSSION QUESTIONS

- How did Nehemiah respond when he heard the condition of Jerusalem? Why do you think he felt this way?
- For whose sins did Nehemiah ask forgiveness? Do you think God accepts the prayers of one individual for an entire group? Why or why not?
- Who did God raise up as a leader in response to Nehemiah's prayers? Do you think He often uses the person who prayed as part of the answer to the prayer? Why?
- Why did Nehemiah survey the city before beginning his work?
- What kinds of tactics did the enemies of the Jews use to disrupt their work? How did Nehemiah and the people overcome each of those strategies?
- What obstacles from among God's people arose to disrupt their work? How did Nehemiah and the people overcome those obstacles?
- If we follow Nehemiah's example, how should we deal with lies or rumors about us?
- How did Nehemiah recognize the schemes against him as the work of his enemies? How can we discern when a disruption or distraction is from God and when it interferes with God's work? How can we discern when a potential alliance is beneficial and when it's a compromise?

- In what ways does the strategy of "working with one hand and holding a weapon with the other" apply to our spiritual life? What does the story of Nehemiah teach us about self-discipline and diligence? What does it teach us about maintaining our focus?
- Why did the people mourn and weep when they heard the law being read? Why did Nehemiah tell them to rejoice instead? How did they respond?
- How do you feel about past mistakes when you realize you've neglected an important part of God's plan for your life? When you realize the truth, how do you feel and what should you do about it?
- Do you know what lasting work God has called you to do? If so, what can you do to renew your commitment to it and maintain your focus? If not, why not ask God to reveal it to you?

QUESTIONS FOR FAMILIES/CHILDREN

- Why was Nehemiah sad about Jerusalem? What did he pray? What did he want to do about the problem?
- What did Nehemiah's enemies do to try to prevent him from working on the city wall? How did Nehemiah respond to them?
- Why do you think Nehemiah was so determined to stick to his work? What did he do to guard against his enemies?
- What lies did Nehemiah's enemies tell about him? How did they try to get him to run and hide?
- What happened when Nehemiah's enemies realized they couldn't stop the work on Jerusalem?
- Why did the people weep when they heard God's Word being read to them? What did they realize they had done wrong? Why did Nehemiah tell them to rejoice?

MEMORY VERSES

All the people had been weeping as they listened to the words of the Law. Nehemiah said, "Go and enjoy choice food and sweet drinks, and send some to those who have nothing prepared. This day is sacred to our Lord. Do not grieve, for the joy of the LORD is your strength."

NEHEMIAH 8:9-10

KEY APPLICATION

God wants to use us to build something lasting for His glory.

27

JESUS' BIRTH
Promises and Prophecies Fulfilled

THEME

Jesus is born in Bethlehem.

PASSAGE/REFERENCE

Luke 1:26-38; 2:1-20; Matthew 1:18-24

BACKGROUND

About four centuries after the last Old Testament book was written, the long-awaited Messiah was born. Prophets had foretold many details about His life and ministry, so expectations for a deliverer often burned brightly in Israel, which was now under Roman domination. But no one knew exactly what kind of Messiah to expect or specifically when He would come. Two of the gospel writers tell us the story of His birth.

PRE-STORY DIALOGUE

You may remember that one of God's promises after Adam and Eve sinned was that He would send someone to tread on the serpent's head. Thousands of years later, God sent Jesus into the world as our Savior. Notice as you listen to this story how special Jesus' birth was. Also think about these questions: What kind of people did God choose to be the earthly parents of His Son? What kind of people did God choose to be the first to receive His good news?

TELL THE STORY

God sent the angel Gabriel to a young woman named Mary, who had never been married. Gabriel greeted her by telling her she was "highly favored" by the Lord and that the Lord was with her. This troubled Mary; she didn't know why she was greeted this way. The angel told her not to be afraid and again said she had found favor with God. He told her she would have a child and that she should name Him Jesus. "He will be great and will be called the Son of the Most High," Gabriel said. He would reign on the throne of King David, His ancestor, and His kingdom would never end.

Mary wondered how this could be, because she was a virgin. Gabriel told her that the Holy Spirit would overshadow her — that He would be the father of the child. Then the angel told her how her relative Elizabeth was going to have a child in her old age (who would be John the Baptist) because "nothing is impossible with God."

"I am the Lord's servant," Mary answered. "May it be to me as you have said." Then the angel left her.

When Joseph, Mary's future husband, found out Mary was pregnant, he planned to quietly send her away. But an angel appeared to him in a dream and explained that the child was conceived by the Holy Spirit. "She will give birth to a son," the angel said, "and you are to give him the name Jesus, because he will save his people from their sins." This fulfilled Isaiah's prophecy that a virgin would give birth to a child, and His name would be Immanuel, or "God with us." Joseph was familiar with the Scriptures and knew of the prophecy. So when he woke up, he did what the angel said and took Mary as his wife.

Several months later, Joseph and Mary had to travel to Bethlehem of Judea, their ancestral town, because Caesar Augustus had ordered a census. While they were there, the time came for the baby to be born. The town was crowded with people registering for the census, so Joseph and Mary had to stay where the animals were kept because there was no room for them in the inn. Mary gave birth to Jesus, wrapped Him in cloth, and placed Him in a manger, the animals' feeding trough.

That night, an angel appeared to shepherds who were out in the nearby fields keeping watch over their flocks. The sight of the angel bathed in God's glory terrified the shepherds, but the angel told them not to be afraid. "I bring you good news of great joy that will be for all the people," he said. He declared that a Savior—the Messiah—had been born that day in Bethlehem, King David's ancestral city. They would recognize the Savior by this: They would find a baby wrapped in cloths lying in a manger. Then more angels suddenly appeared, and they were praising God, saying, "Glory to God in the highest, and on earth peace to men on whom his favor rests."

After the angels left, the shepherds went into Bethlehem to see the baby. They found Mary and Joseph and Jesus, and they spread the word about what they had heard and seen. Everyone who listened to them was amazed. The shepherds returned to the fields praising God, and Mary treasured these things in her heart.

DISCUSSION QUESTIONS

- How did the angel Gabriel greet Mary? Why do you think Mary was "highly favored"? Why was Mary frightened?
- What did Gabriel tell her about Jesus? What did the angel who appeared to Joseph tell him about Jesus?
- In what way was Jesus' birth a miracle? What does the nature of His birth tell us about who He is?
- What plans do you think Mary had for her life? How did God's plan change her life?
- What challenges do you think Mary faced because of God's plan? How would you have felt if you had been in her place?

- What challenges do you think Joseph faced because of God's plan? How would you have felt if you had been in his place?
- How did Joseph first react to the news that Mary was pregnant? How did he respond to the angel's instructions?
- What does Immanuel mean? In what ways does this name for Jesus apply to our lives?
- Why do you think God chose for Jesus to be born in such an out-of-the-way, humble setting? What does this tell us about God's plan?
- When Jesus was born, to whom did the angels first announce the good news? What were these shepherds doing? Why do you think God chose to tell them first?
- What did the angels tell the shepherds? Why was this birth considered "good news"?
- How did the shepherds respond to the angels' good news? How did they respond after they saw Jesus? Who did they tell? In what ways is their response a good example for us?
- How does the story of Jesus' birth relate to the story of Adam and Eve in the Garden of Eden? What had God promised after Adam and Eve sinned? In what ways did Jesus fulfill this promise?
- What does the birth of Jesus show us about God's faithfulness in keeping His Word? What does it show us about His compassion for us?

QUESTIONS FOR FAMILIES/CHILDREN

- Who came to Mary and told her what God was going to do? How do you think Mary felt when she saw this messenger?
- What did the angel tell Mary?
- What made Jesus special and different from other people? Who was His true Father?
- What does the name Immanuel mean?

- Why was Jesus born where the animals were kept? Why didn't God arrange for His Son to be born in a palace? What kind of people did Jesus come to help?
- Who were the first people to visit Jesus after He was born? What were these people doing when the angels announced that Jesus had been born? Why do you think the angels announced the news to them first?
- What did the shepherds do after they had seen Jesus? Whom did they tell?
- What should we do after we know who Jesus is? Whom should we tell?

MEMORY VERSES

All this took place to fulfill what the Lord had said through the prophet: "The virgin will be with child and will give birth to a son, and they will call him Immanuel"—which means, "God with us."

MATTHEW 1:22-23

KEY APPLICATION

Jesus, while remaining God, became fully human for us.

28

JESUS' BAPTISM
A Heavenly Endorsement

THEME

Jesus is baptized by John.

PASSAGE/REFERENCE

Matthew 3:1-6,11-17; John 1:19-34

BACKGROUND

We are told almost nothing about the years between Jesus' birth and the beginning of His public ministry at around age thirty. The only story we have from His early years describes a trip to Jerusalem during which His parents lose track of Him and then finally find Him in the temple listening to the rabbis and asking them penetrating questions. Other than that, all we know is that "the child grew and became strong; he was filled with wisdom, and the grace of God was upon him," and that He "grew in wisdom and stature, and in favor with God and men" (Luke 2:40,52).

PRE-STORY DIALOGUE

John the Baptist had been preaching in the wilderness, and people were flocking to see him. He baptized those who believed his message: that people should turn away from their sin. When Jesus came to Him, John naturally wondered why. As you listen to the story, notice how Jesus answered John's questions—and how God demonstrated that Jesus was His Son.

TELL THE STORY

Just as Isaiah had prophesied, John the Baptist preached in the wilderness in order to prepare the way for the Messiah. He told people, "Repent, for the kingdom of heaven is near." John lived on locusts and wild honey in the desert and wore clothes of camel hair, and people came from everywhere to see him. If anyone confessed his sins, John baptized him in the Jordan River.

Some people thought John might be the Messiah, the Christ, but John assured them he wasn't. He told instead of another who was coming: the true Messiah. "I baptize you with water for repentance," John explained, but the Messiah would baptize people with the Holy Spirit and with fire. He described how the Messiah would come to gather His wheat but burn up the chaff. John said he wasn't worthy even to carry this Savior's sandals.

One day, Jesus came down from Galilee to be baptized by John. John didn't understand this; he felt that *he* should be baptized by Jesus, not the other way around. But Jesus told him this was the right thing to do in order "to fulfill all righteousness," so John agreed to do it.

As soon as Jesus was baptized and came out of the water, heaven opened and God's Spirit came down like a dove, landing on Him. Then a voice from heaven said, "This is my Son, whom I love; with him I am well pleased." This was a sign to John that Jesus was definitely the Christ, because God had told him, "The man on whom you see the

Spirit come down and remain is he who will baptize with the Holy Spirit." John called Jesus "the Lamb of God, who takes away the sin of the world!"

DISCUSSION QUESTIONS

- Who was John and what was his message? What way was he preparing, and for whom?
- In light of his odd clothes and lifestyle, why do you think people were drawn to John? Why did his message affect people's hearts?
- What do you think John meant about Jesus baptizing "with the Holy Spirit and with fire" (Matthew 3:11)?
- Why did Jesus say He should be baptized by John? What do you think He meant by this?
- What happened immediately after Jesus was baptized? What did Jesus and John see? What did the voice from heaven say?
- Why do you think God gave visible and audible signs of His presence at Jesus' baptism? What is the significance of the Father, the Son, and the Spirit tangibly working together at the same event?
- What did John say the Lamb of God would do?
- What is the significance of Jesus' baptism for us today?
- Is a baptism "with the Holy Spirit and with fire" something you have experienced? If so, what is that like? If not, is it something you would like to experience? How do you think God would respond if you asked Him to apply this promise to your life?

QUESTIONS FOR FAMILIES/CHILDREN

- What was John the Baptist like? What did he tell people to do? What did they do when they heard him preach?

- What kinds of things did John say about Jesus? How was Jesus different from John?
- When Jesus came to see John at the river, what did He ask John to do? How did John answer Him? Did John do what Jesus asked?
- What happened when Jesus was baptized? What did the Holy Spirit do? What did God the Father do?
- What did the voice from heaven say about Jesus?
- What animal did John compare Jesus with? What did John say Jesus would do about the world's sins?

MEMORY VERSES

After me will come one who is more powerful than I, whose sandals I am not fit to carry. He will baptize you with the Holy Spirit and with fire.

MATTHEW 3:11

As soon as Jesus was baptized, he went up out of the water. At that moment heaven was opened, and he saw the Spirit of God descending like a dove and lighting on him. And a voice from heaven said, "This is my Son, whom I love; with him I am well pleased."

MATTHEW 3:16-17

KEY APPLICATION

Baptism is the seal of the covenant between God and us.

29

JESUS' TEMPTATION

The Truth Is Tested

THEME

Jesus shows how to withstand temptation.

PASSAGE/REFERENCE

Matthew 4:1-11

BACKGROUND

Jesus had just been baptized and His ministry was now public, but no move of God goes uncontested in a fallen world. The word just given to Jesus from heaven—that He was the beloved Son of God—was now to be challenged. The Spirit led Jesus into the wilderness, where He fasted for forty days and forty nights, just as Moses had done when God gave him the law (see Exodus 34:28) many centuries before.

PRE-STORY DIALOGUE

After forty days of fasting, Jesus was very hungry. And because Satan looks for vulnerable moments in the lives of God's people, Jesus was tempted. As you listen to this story, notice how Jesus handled His temptation. Think of times when you've been tempted, and try to remember how you handled those situations. In what ways can you learn from His response? What would happen if you responded to temptation the way He did? This story shows us how Jesus overcame the Enemy in a very difficult trial.

TELL THE STORY

After Jesus was baptized, the Spirit of God led Him into the desert to be tempted by the Devil. Jesus didn't eat for forty days and nights, so he was very hungry. That's when the tempter came to Him. "If you are the Son of God, tell these stones to become bread," Satan said. But Jesus answered by quoting Scripture: "It is written: 'Man does not live on bread alone, but on every word that comes from the mouth of God.'"

Then the Devil took Jesus to Jerusalem and had Him stand at the highest place on the temple. "If you are the Son of God . . . throw yourself down. For it is written: 'He will command his angels concerning you, and they will lift you up in their hands, so that you will not strike your foot against a stone.'" But Jesus answered, "It is also written: 'Do not put the Lord your God to the test.'"

Finally, Satan took Jesus to a high mountain and showed Him the kingdoms of the world. He offered to give the kingdoms to Jesus if He would bow down and worship Satan. But Jesus told Satan to get away. "It is written: 'Worship the Lord your God, and serve him only.'" So the Devil left Jesus, and angels came to take care of Him.

DISCUSSION QUESTIONS

- Why did Jesus go into the desert? Who led Him there? Why do you think the Spirit did this?
- Why did Satan tempt Jesus at the end of forty days rather than at the beginning? What does this tell us about his strategy?
- In what ways was Jesus just like us? In what ways did He become weak and vulnerable?

- What were the Devil's first words to Jesus? How did those words relate to the last story, of Jesus' baptism? Why do you think Satan chose this fact as a basis for his temptation?
- Why do you think Satan wanted Jesus to turn stones into bread? Could He have done it? Why didn't He?
- What were Jesus' first words to Satan? Why do you think He responded this way?
- Why do you think Satan wanted Jesus to throw Himself off the temple? Why didn't Jesus do it?
- What did Satan's words in this second temptation and Jesus' three responses have in common?
- What offer did Satan make in the third temptation? Why was he able to make this offer? Why didn't Jesus accept it?
- Who came to care for Jesus after the temptations were over?
- Do you think Satan tempts us the same ways he tempted Jesus? What strategies does he use?
- If Jesus is our model, how should we respond when we are tempted? What kind of help can we expect from God when we are tempted?

QUESTIONS FOR FAMILIES/CHILDREN

- How long did Jesus go without eating? How hungry do you think He was?
- Who tempted Jesus?
- What did the Devil try to get Jesus to do? Why didn't Jesus do those things?
- Why was it important for Jesus to know God's Word when He was tempted? Why is it important for us to know God's Word too?
- Who came to care for Jesus after the Devil left?
- In what ways are you tempted to disobey God sometimes? What should you do when you are tempted?

MEMORY VERSES

It is written: "Man does not live on bread alone, but on every word that comes from the mouth of God."

MATTHEW 4:4

It is also written: "Do not put the Lord your God to the test."

MATTHEW 4:7

It is written: "Worship the Lord your God, and serve him only."

MATTHEW 4:10

KEY APPLICATION

We may successfully withstand temptation through God's Word.

30

JESUS CALLS THE DISCIPLES

Becoming a Follower

THEME

Jesus calls people to follow Him.

PASSAGE/REFERENCE

Luke 5:1-11

BACKGROUND

Many people began to gather around Jesus. They followed Him to hear His teaching, to be healed, and to see His miracles. But like many teachers of the time, Jesus called twelve men into a special relationship with Him. They would follow Him everywhere, be trained in His ways, and be taught how to carry out His mission.

PRE-STORY DIALOGUE

Have you ever received news that was so good you dropped everything you were doing? Has someone ever stepped into your life and immediately changed your perspective or your plans? In this story, Jesus encountered several people whose lives were immediately altered by seeing what He did and hearing what He said, and they were never the same afterward. As you listen, imagine how you might have reacted if you were in their place.

TELL THE STORY

Jesus was teaching by the lake—the Sea of Galilee—and everyone was crowding around to hear Him. At the edge of the water were two boats, left there by fishermen who were washing their nets. So Jesus got into one of the boats owned by a man named Simon and asked him to put out from shore a little. He sat down and began teaching people from the boat.

After He finished His teaching, He told Simon to go out into the deep water and let the nets down for a catch. Simon explained that he and his fellow fishermen had been working all night and hadn't caught anything. Still, because Jesus asked him, Simon agreed to give it a try.

When Simon and his men let down the nets, they caught so many fish that the nets began to break. They signaled the fishermen in the other boat to come and help them. They filled both boats with so many fish that the boats almost sank.

All of the fishermen were amazed by this. Simon (also referred to as Simon Peter, or just Peter) was so moved that he fell down at Jesus' knees and said, "Go away from me, Lord; I am a sinful man!" Simon's partners, James and John, were astonished too. But Jesus said, "Don't be afraid; from now on you will catch men." After they pulled their boats up onto the shore, these fishermen left everything behind—their jobs, boats, nets, family, and friends—in order to follow Jesus.

DISCUSSION QUESTIONS

- Where was Jesus teaching? Why was everyone crowding around Him?

- What were the fishermen doing while Jesus was teaching?
- Why did Jesus get into a boat? Whose boat did He get into? What did He ask the owner of the boat to do?
- What did Simon Peter say when Jesus asked him to put out a little deeper and let down his nets? Why was this an unusual request? Why do you think Simon agreed to do it?
- How would you respond if Jesus told you to do something very unusual that contradicted your expertise or experience? Would you trust Him? Why or why not?
- How do you think Jesus knew they would catch so many fish? What did this catch prove to the fishermen about Jesus?
- Why do you think Simon reacted by declaring his own sin and urging Jesus to leave? How did Jesus respond to him?
- What did Jesus mean when He told the fishermen they would now "catch men"?
- What did the fishermen leave behind in order to follow Jesus? How much would you leave behind to follow Him?
- In what ways did Jesus prove to the fishermen that He was trustworthy? Do you think He was trustworthy enough to guide their lives? In what ways has He proven He's trustworthy enough to guide yours?
- What does it look like to follow Jesus fully?

QUESTIONS FOR FAMILIES/CHILDREN

- Why were people crowding around Jesus? What did He do about it?
- Who owned the boat Jesus used? What did Jesus ask the owner to do when He finished teaching?
- Why didn't Simon want to go deeper and let out his nets? Why did he agree to? Do you think he trusted Jesus? Why or why not?

- What happened when the fishermen let down their nets?
- What did Simon say to Jesus when he saw all the fish? How did Jesus answer him?
- What did Jesus mean when He said the fishermen would "catch men"?
- What did Simon and his partners leave behind to follow Jesus? Do you think they trusted Jesus to teach and guide them?
- How can we show that we trust Jesus to teach and guide us?

MEMORY VERSE

Don't be afraid; from now on you will catch men.

LUKE 5:10

KEY APPLICATION

We are to listen to Jesus' call and follow Him.

31

JESUS HEALS THE PARALYTIC

Authority to Forgive and Restore

THEME

Jesus has the power to heal and forgive.

PASSAGE/REFERENCE

Mark 2:1-12

BACKGROUND

Capernaum, the home of the disciples introduced in the last story, served as a home base for much of Jesus' early ministry. When Jesus returned to this city on the Sea of Galilee after traveling throughout nearby villages, a crowd gathered to hear Him. Many people already knew His reputation. He had been called the Son of God by the voice of God at His baptism and "the Holy One of God" (Mark 1:24) by a demon He had cast out of someone, and He had already demonstrated authority over diseases. The people didn't understand exactly who He was, but they knew He was special. The crowd had high expectations.

PRE-STORY DIALOGUE

How far would you go to get your greatest desires and deepest needs met? What obstacles would you be willing to overcome? The friends of one paralyzed man so badly wanted their friend to be healed that they went to great lengths to see the Healer. But when they got to Him, they learned that their friend had an even deeper need. As you listen to this story, try to detect the signs of faith in the people who came to Jesus, notice how He responded to them, and discover how He perceived their deepest needs.

TELL THE STORY

After traveling around to many villages, Jesus returned to Capernaum. When people heard He had come back, crowds gathered around Him. They crowded into the house where He was staying and all around it up to the door so there was no room for anyone to get any closer to Jesus.

Some men were carrying a paralyzed friend to see if Jesus would heal him, but they couldn't get near because of the crowd. So they went up on the roof and dug an opening in it, and then they lowered their friend on his mat down to Jesus. When Jesus saw the faith of these men, He said to the paralytic, "Son, your sins are forgiven."

Some of the religious leaders were there listening to Jesus, and they were offended when He forgave the sins of the paralytic. They didn't say anything about it out loud, but they thought to themselves that Jesus was guilty of blasphemy—because no one can forgive sins but God.

Jesus knew what they were thinking in their hearts, so He brought it out in the open. "Why are you thinking these things?" He asked. "Which is easier: to say to the paralytic, 'Your sins are forgiven,' or to say, 'Get up, take your mat and walk'?" Then to prove that He had authority to forgive sins, He told the paralyzed man to get up, pick up his mat, and go home. And the man did! He got up and walked out in full view of the crowd. Everyone was amazed. They praised God because they had never seen anything like that before.

DISCUSSION QUESTIONS

- What was Jesus doing when the men brought the paralytic to Him? Why couldn't they get near Him?
- What did they expect Jesus to do for their paralyzed friend? What did they do to make sure Jesus saw him?
- Whose faith did Jesus notice — the faith of the paralyzed man or that of his friends? What words would you use to describe this kind of faith? How did Jesus respond to it?
- What specifically did Jesus do first for the paralyzed man? Why do you think this was the first thing He did? What does this tell us about our greatest needs?
- What did the religious leaders think about this? How do you think Jesus knew what they were thinking?
- How did Jesus react to the thoughts of the religious leaders? Did He ignore their thoughts or expose them? Why?
- What did Jesus do to prove He could forgive sins? What does this tell us about who Jesus is?
- How did the crowd respond when the man got up and walked? What would you have thought about Jesus if you had seen what He did?

QUESTIONS FOR FAMILIES/CHILDREN

- What did the friends of the paralyzed man want Jesus to do?
- Why couldn't the men get close to Jesus at first? What did they have to do to see Him?
- How did this show what they believed about Jesus? What did Jesus think about their faith?

- Did Jesus heal the paralyzed man at first? What was the first thing Jesus said to him?
- Did everyone like what Jesus said to the man? What did some of the people think about His words?
- What happened when Jesus told the man to get up and walk? What did the crowd think about this? What would you have thought if you had been there?
- How did Jesus show in this story that He has the power to forgive you and help you with your problems?

MEMORY VERSES

"That you may know that the Son of Man has authority on earth to forgive sins . . ." He said to the paralytic, "I tell you, get up, take your mat and go home." He got up, took his mat and walked out in full view of them all.

MARK 2:10-12

KEY APPLICATION

We may pray for Jesus to heal today according to His will.

32

NICODEMUS'S SECOND BIRTH

Looking to Jesus in Faith

THEME

Jesus teaches the necessity of the second birth.

PASSAGE/REFERENCE

John 3:1-21

BACKGROUND

Though Jesus was very popular among the common people, many of the religious leaders, scholars, and scribes were skeptical of Him or even opposed Him. But some were genuinely interested in His message, as we'll see in this story. As Jesus was speaking to an expert in the law of Moses, He used a story from the life of Moses to describe why He came. Long ago, when God's people had been traveling through the wilderness, they complained against God, so He sent venomous snakes among them. Then He told Moses to put a bronze figure of a serpent on a pole and hold it up. In order to escape the curse and be healed, people who had been bitten had to look up at the bronze serpent. If they did not, they would die.

PRE-STORY DIALOGUE

One of the biggest questions we have as human beings is "What happens after I die?" Why? Because we were created with eternal longings in our hearts. Early and often in Jesus' ministry, He explained how we can have eternal life. One of the people He told was a religious leader who came to Him in secret. This leader knew God's Word, the law that had been given through Moses. But he didn't know the deep things of God's Spirit, and much of what Jesus said surprised him. As you listen to his story, think of how you might have reacted if you had heard Jesus' words for the first time. Would you have understood? Would you have believed?

TELL THE STORY

Nicodemus was a Pharisee, an expert in Jewish scripture and law, and a member of the Jewish ruling council. He came to Jesus one night and confessed that some of his fellow leaders knew that Jesus had been sent by God. "No one could perform the miraculous signs you are doing if God were not with him," he said.

Jesus told him, "No one can see the kingdom of God unless he is born again." Nicodemus didn't know what Jesus meant. He asked how someone could be born when he is old. But Jesus was talking about a different kind of birth. He said that anyone who wasn't "born of water and the Spirit" could not enter the kingdom of God. He explained that there's a difference between a birth in the flesh and a spiritual birth. "You should not be surprised at my saying, 'You must be born again.' The wind blows wherever it pleases. You hear its sound, but you cannot tell where it comes from or where it is going. So it is with everyone born of the Spirit."

Nicodemus still didn't understand. Jesus pointed out that people speak only of what they know about—the things they have experienced—yet Nicodemus, a teacher of Israel, clearly did not understand the Second Birth. Jesus assured Nicodemus He was teaching the things of God—the truths of heaven. He even said He went up to heaven and had come down from heaven. Just as Moses had lifted up a snake in the desert so that people under a curse could look at it and be spared, so must Jesus be lifted up so people could look to Him and have eternal life.

"For God so loved the world that he gave his one and only Son, that whoever believes in him shall not perish but have eternal life," Jesus said. He promised that whoever believes in Him would not be condemned. God didn't send His Son into the world to condemn it; no, God sent His Son into the world to save it. But those who don't believe in Him are condemned because they have rejected God's one and only Son. This Son, Jesus, is the light who has come into the world. Some people love darkness more than light because it keeps their evil deeds hidden. But those who live by the truth come to the light.

DISCUSSION QUESTIONS

- Who was Nicodemus? What did he say he believed about Jesus?
- When did he come to see Jesus? Why do you think he came at that time of day?
- What did Jesus tell Nicodemus he must do to see the kingdom of God? What kind of birth was He talking about?
- What do you think Jesus meant by being "born of the Spirit"? How well did Nicodemus understand this?
- What was Jesus referring to when He said, "The wind blows wherever it pleases"? How do you think this applies to someone who is born of the Spirit?
- How can we be born of the Spirit?
- In what ways is Jesus like the bronze serpent that Moses held up for Israel? What did Jesus say would happen for those who look to Him and believe in Him?

- What did God's love for the world cause Him to do?
- Why did Jesus come into the world: to condemn it or save it? What do we have to do in order to not be condemned? In this story, what are the benefits of believing in Jesus?
- Who is the light that came into the world? Why do some people choose to remain in darkness? Who comes into the light?
- What do light and darkness represent in this story?

QUESTIONS FOR FAMILIES/CHILDREN

- When did Nicodemus come to visit Jesus? Why do you think he came then?
- What did Jesus tell Nicodemus he would have to do in order to see God's kingdom?
- Did Nicodemus understand what Jesus meant? How can we tell whether or not he understood?
- What do you think Jesus meant about being born again? Does it mean being born in a physical body again? What kind of birth is it?
- How does God feel about the world He made and the people in it? What did He do for those He loves?
- What do we need to do to have life forever with God?
- Who is the light that came into the world? In what ways can we show that we love truth?

MEMORY VERSES

I tell you the truth, no one can see the kingdom of God unless he is born again.

JOHN 3:3

For God so loved the world that he gave his one and only Son, that whoever believes in him shall not perish but have eternal life. For God did not send his Son into the world to condemn the world, but to save the world through him.

JOHN 3:16-17

KEY APPLICATION

We must be born again.

33

WOMAN AT THE WELL

A Different Kind of Drink

THEME

Jesus offers refreshing forgiveness.

PASSAGE/REFERENCE

John 4:4-42

BACKGROUND

Jews and Samaritans didn't get along. Many Jews despised Samaritans as a corrupt race of half-breeds (a mixture of Jew and Gentile blood) who had fallen away from the true faith and rejected Jerusalem as the true center of worship. Some Jews would refuse to pass through Samaritan territory when traveling, even if that was the most direct route. But Jesus refused to be governed by ethnic and cultural differences. He showed Samaritans in a positive light (the Good Samaritan and a Samaritan leper who gave thanks, for example); in this session's story, He took time to minister to one needy Samaritan in particular.

PRE-STORY DIALOGUE

As often happened when Jesus had a conversation with people, they spoke on one level while He spoke on another. He always focused on a person's deepest needs and tried to help him or her see deeper spiritual truth. In this story, listen for the different levels of the conversation. What did they talk about on the surface? What was the deeper meaning of their words? How did this normal conversation turn into a life-changing encounter for the woman?

TELL THE STORY

Jesus and His disciples were traveling through Samaria and came to a town called Sychar. The famous landmark, Jacob's well, was there. Jesus was tired from the journey, so He sat down there around noon. The disciples had gone into the town to buy some food.

A Samaritan woman came to get some water from the well, and Jesus asked if she would give Him a drink. This surprised her. "You are a Jew and I am a Samaritan woman," she said. "How can you ask me for a drink?" She said this because Jews and Samaritans didn't get along at all. Jesus told her that if she really knew who she was talking to, she would be the one asking for a drink—a drink of true life.

The woman thought Jesus was talking about water and asked Him how He could possibly give her a drink. He didn't have anything He could use to get water out of this deep well. Where would He get this "living water"? She asked if He was greater than Jacob—a reminder that He was at one of Samaria's most important landmarks, the well where Jacob, the father of Israel, got water for his family and flocks. But Jesus told her that the water in this well was just normal water. Everyone who drank it would get thirsty again later. "Whoever drinks the water I give him will never thirst," He told her. "The water I give him will become in him a spring of water welling up to eternal life."

The woman wanted some of this amazing water. She asked Jesus to give her some so she wouldn't have to keep coming to the well every day. But Jesus changed the subject. "Go, call your husband and come back." She had to tell him that she had no husband. Jesus surprised her by telling her He already knew that. In fact, He told her that she had had five husbands and was now with a man who wasn't her husband.

"I can see that you are a prophet," she answered. So she asked Him the kind of question one would ask a prophet. The Samaritans worshipped on a nearby mountain (Mount Gerizim), and the Jews insisted that Jerusalem was the true place of worship. She asked who was right.

Jesus didn't answer her question directly. He explained that a time was coming when the place of worship wouldn't be the issue—that the Father would be worshipped neither on Mount Gerizim nor in Jerusalem alone. He told her that the Samaritans worshipped in ignorance and that salvation came through the Jews. But true worshippers, He said, will worship the Father in spirit and in truth. "They are the kind of worshipers the Father seeks. God is spirit, and his worshipers must worship in spirit and in truth."

The woman told Jesus she knew the Messiah was coming. "When he comes, he will explain everything to us," she said. Jesus answered, "I who speak to you am he." At that moment, the disciples returned. They were really surprised to see Jesus talking with a woman, but none of them asked Him why He was doing something so unusual. Then the woman left her water jar behind and went back to the town and told people to come out and see Jesus. She asked them if He could be the Christ, as He had told her everything about her past. So they came out to see what was going on.

As they were coming, the disciples tried to get Jesus to eat something, but He told them He had been eating another kind of food that they didn't know about. They asked each other who could have been bringing food to Him. But Jesus said, "My food . . . is to do the will of him who sent me and to finish his work." Jesus explained that just as physical crops ripen and get ready for harvest, so do spiritual crops.

"Open your eyes and look at the fields!" He told them. "They are ripe for harvest." Jesus explained that a lot of people had done the hard work of sowing spiritual seeds among these people, but now it was time for His disciples to reap the spiritual harvest. Many of the Samaritans who came out to see Jesus believed in Him because of the woman's testimony. So He stayed there two more days—they pleaded with Him to tell them more—and when they had heard His words for themselves, many there became believers. They exclaimed, "We know that this man really is the Savior of the world."

DISCUSSION QUESTIONS

- Where did Jesus stop for a rest on His journey? What was noteworthy about this place?
- Who did Jesus meet at the well? What did He ask her to do?
- Why was the woman surprised that Jesus asked her a question? What did she say? How did Jesus respond to her?
- What kind of water did the woman think Jesus was talking about? What kind of water was He really talking about? What do you think He meant by "living water"?
- According to Jesus, what would happen for those who drank this kind of water? How satisfying would it be? What would occur inside of them?
- Did the woman want this kind of water? How did she respond? How would you have responded to a man who described this kind of water to you?
- What did Jesus tell the woman to do when she asked for His living water? What did she have to admit to Him?
- What did Jesus say that made the woman think He was a prophet? How much do you think God knows about our lives? How closely do you think He watches over us?
- When she discovered that Jesus was a prophet, what did she ask Him?

- How directly did Jesus answer her question? What did He say about worship? What kind of worshipper does God seek? What do you think it means to worship in spirit and in truth?
- Why were the disciples surprised when they returned and saw Jesus talking to the woman?
- What did the woman do when Jesus told her He was the Messiah?
- When the disciples tried to get Jesus to eat, what did He say about food? What do you think He meant?
- What did Jesus say about the fields and the harvest? What kind of harvest was He talking about? What was happening with the people in town as He talked about this harvest? What role do those who follow Jesus play in His harvest?
- How did the townspeople who came out to see Jesus respond to Him? What did they ask Him to do? What was the result of His ministry there?
- How would you describe the conversation Jesus had with the woman? In what ways did He get to the real issues and focus on the woman's real needs? Do you see any evidence in the story that she received what He promised?
- What kind of water would quench your desires? How do you think Jesus would tell you to get that water? What do you need to do to find satisfaction and fulfillment in life?

QUESTIONS FOR FAMILIES/CHILDREN

- Where did Jesus stop when He was traveling? Who did He meet there? What did He ask this person for?
- Why did this woman think it was strange for Jesus to ask her a question? What did He tell her she would do if she really knew who she was talking to?
- What kind of water did the woman think Jesus was talking about? What kind of water was He really talking about? What

do you think He meant by "living water"?

- What happens to somebody who drinks Jesus' living water? How do you think we can get that kind of water?
- How much did Jesus know about this woman's past? How much do you think God knows about our lives?
- What kind of worshipper is God looking for? Is He picky about where we worship or what time we worship? What does He want our hearts to be like when we worship?
- Who did Jesus tell the woman that He really was? Did she believe Him? Where did she go when He told her this?
- What did Jesus say His "food" was? What do you think He meant?
- What kind of harvest was Jesus talking about when the townspeople were coming to Him? Did these people believe Him when He taught them?

MEMORY VERSES

Whoever drinks the water I give him will never thirst. Indeed, the water I give him will become in him a spring of water welling up to eternal life.

JOHN 4:14

A time is coming and has now come when the true worshipers will worship the Father in spirit and truth, for they are the kind of worshipers the Father seeks. God is spirit, and his worshipers must worship in spirit and in truth.

JOHN 4:23-24

KEY APPLICATION

We may experience Jesus' refreshing forgiveness today.

34

STORM STILLED

Fear, Faith, and the Power of Jesus

THEME

Jesus shows His power over nature.

PASSAGE/REFERENCE

Mark 4:35–41

BACKGROUND

Jesus frequently used the Sea of Galilee as a classroom for His disciples. That's where He helped them catch a multitude of fish in one of our earlier stories. That's where He walked on water. And that's where He taught them a lesson about His power over nature, as we'll see in this session. Sudden squalls were common on this sea—they still are today—and they could often be very violent and life threatening. But this sort of storm was a perfect situation for Jesus to teach a lesson about fear and faith.

PRE-STORY DIALOGUE

In the midst of difficult circumstances, we often pray to God. Sometimes we wonder if He's *able* to meet our needs, but usually we question whether He's *willing* to do so. In this story, we'll see that Jesus was both willing and able to help His disciples—and even when they thought He didn't care, He really did. As you listen, think about any storms that might be going on in your life. Does Jesus want to intervene in them? If so, how? Now see how He responded one day when His disciples panicked.

TELL THE STORY

After a day of teaching at the lake, Jesus told His disciples that it was time to go to the other side. They left the crowds behind, got in the boat, and set sail for the far shore along with some other boats. Suddenly, a furious storm came up and endangered the boat. Waves were crashing over it and filling it with water, but Jesus was in the back of the boat sleeping through all of the chaos.

The disciples finally woke Jesus and asked Him, "Don't you care if we drown?" Jesus got up and told the wind and the waves to be quiet. Suddenly, the wind died down and the waves stopped crashing. Everything was calm.

Jesus turned to His disciples and asked, "Why are you so afraid? Do you still have no faith?" But they were terrified by what they had just seen. They asked each other who this man could possibly be. "Even the wind and waves obey him!" they marveled.

DISCUSSION QUESTIONS

- Why were Jesus and the disciples in a boat? Who decided that they should go?
- What happened when they were out at sea? How serious was the situation?
- What did the disciples think about their situation? What was Jesus doing while the disciples were dealing with the crisis?
- When Jesus woke up, what did the disciples accuse Him of?

Do you think He cared about their circumstances? Why or why not?

- How worried was Jesus about this situation? What did He do to fix it? What happened when He spoke?
- What questions did Jesus ask the disciples? What did He expect them to think and believe?
- If you were one of the disciples, how do you think you would have answered Him? How did they respond? Why do you think they were terrified?
- Does Jesus promise that we won't have storms in our lives? What does He expect us to think and believe when we're going through a crisis?
- Do you ever feel as if God doesn't care about what's going on in your life — that maybe He's asleep during your crisis? What does this story say about that?
- What storm is going on in your life right now? How do you think Jesus might want to deal with it? What does He want your attitude to be in this situation?
- What does this story show us about Jesus' authority? What does it show us about His compassion for those who love Him? What does it show us about how to deal with fear in our lives?

QUESTIONS FOR FAMILIES/CHILDREN

- What happened when Jesus and the disciples were in a boat out at sea? Were they in danger? How serious was their situation?
- What was Jesus doing while this was going on? Do you think He cared about what the disciples were going through? Did they know He cared?
- How did Jesus fix the problem? What happened when He spoke?

- What did Jesus ask the disciples? Did He want them to be afraid or to trust Him? Why?
- When you're afraid of situations in your life, what do you think Jesus wants you to do? Do you think you can trust Him to help?
- What kind of problems do you go through that you would like Jesus to help you with? Do you think Jesus cares about those problems? In what ways do you think He might want to help you?

MEMORY VERSE

Why are you so afraid? Do you still have no faith?

Mark 4:40

KEY APPLICATION

Jesus is Lord over all creation, which we must honor as His.

35

CROWD FILLED
The Bread That Satisfies

THEME

Jesus shows His power to meet human needs.

PASSAGE/REFERENCE

John 6
Focus: John 6:1-5, 24-40

BACKGROUND

Crowds often followed Jesus for days at a time, and sometimes that meant being out in the countryside away from their homes. Whenever this was the case, Jesus had compassion on those who had come to hear Him. On at least a couple of occasions, as a day of teaching and healings drew to a close, the people were hungry and too far from home to get food. This wasn't a major hardship — they wouldn't have starved by any means — but Jesus wanted them to be nourished in every way during their time with Him.

PRE-STORY DIALOGUE

What do you hunger for? What are your deepest, most persistent needs?

Whatever they are, we've seen how Jesus can meet them. But as is often the case, Jesus gave a physical picture of His spiritual blessings. That's what He did with the woman at the well—He quenched her spiritual thirst with living water. And He will do that with us, too. As you listen to the story, know that Jesus wants to meet all of your needs, both physical and spiritual. Think about the many ways His miracle of multiplying food might apply to your life.

TELL THE STORY

Jesus was on the far shore of the Sea of Galilee, and crowds were following Him because they had seen Him heal so many people. He and the disciples went up on a mountain and sat down, and when the crowd followed, Jesus asked Philip if there was anywhere to buy bread for all these people. (He was really just testing Philip because He already knew He was going to do a miracle.) Philip answered that it would be impossible to feed so many people; even if they saved up for eight months, it would be barely enough for everyone to have one bite. But Andrew, Simon Peter's brother, pointed out a boy with five loaves of bread and two small fish. He knew it wasn't much, but it was at least something.

Jesus told the disciples to have the people sit down. So all five thousand men—and who knows how many women and children—sat down in the grassy fields. Jesus took the boy's loaves, thanked God for them, and started passing out portions to everyone there. He did the same with the fish. And somehow everyone had as much as they wanted.

After they finished eating, Jesus told the disciples to gather up the leftovers—and there was enough to fill twelve baskets! The people began to talk, saying Jesus must surely be the prophet everyone was expecting to come, the one who could conquer their enemies. But Jesus could see that the crowd wanted Him to be their king, so He went off to a mountain by Himself.

Later, after Jesus had sent the disciples off to the other side of the lake in a boat, and after He had come to them walking on the water, the crowd who had been fed went searching for Him. When they found Him on the other side of the lake, they asked Him how He got there. Jesus didn't answer their question, but He did tell them He knew why they were searching: He had satisfied their hunger. "Do not work for food that spoils," He told them, "but for food that endures to eternal life, which the Son of Man will give you."

The people asked Jesus how they could do the works of God. He explained that "the work of God" was to believe in Him. Then they asked Him for a sign. How would He prove it to them? After all, their forefathers had eaten manna from heaven, a visible miracle that all could see, proving that Moses was the man God had sent. What sign could He show them?

Jesus assured them that Moses had not given bread to Israel in the wilderness; it was God, the Father of Jesus, who had done that. In fact, Jesus pointed out that *He* was the bread that comes down from heaven. He would give life to the world.

The people wanted this kind of bread. Jesus told them, "I am the bread of life. He who comes to me will never go hungry, and he who believes in me will never be thirsty." Jesus went on to explain that even though many had seen Him and still not believed, the Father would give Him many people, and He would never drive them away. He said He came down from heaven to do God's will, not His own—and God's will was to give people to the Son, none of whom would be lost and all of whom would be raised up in the end. Everyone who looks to Jesus and believes in Him will have eternal life and be raised up from death.

DISCUSSION QUESTIONS

- What did Jesus ask Philip when He saw all the people coming up the mountain? Why did He ask this?

- How did Philip answer? What did Philip think about Jesus' question?
- What did Andrew say about the situation? Why do you think Andrew even mentioned such a small amount of food? Who showed more faith in this situation: Philip or Andrew?
- How many people were there? What did Jesus do after Andrew answered Him? If you were one of the disciples, what would you have thought when they started passing out food?
- How much did everyone get to eat? How much was left over? Why do you think Jesus wanted the miracle to produce more than enough?
- What did the people want to do with Jesus when they saw this miracle? How did Jesus respond? Why?
- What kind of food did Jesus say to work for? What do you think He meant?
- What did Jesus say was "the work of God"?
- What did the people want as proof that Jesus was who He said He was? What Old Testament story did they refer to as the kind of sign they wanted?
- How did Jesus respond to their request? In what ways did He compare Himself with the Old Testament miracle they remembered? In what ways was He better than that miracle?
- What or who is the bread of life? What happens to those who eat this bread? What do you think it means to eat the bread of life?
- What promises did Jesus make to those who believe in Him?
- What does this story teach us about Jesus' desire to meet human needs?
- What does this story tell us about how God uses what we offer Him? How much of doing His work is our part? How much is His part?

QUESTIONS FOR FAMILIES/CHILDREN

- What need did the crowd have that Jesus wanted to meet? Why do you think He wanted to meet their need?
- What did Jesus ask Philip? What did Philip think about the idea? What did Andrew say about it? Who do you think showed more faith: Philip or Andrew?
- What did Jesus do with the five loaves and two fish? How many people did He feed? How much was left over?
- Why did Jesus want to be by Himself after this miracle? What did the people want to do with Him?
- What kind of work does Jesus want us to do? Why do you think God is pleased when we believe in Jesus?
- What food did Jesus compare Himself to? Who is the bread of life? What happens to people who "eat" this food?
- What promises did Jesus give those who believe in Him? What does He do for them? In what ways does He promise to take care of them?

MEMORY VERSES

The work of God is this: to believe in the one he has sent.

JOHN 6:29

Then Jesus declared, "I am the bread of life. He who comes to me will never go hungry, and he who believes in me will never be thirsty."

JOHN 6:35

KEY APPLICATION

Every need we experience is known—and may be met—by Him.

36

LAZARUS RAISED

Victory over Our Worst Enemy

THEME

Jesus shows His power over death.

PASSAGE/REFERENCE

John 11:1-45

BACKGROUND

Jesus had a close friendship with a family in Bethany: a brother and sisters named Lazarus, Mary, and Martha. On one occasion, He was teaching in their home when a conflict arose between Martha, who was busy with hospitality, and Mary, who was sitting and listening to Jesus teach. Jesus commended Mary's desire to learn from Him (see Luke 10:38-42). Some time later, their brother Lazarus was very sick, so Mary and Martha naturally sent word to their miracle-working friend.

PRE-STORY DIALOGUE

What do you fear more than anything else? If you're like most people, the knowledge that we will die causes a lot of anxiety and dread. As you listen to this story, consider what it shows us about how Jesus overcomes our fear of death. What authority does He have over it? What promises does He give us about life after death? As you think about these things, ask yourself how our lives can change when we no longer fear death and instead look forward to eternal life.

TELL THE STORY

Lazarus, one of Jesus' friends from Bethany, was very sick. His sisters, Mary and Martha, sent word to Jesus to see if He could come help them or even heal Lazarus — "the one you love," they reminded Him. When Jesus got the message, He told His disciples that Lazarus's sickness would not end in death. In fact, God would get glory from it. But Jesus stayed where He was for two more days.

Finally, Jesus headed back toward Judea, where Lazarus was — even though some of the religious leaders had tried to kill Him last time He was there. But Jesus didn't let the disciples talk Him out of it. He was walking by the "light" God had given Him and knew it was okay to go. Jesus told His disciples that Lazarus had fallen asleep and He was going to wake him up. The disciples didn't understand; they thought Jesus was talking about natural sleep. But Jesus knew Lazarus had already died, and He told them plainly. He even said He was glad He wasn't there when it happened. This would be an occasion for the disciples to learn about faith and believe in Jesus even more. (Thomas, however, thought it was a dangerous trip and figured they might get killed.)

When they arrived, Jesus found out that Lazarus had already been in the tomb four days. Martha went out to meet Him, but Mary stayed inside. Martha wondered why Jesus hadn't come sooner. "If you had been here, my brother would not have died," she said. Still, she had faith that Jesus would do something good. Jesus assured her that Lazarus would rise again. Martha thought He was talking about the resurrection at the last day. But Jesus told her, "I am the resurrection and the life. He who believes in me will live, even though he dies; and whoever lives and believes in me will never die." He asked her if she believed this. She said she did—and that she believed He was the Christ, the Son of God.

Martha went back inside and told Mary that Jesus was asking for her, so Mary got up and quickly went to see Him. Jesus was still outside the village where Martha had met Him. Some of the people who had come to visit the family saw her get up quickly and thought she was going to the tomb to mourn, so they followed her. When Mary saw Jesus, she said the same thing as her sister: "If you had been here, my brother would not have died." When Jesus saw her crying, along with everyone who had followed her, He grieved with them. He asked where Lazarus was buried, and they told Him to come and see. And Jesus cried, too.

When the people saw Jesus crying, some thought it was because He loved Lazarus so much. Others wondered why a man who could do miracles didn't do anything to save His friend. But Jesus, still deeply moved, came to the tomb, a cave with a stone blocking the entrance. Jesus told them to take away the stone.

Martha protested. She said Lazarus would have a bad odor by now because he had been buried for four days. But Jesus said, "Did I not tell you that if you believed, you would see the glory of God?" And they took away the stone.

Jesus looked up and prayed. He thanked God for hearing Him. (He knew God always heard Him, of course, but He prayed out loud so everyone else could hear and believe in Him.) Then Jesus called out in a loud voice, "Lazarus, come out!" Lazarus came out, still wrapped in burial linen and with a cloth covering his face. Jesus told the people there to take off Lazarus's grave clothes and let him go. Many people who saw this put their faith in Jesus.

DISCUSSION QUESTIONS

- What was the relationship between Jesus and Mary, Martha, and Lazarus? How did Mary and Martha describe Jesus' attitude toward Lazarus?

- What did Jesus tell the disciples when He heard about Lazarus's sickness? How did He say it would end?
- What did Jesus do when He heard that Lazarus was sick? Did He go to him right away? Why or why not?
- How did Jesus describe Lazarus's condition to the disciples? What did He say He was going to do for Lazarus? What did the disciples think He was talking about?
- Did Jesus know what had happened to Lazarus? Why did He say He was glad He wasn't there?
- Why were Thomas and some of the other disciples concerned about going back to Judea? Why do you think Jesus went anyway?
- How long had Lazarus been in the tomb?
- Who came out to meet Jesus first? What did she say? What did she believe about life after death? Do you think she knew what Jesus was about to do? Why or why not? What did Jesus tell her to do?
- How did Jesus describe Himself to Martha? What did He say about those who believe in Him?
- What did Mary say when she came out to see Jesus? How did Jesus respond to her and to everyone around her who was crying?
- What does Jesus' reaction tell us about His compassion for us? Why do you think He grieved if He already knew He was going to raise Lazarus?
- What did Jesus say Martha would see if she believed? In what way did she see this?
- Why did Jesus pray out loud? What happened when He called out to Lazarus? How did the people react to this miracle?
- What does this story tell us about Jesus' authority over death? What does it tell us about our own life after death? How can we have eternal life?
- How does this story comfort us when we grieve those who

have died? How does it change our perspective as we live and look toward the future?

QUESTIONS FOR FAMILIES/CHILDREN

- Who is the friend Jesus loved in this story? What happened to this friend?
- Did Jesus go see this friend when He found out the news about his sickness? Why or why not?
- What did Jesus tell the disciples He was going to do? How was this miracle like waking up somebody who is asleep?
- Was Lazarus still alive when Jesus arrived in Bethany? What did his sisters tell Jesus? What had they wanted Jesus to do?
- If people believe in Jesus, what happens to them when they die? Do they remain dead, or will they live again?
- Why do you think Jesus cried when He saw Mary and her friends crying? How do you think He feels when we cry?
- What happened when Jesus prayed and then called out to Lazarus with a loud voice? What did Lazarus do?
- What would you have thought if you had been there? Would you have believed in Jesus when you saw Lazarus come out?
- Does this story help you not to feel afraid? Why or why not? Which has more power: death or Jesus?

MEMORY VERSES

I am the resurrection and the life. He who believes in me will live, even though he dies; and whoever lives and believes in me will never die.

JOHN 11:25-26

KEY APPLICATION

We need not fear death because Jesus has overcome it.

37

ZACCHAEUS PRAISED

A Life-Changing Encounter

THEME

Jesus praises repentant sinners.

PASSAGE/REFERENCE

Luke 19:1-10

BACKGROUND

Jews hated tax collectors. They were considered traitors because they were usually fellow Jews who chose to serve the hated Roman government in order to make money. In fact, they often made more money than they should have; Romans gave them authority to collect as much extra as they needed for themselves. When Jesus called a tax collector—Levi (or Matthew)—to be one of His disciples, many were surprised that He would associate with such a sinner. And when He saw a tax collector in the crowd at Jericho and then invited Himself to the sinner's home for a meal, many were very offended.

PRE-STORY DIALOGUE

Do you think Jesus loves most people but only puts up with you? Surprisingly, a lot of people feel this way, usually because they don't feel worthy of His love. As you listen to this story, notice the kind of person Jesus chose to spend time with. Notice also how spending time with Jesus changed this man's life. Ask yourself if you want this kind of relationship with Jesus—and see what qualifies a person to have it.

TELL THE STORY

Jesus was traveling through Jericho, and crowds were surrounding Him as He passed through the town. A man named Zacchaeus was there. This high-ranking tax collector was very wealthy and very short. He couldn't get a glimpse of Jesus because he couldn't see over the crowd, so he ran ahead to where he thought Jesus would pass by and climbed a sycamore tree to have a good view.

When Jesus got to that spot, he noticed Zacchaeus and looked up at him. "Zacchaeus, come down immediately," He said. "I must stay at your house today." So Zacchaeus climbed down the tree and gladly welcomed Jesus into his home.

Many of the people who saw this started to grumble about it. They knew Zacchaeus's reputation. Many of them may have felt more worthy to visit with Jesus than Zacchaeus was. "He has gone to be the guest of a 'sinner,'" they said. But Zacchaeus told Jesus he would give half his possessions to the poor and give back everything he had ever gained by cheating people. In fact, he would pay them back four times the amount.

Jesus called Zacchaeus a "son of Abraham"—a true Jew—and declared that salvation had come to his house that day: "For the Son of Man came to seek and to save what was lost."

DISCUSSION QUESTIONS

- How does this story describe Zacchaeus? How do you think the people of Jericho felt about this tax collector? How had he become so wealthy?
- Why couldn't Zacchaeus see Jesus? Why do you think he wanted to?
- What did Zacchaeus do in order to see Jesus? What does this demonstrate about his desire or his faith? How desperately do you want to see Jesus? In what ways do you need to persevere to know Him better?
- What did Jesus say when He saw Zacchaeus? What did He tell Zacchaeus to do? What did He want to do with Zacchaeus?
- How did Zacchaeus respond to Jesus' request? How did other people respond to it?
- Do you see any kind of person as the type Jesus would want nothing to do with? What does this story say about that?
- What did Zacchaeus decide to do after talking with Jesus? How was this different than his life before he met Jesus? Had his heart changed? How can we tell if it did?
- Do you think Zacchaeus earned forgiveness by giving away his money? Why or why not? According to other stories we've heard recently, what does someone need to do to be saved? In what way did Zacchaeus's repentance demonstrate what he truly believed?
- What does God want us to do when we've wronged someone? How can we try to make things right?
- What did Jesus say about Zacchaeus's household? What did He call Zacchaeus?
- What did Jesus say about His mission? Why did He come? Who is He seeking?
- According to this story, who is qualified to receive Jesus? What happens when someone does?

QUESTIONS FOR FAMILIES/CHILDREN

- Did people like Zacchaeus? Why or why not?
- Do you think Jesus liked him? Why?
- Why couldn't Zacchaeus see Jesus? What did he do in order to see Him?
- What did Jesus do when He saw Zacchaeus? How do you think Zacchaeus felt about having Jesus over to his house? How did the other people feel about it?
- What did Zacchaeus want to do with his money after he met Jesus? Why do you think he changed his mind about his money? What do you think had happened in his heart?
- What do you think God wants us to do when we've done wrong things to people?
- What kind of person did Jesus come to help and to save? Was Zacchaeus that kind of person?
- Do you think there's any kind of person Jesus wouldn't want to help? Why or why not?

MEMORY VERSE

The Son of Man came to seek and to save what was lost.

LUKE 19:10

KEY APPLICATION

As we repent and make restitution toward others, God is pleased.

38

DEMONIAC DELIVERED

The Good News of Freedom

THEME

Jesus alone can deliver from Satan's power.

PASSAGE/REFERENCE

Mark 5:1-20

BACKGROUND

Jews did not expect the Messiah to have much to do with Gentiles. But even though Jesus did most of His ministry among Jews, He sometimes found greater faith or greater opportunities for ministry among Gentiles. In this story, Jesus encounters a man in pagan territory who not only was probably a Gentile but also lived among tombs, was tormented by demons, and was surrounded by pigs. In Jewish eyes, this was a very unlikely place for God to work.

PRE-STORY DIALOGUE

Many people feel enslaved. We can be oppressed by serious addictions, confined by harmful relationship or behavior patterns, or even just trapped by our circumstances. And sometimes Satan directly attacks us. In this story, we encounter a man who suffered from the worst kind of enslavement. He was tormented by demons and forced to live among graves. As you listen, ask yourself: If Jesus could free someone like that, is there anything in your life too difficult for Him to overcome? Can any power come against you that is more powerful than Him? Be encouraged as you hear how Jesus radically changed one man's life.

TELL THE STORY

Jesus and the disciples went to the far side of the lake to the region of the Gerasenes, an area populated with non-Jews who had many pagan beliefs. When Jesus got out of the boat, a man with an evil spirit came out from the nearby tombs. Though many had tried to chain him up, he had been living in the graveyard because no chains could hold him. He was too violent and strong to live with people. So he spent all his time at the tombs and in the hills, and he would often yell and cut himself.

When this man saw Jesus, he ran up to Him and fell on his knees. He screamed, "What do you want with me, Jesus, Son of the Most High God?" He begged Jesus not to torture him because Jesus had been ordering the evil spirit to come out of him.

Jesus asked the demon, "What is your name?" But instead of a name, a spirit only told him that there were many spirits in the man—as many as in a Roman legion of soldiers. They kept begging Jesus not to send them away. Instead, they pleaded for Him to send them into the pigs on a nearby hill. Finally Jesus agreed to that, and as soon as the evil spirits left the man and went into the pigs, the whole herd of two thousand ran down the steep hill into the lake and drowned.

The pig farmers ran off to tell everyone in town what had happened, and many people came out to see. When they arrived, the demon-possessed man was sitting there in his right mind. Those who had witnessed the incident explained everything that had happened. The people were afraid and begged Jesus to leave.

As Jesus was getting into the boat, the man who had been tormented by demons pleaded to go with him, but Jesus told him no. He sent the man back home to tell his whole family what God had done and how merciful God had been. So the man went all around the region telling people what Jesus did, and everyone was amazed.

DISCUSSION QUESTIONS

- What kind of man did Jesus encounter on the other side of the lake? How is he described? What kind of torment did he experience? How much hope did the community have for him?
- Why did he come to Jesus? What had Jesus been saying to him? What did he scream at Jesus?
- What question did Jesus ask this man? What answer did He get?
- Why do you think the demons wanted to be sent into pigs rather than simply cast out? Did Jesus grant their request?
- How many pigs were there? What happened when the spirits entered the pigs? How did the pig farmers react to this?
- What happened when the townspeople heard about the incident? When they came out to see Jesus, what was the demon-possessed man doing? How had he changed?
- Why do you think the people were afraid when they realized what had happened? Why did they ask Jesus to leave?
- What did the man who had been delivered want to do? What did Jesus tell him to do? How did he carry out Jesus' instructions? What was the result of his ministry?

- What does this story teach us about Jesus' compassion for people in pain? What does this story tell us about the kind of freedom He wants us to have?
- What does this story tell us about Jesus' authority over the Enemy? How does His authority over Satan apply to our lives? In what ways can Satan affect us? What can we ask and trust Jesus to do when we are under spiritual attack?
- What does this story tell us about who is qualified to give their testimony about Jesus? What were this man's qualifications? What are ours?

QUESTIONS FOR FAMILIES/CHILDREN

- What kind of man did Jesus encounter when He got out of the boat? What was this man like? What kinds of things did he do?
- Why did this man act so strangely? What was his problem? Who was controlling him?
- What did the spirits inside the man ask Jesus to do? What did Jesus order them to do?
- What happened when the spirits left the man and entered the pigs? What would you have thought if you had seen this?
- What was the man like after Jesus did this? How did the townspeople react when they heard the story and saw the man? Why do you think they were afraid?
- What did the man want to do for Jesus? What did Jesus tell him to do?
- What does this story teach us about Jesus' compassion for people with big problems? What does it teach us about His power over evil?

MEMORY VERSE

Go home to your family and tell them how much the Lord has done for you, and how he has had mercy on you.

MARK 5:19

KEY APPLICATION

If we're attacked by Satan, Jesus has power to free us.

39

LEARNING TO PRAY

Priorities, Promises, and Persistence

THEME

Jesus teaches how to pray.

PASSAGE/REFERENCE

Matthew 6:5-13; Luke 11:1-13

BACKGROUND

The disciples could tell that Jesus had an unusual prayer life. Sometimes He would go off at night to pray, and they would come looking for Him later. And when He prayed, things happened: God answered. Miracles occurred. They wanted to know the secret of how to communicate with God as Jesus did.

PRE-STORY DIALOGUE

Do you ever feel like your prayers go no further than the ceiling? Or that your prayers don't have the power God's Word says they should have? Or that other people experience more answers than you do? The disciples seemed to feel this way, too, so they asked Jesus how to pray.

As you listen to His answer, see if He emphasized the same aspects of prayer that you do when you pray. How closely do your prayers line up with His? How do your attitudes about prayer fit the attitudes He describes?

TELL THE STORY

One day after Jesus finished praying, one of His disciples asked Him to teach them how to pray. After all, John the Baptist taught his disciples about prayer; Jesus' disciples wanted to learn too. So Jesus gave them an example of what prayer should include:

> *Our Father in heaven,*
> *hallowed be your name,*
> *your kingdom come,*
> *your will be done*
> *   on earth as it is in heaven.*
> *Give us today our daily bread.*
> *Forgive us our debts,*
> *   as we also have forgiven our debtors.*
> *And lead us not into temptation,*
> *but deliver us from the evil one.*

Jesus told His disciples not to pray like hypocrites—in other words, don't try to impress other people or to be seen as "spiritual." People who do that already have their reward: the opinions of others. Real prayer is the kind you would do if you were in private. In fact, that's often where the most effective prayer takes place—behind closed doors. God sees what is done in secret and rewards it. Jesus also said not to go on and on with repetitive words, as if getting God's attention depends on the number of words you speak. He already knows what we need even before we ask.

Luke 11:5

→Then Jesus told a story to illustrate prayer. Imagine a traveler on a long journey arriving at the home of his host late at night, He said. The host has nothing to feed his visitor, and not wanting to be rude, he goes to a neighbor at midnight to ask for some bread. But the neighbor has already turned off the lights and gone to bed. "Don't bother me," he says. "The door is already locked, and my children are with me in bed. I can't get up and give you anything." But the man keeps on knocking persistently. And because of his boldness, the neighbor finally gets up and gives him as much as he needs.

Jesus said the point was this: "Ask and it will be given to you; seek and you will find; knock and the door will be opened to you." In other words, prayer *will* be answered, one way or another.

And the answer will be good. Jesus pointed out that no good father gives his child a snake when the son really asked for a fish. No father would give a scorpion instead of an egg. So if imperfect human fathers would give good gifts to their children, certainly God the Father would give good gifts to His children. And He'll especially give the Holy Spirit to anyone who asks Him.

DISCUSSION QUESTIONS

- What did the disciples ask Jesus? Why do you think they wanted to know?
- In Jesus' model prayer, how did He address God? Why do you think He wants us to address God this way?
- What are the first requests in this prayer focused on? Do you think most people focus first on God's kingdom when they pray? Why or why not?
- How would you describe the other requests in this prayer? What does Jesus tell us to ask for? Are these the kinds of things you ask for when you pray? Why or why not?
- Do you think the requests in this example prayer are the only ones we are allowed to pray for? Or does it simply give us an

idea of our priorities in prayer? How do you think we should follow its example?

- Do you think Jesus meant for us to repeat this prayer as a formula?
- What attitudes did Jesus tell us to have when we pray? How aware should we be of other people listening when we pray? How many words should we use when we pray? Why?
- In the story of the man asking for bread at midnight, what finally caused the neighbor to answer? Did Jesus tell us this parable to show us that God is reluctant to give us good things? What is the point of this parable? How does it apply to our prayers?
- What did Jesus promise to those who ask, seek, and knock? What do you think He meant by "the door will be opened"?
- What kind of answers can we expect when we pray? What kind of heart does the Father have toward His children?
- What gift did Jesus especially promise to those who pray persistently? In what ways have you prayed for the Holy Spirit to fill your life?
- What does this passage of Scripture teach us about God's priorities for our prayers?
- How certain can we be that God will answer us? How certain can we be that He will answer us with something good?

QUESTIONS FOR FAMILIES/CHILDREN

- What name did Jesus call God when He taught us to pray? What kind of Father do you think God is? How much do you think He loves His children?
- What did Jesus ask for in the example prayer He gave us? Should we ask for these things too? Why or why not?
- Did Jesus tell us to try to impress other people when we pray? Who should we be thinking about when we pray?

- Do we have to use a lot of words to explain to God what we need? Why or why not?
- In the story of the man asking for bread at midnight, what did he do that caused the neighbor to get up and answer? How do you think that applies to our prayers?
- What did Jesus promise to those who ask, seek, and knock? What will God do for them?
- How do we know that God gives good things to His children?
- How can we know that God will answer our prayers?
- Who does God promise to send to us to help us?

MEMORY VERSES

So I say to you: Ask and it will be given to you; seek and you will find; knock and the door will be opened to you. For everyone who asks receives; he who seeks finds; and to him who knocks, the door will be opened.

LUKE 11:9-10

KEY APPLICATION

Prayer is vital to our growing relationship with Jesus.

40

SEEKING THE LOST

An Unexpected Mission

THEME

Jesus teaches how He seeks the lost.

PASSAGE/REFERENCE

Luke 15

BACKGROUND

The Pharisees had high standards for ritual holiness, including careful hand washing and avoiding contact with common and ritually unclean people. So when they saw Jesus carelessly eating with known "sinners," they were shocked. This was not appropriate behavior for a rabbi, particularly one that kept implying that He was the Messiah. In their minds, He was contradicting His own mission; they thought the Messiah was coming to establish the righteous in Israel and rebuke the unrighteous by setting up His kingdom. Jesus had to inform them of the real reason He came.

PRE-STORY DIALOGUE

Many people believe God is stingy with His blessings — that He only gives them out when we've performed well enough to earn them. Even those who know about God's grace often assume God is holding out on them. But according to Jesus, that isn't God's attitude at all. Do you know what God's attitude toward you is? As you listen to these three parables, notice how God is portrayed. What does He think of you? To what lengths would He go in order to bring you closer to Him? Then ask yourself: How does He want us to view those who have strayed from Him? How can we help Him in His mission?

TELL THE STORY

A lot of people were gathering around Jesus, even corrupt tax collectors and other sinners. Apparently Jesus had no concerns about eating meals with them. This bothered the Pharisees, who were so careful to obey ritual laws that they avoided contact with unclean people. So Jesus started telling stories, or parables, to address their concerns.

In the first parable, Jesus reminded them that a good shepherd would leave his herd in order to go find one missing sheep. He wouldn't just return home, content with having ninety-nine of his one hundred sheep. He would go search for the missing sheep and joyfully carry it back to safety when he found it. His friends would rejoice with him too. Likewise, heaven celebrates when a lost sinner repents and comes to God.

Or, for another example, what about a woman who has ten silver coins but loses one? Would that woman be content with having nine out of ten? Jesus pointed out that she would light a lamp and search high and low until she found the missing one. And her friends would rejoice with her too. The angels rejoice like that over just one sinner who repents.

Then Jesus told about a man who had two sons. The younger son asked his father to give him his inheritance, even before the father died. And the father actually did it; he divided his estate between his two sons and gave the younger one his inheritance. So the younger son gathered up all his possessions and took off for another country. But it didn't take long for him to run out of money. He squandered his inheritance on a reckless lifestyle. And after he spent everything, a famine hit the whole country, and he lived in poverty.

This son got a job feeding pigs in the far country. He would have even eaten the pig's food if he could have, but no one gave him anything to eat. Finally, he came to his senses. He realized that his father's hired hands back home were living better than he was. He decided to go back, apologize to his father for being so unworthy, recognize that he would no longer be considered a son, and ask for a job with the other workers. So he got up and started the journey home.

While he was still a long way off, his father saw him and was filled with compassion for him. He ran to his son, threw his arms around him, and started kissing him. The son started his speech: "Father, I have sinned against heaven and against you. I am no longer worthy to be called your son." But the father was too excited. He called his servants to bring the best robe, a ring, and some sandals to put on his poor son. He dressed him like part of the family again, and he told the servants to get ready for a party—to kill the best calf and prepare a feast. "For this son of mine was dead and is alive again; he was lost and is found." So they all began to celebrate.

The older son was working out in the fields while all this was going on; when he came back to the house, he heard the noisy celebration. He asked one of the servants what was going on, and when he found out, he was furious. He refused to go to the party. His father came out to plead the younger son's case, but the older son wouldn't listen. "All these years I've been slaving for you," he said. "Yet you never gave me even a young goat so I could celebrate with my friends. But when this son of yours who has squandered your property with prostitutes comes home, you kill the fattened calf for him!"

The father reminded the older son that he had always been with him, that he already had access to everything—all the family privileges and possessions. But the younger son might as well have been dead, and now he's alive again. That's worthy of a huge celebration.

DISCUSSION QUESTIONS

- What was Jesus doing that caused the Pharisees to grumble? Why did they disapprove of Him?
- What did Jesus do to explain why He ate with "sinners"? Did He argue? Give them a point-by-point rebuttal? How did He make His case?
- What did Jesus compare Himself to in the first story? What did He compare lost people to? What does a shepherd do for his sheep?
- What happens in heaven when someone comes back to God?
- What did Jesus compare Himself to in the second story? What did He compare lost people to? What does a woman do to find a lost coin?
- How do you think Jesus wants us to feel about those who have strayed from Him? How do you think He wants us to feel when they return to Him?
- What did the younger son ask his father to do? What do you think the father thought about this request? How did he respond to it?
- What did the son do when he got his father's inheritance? How did he end up in poverty? What do you think the people listening to Jesus thought about this young man's behavior?
- What caused the son to change his mind? Was it guilt? Love for the father? A moral decision? Why did he decide to go back?
- What was the son planning to say when he met his father again? How did he expect his father to view him?

- What did the father do when he saw the son returning? How quickly did he react? What emotions did he display? What did he tell the servants to do?
- Did the father react the way his son expected him to? How do you think the son felt when he saw his father's reaction?
- Where was the older son when his younger brother returned? How did he respond when he heard what had happened? How would you have felt if you were in his place?
- What did the father do to reach out to the older son? What were his reasons for celebrating the younger son's return?
- Who does the older brother represent in this story? Who does the younger brother represent? Who does the father represent?
- What does this story tell us about God's heart for those who are lost? According to this story, what does God think of those who try to obey His rules but don't understand His heart?

QUESTIONS FOR FAMILIES/CHILDREN

- Why were some people upset with Jesus? What was He doing that they didn't like?
- In Jesus' first story, what does a good shepherd do when he loses a sheep? How is Jesus like that good shepherd? Who rejoices when someone returns to God?
- In Jesus' second story, what does a wise woman do when she loses a coin? How is Jesus like that woman?
- In Jesus' third story, what did the younger son ask his father for? Why do you think he did that? How do you think the father felt about it?
- What did the younger son do with all his money? How did he end up poor?
- What happened when the son went back home to see his father? Did his father send him away? How did the father feel about his son's return?

- What did the older brother think of the celebration? Why did he feel this way?
- What did the father say to the older brother to explain things to him?
- From these stories, what do we know about God's heart? How does He feel about those who are lost?
- What does God want us to think about those who are lost? How can we show love to people who don't know Him?

MEMORY VERSES

Suppose one of you has a hundred sheep and loses one of them. Does he not leave the ninety-nine in the open country and go after the lost sheep until he finds it?

Luke 15:4

There is rejoicing in the presence of the angels of God over one sinner who repents.

Luke 15:10

KEY APPLICATION

Our Savior enlists us to reflect His heart and work for the lost.

41

REVEALING THE KINGDOM

God's Reign Now and Forever

THEME

Jesus teaches about the kingdom of God.

PASSAGE/REFERENCE

Matthew 5:3-10; 13:24-50; 18:1-5; Luke 20:27-36; John 14:1-3

BACKGROUND

Jesus came preaching the "good news of the kingdom" (Matthew 4:23), and one of the priority requests He told His disciples to pray for was that God's kingdom would come on earth as it is in heaven. What kingdom was He talking about? He meant more than a restoration of the kingdom of Israel under David and Solomon. It's wherever God rules and reigns, whether in heaven or this fallen world. In fact, this kingdom is referred to more than one hundred times in the Gospels. It's considered one of the primary messages Jesus preached. And though we only see the kingdom in part now, we are encouraged to look forward to it forever.

PRE-STORY DIALOGUE

Do you want God to rule in your country? What about in your work-place or your home? Or, more specifically, in every detail of your life? Those seem like easy questions to answer, but the truth is ever since the Garden of Eden, we human beings have wanted to rule our own lives. Perhaps we don't think God will allow us to enjoy life the way we want to, or maybe we just prefer our own goals and agendas. As you listen to this story, think about what life in God's kingdom is really like. What would His rule and reign mean in your life today? In what ways do you look forward to experiencing His kingdom in eternity? What will it be like when we're with Him in heaven?

TELL THE STORY

Jesus taught His disciples about the attitudes and character of His kingdom. He said the kingdom belongs to those who are poor in spirit. He blessed those who mourn, who are meek, who hunger and thirst for righteousness, who are merciful, who are pure in heart, who are peace-makers, and who are persecuted for the sake of righteousness.

Jesus also told many parables about the kingdom of heaven. It's like a mustard seed that starts out smaller than other seeds but grows into a plant large enough for birds to nest in it. Or it's like the yeast a woman puts into bread dough—just a little is enough to leaven the whole batch. Jesus often taught in parables like this in order to fulfill prophecy about the way He would teach and also to get His message across to those with open hearts while obscuring it from those who would reject or abuse it.

Jesus also told the disciples another parable about the kingdom of God. It's like a man who sowed good seed into a field, He said. While everyone was asleep, the man's enemy came and sowed weeds among the wheat, and both wheat and weeds grew up together. The man told his servants that an enemy must have done this, but he didn't allow the servants to pull the weeds because the wheat could be uprooted too. He let both grow until the harvest. Then the harvesters could gather the weeds for burning and separate the wheat to be stored in a barn.

The disciples asked Him to explain the parable of the weeds in the field. Jesus said the sower was the Son of Man—Himself, the field was the world, and the good seed represented the children of His kingdom. The weeds were the children of the Evil One, and the Devil sows them into the world. But both the children of God and the children of evil grow up together and will be harvested by angels at the end of time. Jesus warned that the weeds would be put into a fire. He would send angels to sort out from God's kingdom everything that causes sin and everyone who does evil. The children of evil will be thrown into a furnace, where there will be weeping and gnashing of teeth. But the righteous will shine like the sun in God's kingdom.

Jesus said the kingdom was like treasure hidden in a field—so valuable that a man who found the treasure would sell all he had just so he could own this one field. He said it was like a merchant who found a priceless pearl and sold everything he had in order to get it. Or it was like a fishing net that caught all kinds of fish, but when the fishermen pulled it in, they kept the good fish and threw out the bad. That's what the end of the age will be like—angels will separate the wicked from the righteous.

Later, the disciples asked Jesus who would be the greatest in the kingdom. Jesus said those who are great are those who become like little children—humble and accepting.

Once some Sadducees, religious leaders who didn't believe in the afterlife, tried to trick Jesus by asking Him about the kingdom. They described a woman who was married and widowed seven times. Who would be her husband in the kingdom of God? Jesus said those in the resurrection wouldn't marry; they would be like angels. They are God's children.

The night before He was crucified, Jesus urged His disciples not to be distressed. He said there was plenty of room in His Father's house.

He was going to prepare a place for those who believe. And He promised to come back and take those who believe to be with Him. That's when we'll see the kingdom fulfilled.

DISCUSSION QUESTIONS

- What are the attitudes and characteristics of those who inherit God's kingdom? Are these the same qualities our culture cultivates and honors? Why or why not? Why do you think God desires qualities like these?
- How is the kingdom of heaven like a man who sowed seeds into a field? Who sowed the good seeds? What do they represent? What do the weeds represent? Who sowed the bad seeds? When do the wheat and weeds get separated? What happens to each?
- In what ways is the kingdom of heaven like a mustard seed? In what ways is it like yeast?
- How valuable is the kingdom of heaven? What would a treasure hunter or a pearl merchant give up in order to gain the kingdom?
- How is the kingdom like a fishing net? What happens when the net is dragged to shore? Why is this a good picture of the end of the age? Who will separate the wicked from the righteous?
- Who should we become like in order to be great in God's kingdom? Why?
- How is life in the kingdom of heaven different than it is right now on earth?
- How much room is in God's kingdom? How exclusive is it? What is Jesus doing now for those who will go to heaven? Who gets to enter the kingdom?
- From the descriptions in this story, how desirable is the kingdom to you? Do you think the kingdom is for right now

or only for later? In what ways can we experience it now? In what ways must we wait for its fulfillment?

QUESTIONS FOR FAMILIES/CHILDREN

- How did Jesus describe people who had the right attitudes for the kingdom of heaven?
- What did Jesus compare the kingdom of heaven to? How many descriptions of it can you remember?
- In one parable of the kingdom, what did the good wheat and the bad weeds represent? Does God separate those people right away? When does that happen?
- How do people feel when they miss out on God's kingdom?
- What does a mustard seed do that the kingdom of heaven also does? What does yeast do to bread that the kingdom also does?
- In what ways is the kingdom like a valuable treasure or a fine pearl? What are those things worth? What would someone give up for God's kingdom?
- Why is it good for people to be like children? What attitudes do children have that can make people great in God's kingdom?
- How is the kingdom like a fishing net? What happens when all the fish get pulled to shore?
- Do people get married in heaven? Who does Jesus compare people in heaven to?
- How much room is there in God's house? What is Jesus doing for us before we get to heaven?

MEMORY VERSES

Blessed are the poor in spirit, for theirs is the kingdom of heaven.

MATTHEW 5:3

The kingdom of heaven is like treasure hidden in a field. When a man found it, he hid it again, and then in his joy went and sold all he had and bought that field.

MATTHEW 13:44

Do not let your hearts be troubled. Trust in God; trust also in me. In my Father's house are many rooms; if it were not so, I would have told you. I am going there to prepare a place for you. And if I go and prepare a place for you, I will come back and take you to be with me that you also may be where I am.

JOHN 14:1-3

KEY APPLICATION

We're to seek God's kingdom and righteousness above all.

42.

DECLARING THE KING

A Foundation for the Church

THEME

Jesus is declared to be Messiah, the Son of God.

PASSAGE/REFERENCE

Matthew 16:13-23

BACKGROUND

At the far northern part of Israel, above the Sea of Galilee, Jesus had been going from town to town teaching and healing. The disciples had been with Him for at least a couple of years and had not only seen many miracles but also had heard what people were saying about Jesus. Although there had been much speculation, few people knew exactly what to make of this man. He didn't fit most people's expectations of what the Messiah should look like.

PRE-STORY DIALOGUE

Perhaps the most important thing about a person is what he or she thinks of Jesus. Who is this unusual man? A good teacher? A prophet? Or something more? If He wasn't truly God's Son, He misled a lot of people. But if He was truly God's Son, we should listen carefully to what He says and follow Him without reservation. As you listen to this story, notice the struggle His disciples had with how to perceive Jesus. But also notice the conclusion the disciples came to—and how Jesus surprised them after that.

TELL THE STORY

When Jesus was in Caesarea Philippi, He asked the disciples what people were saying about Him. Who did they think He was? They reported that some people thought He was John the Baptist—John had been killed earlier, but they thought maybe he had come back to life. Others thought He was Elijah, who had ascended to heaven without ever dying. And some said He was another one of the old prophets, perhaps Jeremiah, who had returned.

"What about you?" Jesus asked His disciples. "Who do you say I am?" Peter spoke up: "You are the Christ, the Son of the living God." Jesus blessed him for saying this and assured him that his statement was a revelation from God. Jesus said He would build His church on this rock, and the gates of hell would not overcome it. "I will give you the keys of the kingdom of heaven," He said. "Whatever you bind on earth will be bound in heaven, and whatever you loose on earth will be loosed in heaven." And then He warned them not to tell anyone He was the Messiah.

Now that the disciples understood Jesus was the Messiah, He began explaining that He would have to go to Jerusalem and suffer—that the religious leaders would kill Him, but He would come to life after three days. Peter pulled Him aside and tried to correct Him. He said such a thing would never happen, but Jesus responded harshly. "Get behind me, Satan!" He said. He called this idea a stumbling block. "You do not have in mind the things of God, but the things of men."

DISCUSSION QUESTIONS

- What did Jesus ask the disciples? Why do you think He wanted to know what other people thought?
- What were some of the ideas about Jesus? Who did people think He was?
- When Jesus asked the question, do you think most of His disciples knew the answer? Which one gave the answer? What did this disciple say?
- How did Jesus respond to this answer? According to Jesus, how had Peter gotten his information?
- What did Jesus say He would build His church on? What do you think He meant by this? What did He say about the strength of His church? What specifically will not be able to overcome it?
- What did Jesus say He would give His disciples? What do you think Jesus meant by this? What would they be able to do with this gift?
- What did Jesus warn His disciples not to say? Why do you think He didn't want them to talk about this?
- What did Jesus say would happen when He went to Jerusalem? How would He be treated? What would be the end result?
- What did Peter say to Jesus when he heard Jesus' prediction? Why do you think he disagreed with Jesus?
- How did Jesus respond to Peter's words? Why? Whose plan was it for Jesus to go to Jerusalem and suffer and die?
- Why is it important for us to recognize who Jesus is? Why is it important for us to publicly confess who Jesus is?

QUESTIONS FOR FAMILIES/CHILDREN

- Who did people think Jesus might be? Who did the disciples say He was?
- How did Peter know who Jesus was? Who revealed that information to him?
- How strong did Jesus say His church would be?
- What kind of keys did Jesus give His disciples? What would they be able to do with these keys?
- What did Jesus say would happen to Him when He went to Jerusalem?
- What did Peter think about this? What did he say to Jesus? How did Jesus respond to Peter?
- What does this story tell us about Jesus? Why is it important for us to know who He is? Do you think it's important for us to say who He is as Peter did? Why?

MEMORY VERSE

I will give you the keys of the kingdom of heaven; whatever you bind on earth will be bound in heaven, and whatever you loose on earth will be loosed in heaven.

MATTHEW 16:19

KEY APPLICATION

We are to use every opportunity to express our faith in Jesus as Lord.

43

HEAVEN OR HELL
The Great Divide

THEME

Jesus teaches only heaven or hell follows death.

PASSAGE/REFERENCE

Luke 16:19-31

BACKGROUND

Jesus often taught that the first will be last and the last will be first. In other words, as it's said many places in Scripture, the humble will be lifted up and the proud will be made low. This truth is applied in various situations in the Bible (most of them having to do with status and wealth and the complacent or arrogant attitudes that so often come with them). In this story, Jesus' parable illustrates this theme as it plays out in eternity.

PRE-STORY DIALOGUE

What happens when we die? We've already learned in other stories that those who believe in Jesus will live, even though they die. Faith in Him leads us to eternal life. In this story, Jesus shows us both sides of the equation: someone who has gone to be with God, and someone else who will spend eternity apart from God. As you listen, notice how many possibilities there are for where we spend eternity. Also notice what life is like in each place.

TELL THE STORY

Jesus told a parable to His disciples. There was once a rich man who dressed in all the finest clothes and lived in luxury every day. Lying outside his home was a beggar named Lazarus, who was covered in sores and would have given anything just to have a few scraps from the rich man's table. Dogs would come and lick his sores as he lay there.

One day the beggar died, and God's angels came and carried him to heaven, where Abraham was. Then the rich man died too, but he went to hell and was in torment. He looked up, and as he saw Abraham far away, he noticed the beggar Lazarus by his side. The rich man called out to Abraham, "Have pity on me." He asked Abraham to send Lazarus to dip his finger in water and cool his tongue. "I am in agony in this fire," he cried.

Abraham reminded the rich man that he had already received his good things during his lifetime. But because Lazarus received bad things, he was now being comforted in heaven while the rich man was in agony. Even if Abraham wanted to send Lazarus, it wouldn't matter; there is a huge chasm between heaven and hell, and no one can cross it. There's no going back and forth.

So the rich man begged Abraham to send Lazarus to his father's house to warn all of his brothers about the torment they might face in hell. But Abraham said, "They have Moses and the Prophets; let them listen to them."

Still, the rich man pleaded. "If someone from the dead goes to them, they will repent," he argued.

Abraham disagreed. "If they do not listen to Moses and the Prophets, they will not be convinced even if someone rises from the dead."

DISCUSSION QUESTIONS

- What kind of lifestyle did the rich man live? Do you think he cared about the beggar outside his door? What evidence is there in the story about whether or not he was concerned?
- How did Jesus describe Lazarus the beggar? What was his life like?
- How do you think the storyteller, Jesus, expects His listeners to react to this situation of a rich man who hardly notices the poor man outside his door?
- Where did Lazarus go when he died? What was the afterlife like for him? Where did the rich man go? What was the afterlife like for him?
- What did the rich man first ask Abraham to do? Why wouldn't Abraham do it? What reasons did he give?
- After Abraham denied his request, what did the rich man then ask him to do? How did he expect his family members to respond to a visit from Lazarus?
- What did Abraham say about how the rich man's family would respond? What did they really need to do to go to heaven?
- Do you think this story teaches that rich people go to hell and poor people go to heaven? Why or why not?
- How does Jesus expect us to respond to the truth of Scripture? Does the story imply that that response is enough to save us?
- Who do you think Jesus was really talking about when He said, "Even if someone rises from the dead"?
- What does this story teach us about the kinds of people who believe in Jesus and those who don't? What attitudes do we need to have in order to be open to truth?
- What does this story teach us about caring for the poor?
- What does this story teach us about heaven and hell? What is the afterlife like? How many possibilities are there for us when we die? How permanent is our situation?

QUESTIONS FOR FAMILIES/CHILDREN

- How did the rich man in this story live? How did the poor man live? Did the rich man take care of the poor man? How can we tell?
- Where did each man go when he died? What was life like for them in those places?
- What did the rich man ask when he saw Lazarus with Abraham? What did he want Abraham to let Lazarus do for him?
- How did Abraham answer? What reasons did he give?
- What did the rich man want Lazarus to do for his family? What did Abraham say about that? Would a visit from Lazarus cause them to believe? What did they have that should cause them to believe already?
- What two places can someone go to when he or she dies? Can a person go back and forth from one to the other?
- What do we need to believe in order to go to heaven?

MEMORY VERSE

If they do not listen to Moses and the Prophets, they will not be convinced even if someone rises from the dead.

LUKE 16:31

KEY APPLICATION

God sets heaven and hell before us, with no other options.

44.

WASHING THEIR FEET

Greatness Through Serving

THEME

Jesus serves by washing the feet of His followers.

PASSAGE/REFERENCE

John 13:1-17

BACKGROUND

Most of those who believed Jesus to be the Messiah expected Him to set up a visible earthly kingdom — to establish Israel's independence from Rome and to begin governing a kingdom known for its justice and peace. And with all His talk about the "kingdom of heaven" — well, it seemed that this was His plan. What people didn't expect, however, was for this King to serve in humility and even offer Himself up as a sacrifice. They would soon see some dramatic portraits of a very unusual King.

PRE-STORY DIALOGUE

In what ways do you want to be great? What efforts do you make to seek greatness? We all have a desire to make a difference, but God's definition of greatness is much different from the world's. As you listen to this story, notice the humility of Jesus and see how He valued others. At the end of this story, what does He tell His disciples—and us—to do?

TELL THE STORY

It was time for the Passover feast in Jerusalem, and Jesus knew it was also time for Him to leave the world and go to the Father. On His last night, He gave His disciples a picture of His love for His followers. It happened while the evening meal was being served.

The Devil had already put it into Judas's mind to betray Jesus, and Jesus knew that. But He also knew that all things were under God's power, that He had come from God, and that it was time to go back. So Jesus got up from the table, took off His normal robe, and wrapped a towel around His waist like a servant. He poured water into a bowl and started washing His disciples' feet and drying them with the towel.

Simon Peter was baffled by this, so when Jesus finally got around to him, Peter asked Jesus if He was really going to wash his feet. "You do not realize now what I am doing," Jesus answered, "but later you will understand." But Peter was adamant: "You shall never wash my feet." Jesus told Peter that if he didn't let Him wash his feet, he could have no part with Jesus. If that was the case, Peter answered, he wanted it all: "Not just my feet but my hands and my head as well!" Jesus told him that wasn't necessary. A person who has already had a bath only needs to wash his feet after walking somewhere, He said. He told His disciples they were already clean—with one exception; He added that because He knew Judas was going to betray Him.

When Jesus finished washing their feet, He took off His servant clothes and put His regular clothes back on. "Do you understand what I have done for you?" He asked. He told them it was right for them to call Him "Teacher" and "Lord," but now they should follow His example. They should wash each other's feet too. Servants aren't greater than their master, so if the Master served His followers, His followers should be the servants of other people too. "Now that you know these things, you will be blessed if you do them."

DISCUSSION QUESTIONS

- What did Jesus know about God's timing that His disciples didn't know yet?
- When did Jesus demonstrate His love for them? What were they about to do together?
- What did Jesus do with regard to His clothing before He washed the disciples' feet? What was symbolic about that?
- What did Simon Peter say when it was his turn for Jesus to wash his feet? Why do you think he said this?
- What did Jesus say to convince Peter that he should have his feet washed? What did Peter say when he realized it was necessary? How did Jesus respond to Peter's request? What do you think His response meant?
- What did Jesus mean when He told the disciples they were already clean? How do we become clean spiritually?
- Why did Jesus tell the disciples He was truly their Master and Lord? What was He telling them they would need to do?
- Do you think Jesus literally meant for His disciples to wash each other's feet? How can we follow Jesus' example in washing the feet of others?
- According to Jesus, what happens to us if we do these things?

QUESTIONS FOR FAMILIES/CHILDREN

- What did Jesus do to show the disciples how He cared for them?
- Why was it considered unusual for someone like Jesus to behave as a servant? How do you think the disciples felt about their master helping and serving them?
- What did Peter say when Jesus tried to wash his feet? What did he say after Jesus told him it was necessary?
- What do you think Jesus meant when He said the disciples were already clean? Was He really talking about baths? How can we be clean spiritually?
- What did Jesus say the disciples should do for each other? What are some of the ways people can serve each other? How have people done that for you? How have you done that for others?
- What did Jesus say would happen for those who served each other?

MEMORY VERSES

Now that I, your Lord and Teacher, have washed your feet, you also should wash one another's feet. I have set you an example that you should do as I have done for you.

JOHN 13:14-15

KEY APPLICATION

We are to serve one another as Jesus has served us.

45

LAST SUPPER
Celebrating a Greater Deliverance

THEME

Jesus points to His death with the bread and cup.

PASSAGE/REFERENCE

Luke 22:1-23

BACKGROUND

We saw in the Passover story in the Old Testament that God miraculously delivered Israel from Egypt. The final plague on Egypt was the death of the nation's firstborn sons; the only thing that protected a household on that night was the blood of a sacrificed lamb. As Jesus celebrated the Passover feast with His disciples, He pointed to the symbolism of that deliverance long ago and showed how that event served as a picture of what He was about to do.

PRE-STORY DIALOGUE

The time for Jesus' crucifixion was approaching. The disciples didn't understand what was about to happen, but they probably noticed Jesus' sense of urgency to teach them some important truths. In this story, notice the things He wanted them to remember. What sacrifice was He about to make? On whose behalf would this sacrifice be made? The events of that night and the next three days would change history forever, and we still remember them today.

TELL THE STORY

The Passover feast was about to begin, and the religious leaders in Jerusalem were busy trying to think of ways to get rid of Jesus. They were afraid of doing anything to Him while all the people were crowding around Him—that could have caused a riot. About this time, Satan inspired Judas, one of Jesus' disciples, to turn Jesus over to the authorities. Judas went to the chief priests and the officers of the temple guard, and they came up with a plan together. The leaders were delighted and offered Judas money. They struck a deal, and Judas began looking for a good opportunity to hand Jesus over when the crowd wasn't around.

As the day for sacrificing the Passover lamb approached, Jesus sent Peter and John to go make preparations for the Passover meal. When they asked where they should prepare it, Jesus told them they would meet a man carrying a jar of water when they entered the city. They were to say to him, "The Teacher asks: Where is the guest room, where I may eat the Passover with my disciples?" Then the man would show them a furnished upper room of a house. When Peter and John entered the city, that's exactly what happened, so they prepared the meal as Jesus had told them.

At the meal, Jesus and the disciples reclined at the table. "I have eagerly desired to eat this Passover with you before I suffer," He told them, saying He would not eat it again until the kingdom of God was established. Then He took the Passover cup, gave thanks to God, and told His disciples to divide it among themselves. "I will not drink again of the fruit of the vine until the kingdom of God comes," He said.

After that, Jesus took the unleavened Passover bread, gave thanks, broke it, and handed it out to His disciples. "This is my body given for you," He said. "Do this in remembrance of me." In the same way, He picked up the cup again after the supper and said, "This cup is the new covenant in my blood, which is poured out for you."

Then Jesus told the disciples that He would be betrayed to the authorities and that the hand of the betrayer was on the table—in other words, it was someone right there at the meal. Jesus said this betrayal would be part of God's plan, but woe to the one who betrayed Him. The disciples started to ask each other who it could be.

DISCUSSION QUESTIONS

- What feast was about to take place in Jerusalem? Do you remember the story of how this feast began? What did it signify?
- What were the religious leaders looking for an opportunity to do? Why were they afraid of the crowds?
- What did Judas plan to do? Why was he inspired to do this? Who did he conspire with?
- What did Jesus send Peter and John to do? How did they know where to set things up?
- What did Jesus say He eagerly desired to do? When was the next time He would be able to do it?
- What does the Passover bread symbolize? What does the fruit of the vine symbolize?
- What was about to happen to Jesus' body and blood? Why was that significant for His followers?
- What do you think Jesus meant by a "new covenant"?
- Who did Jesus warn about after they finished their meal? Did Jesus think He would be betrayed against God's will? What did He say about the betrayer?
- How did this Passover compare with the first Passover when God used Moses to deliver the Israelites? What kind of

sacrifice did Jews have to make at the time of the Exodus? What kind of sacrifice would be made at this Passover?

- What kind of deliverance did Jesus provide? What are His followers delivered from? How can we take part in this freedom He secured for us?
- How do we commemorate this story today? Why do you think it's important to do so?

QUESTIONS FOR FAMILIES/CHILDREN

- What did the religious leaders want to do to Jesus? Why were they afraid? Who decided to help them?
- What kind of holiday were the people in Jerusalem about to celebrate? What did Jesus send Peter and John ahead to do? How did they know what to do and where to set things up?
- What was Jesus eager to do with His disciples? When would He be able to do this again?
- When Jesus broke the bread, what did He say it represented? When He drank from the cup, what did He say it represented?
- Do you remember the story of the Exodus, when the first Passover happened? How were the Jews set free in that story?
- What do you think Jesus wanted to set His disciples free from?
- Who did Jesus warn about after they finished their meal? What was this person about to do?
- How do we remember this story in our churches today? Why do you think it's important to do that?

MEMORY VERSES

He took bread, gave thanks and broke it, and gave it to them, saying, "This is my body given for you; do this in remembrance of me." In the same way, after the supper he took the cup, saying, "This cup is the new covenant in my blood, which is poured out for you."

LUKE 22:19-20

KEY APPLICATION

We must regularly remember Christ's death for us.

46

PRAYED, BETRAYED
The Moment of Crisis

THEME

Jesus is betrayed while praying in the garden.

PASSAGE/REFERENCE

Luke 22:39-62

BACKGROUND

Just a week earlier, Jesus had been welcomed by a crowd waving palm branches and shouting things like, "Hosanna to the Son of David!" and "Blessed is he who comes in the name of the Lord!" (Matthew 21:9). There were high expectations for this Messiah. And the disciples were already talking about who would be the greatest in the kingdom this Messiah was about to establish. When Jesus indicated that things might not go as they expected, Peter was adamant that nothing would keep him from following Jesus. But Jesus told him that Satan would sift him like wheat and that Peter would deny Him. Peter, the other disciples, and the people of Jerusalem had little idea of what was about to come.

PRE-STORY DIALOGUE

How do you feel when you are in danger? Are you confident that God is taking care of you even when things appear to be going wrong? Jesus knew He was about to face the most difficult circumstances imaginable — rejection, pain, humiliation, and death — but He kept His focus on God and His plan. As you listen to this story, think of how you might have reacted to the night's events if you were one of the disciples. Would you have fled or remained with Jesus when the trials came? It's an important question to consider; life offers us that choice often.

TELL THE STORY

Jesus and His disciples went up to the Mount of Olives right outside of Jerusalem. When they got there, He told them to pray that they wouldn't enter temptation. Then He separated Himself from them a little and knelt down to pray. He asked God, "Father, if you are willing, take this cup from me; yet not my will, but yours be done." An angel came and strengthened Him. But Jesus was in anguish, and He prayed so intensely that His sweat was like drops of blood.

When He went back to the disciples, He found them asleep; they were exhausted from sorrow. He asked them why they were sleeping and again told them to pray so they wouldn't fall into temptation. At that moment, a group of people came up to Jesus; Judas was leading the way. He came up to Jesus to kiss Him. "Are you betraying the Son of Man with a kiss?" Jesus asked him.

When the disciples realized what was going on, they asked if it was time to pull out their swords. One even cut off the ear of the high priest's servant. But Jesus stopped them. "No more of this!" He ordered. And then He healed the man's ear.

Jesus spoke to the people there — the priests, elders, and temple officers. "Am I leading a rebellion, that you have come with swords and clubs?" He asked. He pointed out that He had been highly visible ever since He had been in Jerusalem—right there in the temple courts and out in the streets—yet they waited until darkness to do anything to Him. He was implying that they were people in spiritual darkness. They seized Him, led Him away, and took Him to the high priest's quarters. Peter followed along at a distance.

In the courtyard of the high priest's house, a servant girl saw Peter sitting near the fire. She recognized him as someone who had been with Jesus. But Peter denied it and told her he didn't know Jesus at all. Then someone else saw him a little later and said the same thing. Again, Peter denied being associated with Jesus. About an hour later, a third person suggested that Peter was one of the disciples; Peter was a Galilean after all, so he fit the part. But Peter said he didn't know what any of them were talking about. Just then, a rooster crowed, and Jesus looked out into the courtyard directly at Peter. Peter remembered what Jesus had predicted: Before the rooster crowed the next day, he would have denied Jesus three times. And Peter went out and wept bitterly.

DISCUSSION QUESTIONS

- Where did Jesus and the disciples go? What did Jesus tell them to do? Did they do that?
- Did Jesus tell His disciples to pray that they would be able to resist temptation or that they would not enter into it in the first place? Do you think many Christians pray this way? Why or why not? What kinds of temptations do you think He was expecting His disciples to face?
- What did Jesus pray when He was by Himself? Why did He make this request? What was God's will in this situation?
- Who came to minister to Jesus? How intensely did He pray?
- What did Jesus find when He returned to the disciples? What were they doing? Why do you think they hadn't followed His instructions very carefully? What did He say to them?
- Who came to see Jesus while He was talking with the

disciples? Who was leading them? Why did they come at night?

- What did the disciples want to do when they realized what was going on? Why do you think they wanted to do this? What were they expecting to happen?

- What happened to the high priest's servant? What did Jesus do to help him? Why do you think Jesus did this for one of His enemies?

- How much resistance did Jesus put up when Judas and the religious leaders came to get Him? What did He say to them? What did He do when they tried to seize Him?

- Where did they take Him? Who followed? What do you think the other disciples did?

- What happened in the courtyard of the high priest's quarters? Why do you think Peter denied knowing Jesus? What do you think he was feeling when people kept asking him if he was one of Jesus' followers? How did he feel about his answers afterward?

- How do you think Jesus responded to Peter later? How do you think He would have responded to Judas later? Which one was forgiven? Why?

- What does this story teach us about God's will in a crisis? Is it always His will to rescue? Does God's will always look like we think it should? What was God doing through Jesus' situation?

- What does this story teach us about fear and faith in a crisis? Who demonstrated fear in this story? Who demonstrated faith?

- How would you have reacted if you were one of the disciples in the garden while Jesus prayed? What about when the leaders came to seize Jesus? How would you have responded if you were in Peter's place in the courtyard? Why?

QUESTIONS FOR FAMILIES/CHILDREN

- Where did Jesus and the disciples go at the beginning of this story? What did Jesus do when they got there? What did the disciples do?
- Why do you think Jesus prayed so intensely? What did He ask God? What do you think God's answer was?
- Who came to get Jesus? Why were they coming for Him?
- What did the disciples want to do when the people came to seize Jesus? Did they know Jesus was planning to let things happen the way they did?
- What happened to the high priest's servant? How did Jesus help him? Why do you think He did this for one of His enemies?
- Where did the religious leaders take Jesus? Who followed? Why do you think this person wanted to follow?
- What did people keep asking Peter in the courtyard? How did Peter answer? How did Peter feel about his answers later?
- Who showed fear in this story? Who showed faith? Which emotion do you feel more when things seem to be going wrong: fear or faith? What does God want us to believe when we go through hard times?

MEMORY VERSE

Father, if you are willing, take this cup from me; yet not my will, but yours be done.

LUKE 22:42

KEY APPLICATION

We must avoid betraying our Savior, but forgiveness is offered.

47

TRIED, CRUCIFIED
The Ultimate Sacrifice

THEME

Jesus is tried and crucified to pay sin's penalty.

PASSAGE/REFERENCE

Luke 22:63–23:56

BACKGROUND

The Jewish leaders didn't have the authority to put Jesus to death. Judea was a Roman colony; only the Roman governor could issue a death sentence. But Jesus knew that's what would happen. In fact, He had predicted several times that He would be crucified and then be raised on the third day. The disciples still didn't get it. As soon as Jesus was seized by the religious leaders, most of them fled. One who didn't flee denied Him. And all the hopes of those who had followed Him suddenly crumbled.

PRE-STORY DIALOGUE

The Scriptures had described this kind of Messiah—one who would be "pierced" and "crushed" for our sins (Isaiah 53:5). In the Garden of

Eden, God had told Adam and Eve there would be necessary consequences for disobedience. For centuries, Jews had made blood sacrifices of animals as a picture of that cost of sin. Now Jesus would shed His blood as a once-for-all payment for our rebellion. As you listen to this story, think about the high cost of sin. Notice the great lengths God went to in order to bring us back to Him. And ask yourself what it would be like to really know and believe deep in your heart that all of your sins have been completely covered and wiped away forever.

TELL THE STORY

The guards began mocking and beating Jesus. They blindfolded Him, saying He ought to know which one was hitting Him if He was a prophet. They said a lot of other insulting things, but He did not resist them.

Then the council of leaders met first thing in the morning. They demanded that Jesus tell them if He was the Messiah. Jesus said they wouldn't believe if He told them, but then He referred to a messianic verse from Scripture: "From now on, the Son of Man will be seated at the right hand of the mighty God." So they asked if He was the Son of God, and Jesus told them they were right. They thought that blasphemy alone was enough evidence to convict Him, so they led Him away to Pilate, the Roman ruler of Judea. They told Pilate that Jesus had been telling people not to pay taxes and was claiming to be the real king.

"Are you king of the Jews?" Pilate asked Jesus.

"Yes, it is as you say," Jesus answered.

But Pilate wasn't concerned. He said he found no basis for criminal charges against Jesus. So the religious leaders began telling him how Jesus had been stirring everybody up, even when He lived in Galilee. When Pilate found out He was a Galilean, he decided to send Jesus to Herod, who was the ruler over that region. Herod happened to be in Jerusalem at the time.

Herod was delighted to see Jesus because he had heard a lot about Him. He wanted to see Jesus do one of His miracles. He asked Jesus lots of questions, and the religious leaders stood there accusing Him of all sorts of things, but Jesus gave no answer. So Herod and his soldiers mocked Him and sent Him back to Pilate.

Pilate told the Jewish leaders that neither he nor Herod had found any reason Jesus should be executed, so he said he would punish Jesus and let Him go. But the leaders demanded crucifixion for Jesus and insisted that Pilate let Barabbas go instead. (Barabbas was being held on charges of instigating a rebellion and killing someone.) Pilate kept trying to release Jesus because he couldn't find evidence of any actual crime. But the leaders and the crowd kept shouting at him and finally convinced him. Pilate released Barabbas and convicted Jesus.

As Jesus was being led to the place of crucifixion, His accusers forced Simon of Cyrene to help Him carry the cross. A lot of people followed this procession, including women mourning and weeping for Him. Jesus told them not to weep for Him — that things would get worse for them in their land after He had gone.

Two other criminals were crucified with Jesus at a place called "the Skull." They executed one man on Jesus' right and the other on His left. Jesus prayed for the executioners: "Father, forgive them, for they do not know what they are doing." Some people stood there sneering at Him; even the rulers did this. They mocked Him, saying, "He saved others; let him save himself if he is the Christ of God, the Chosen One." Some of the soldiers mocked Him too.

Someone nailed a sign above Jesus on the cross: "THIS IS THE KING OF THE JEWS." One of the criminals also being crucified kept insulting Him. But the other criminal rebuked the one hurling insults, pointing out that they were being punished fairly but that Jesus had done nothing wrong. He made a request to Jesus: "Remember me when you come into your kingdom." Jesus assured this man that they would be in paradise together that very day.

Darkness covered the land for three hours in the afternoon, and the curtain in the temple in Jerusalem was ripped in two. Jesus cried out in a loud voice, "Father, into your hands I commit my spirit." Then He breathed His last breath. The centurion in charge, seeing what had happened, praised God and said, "Surely this was a righteous man." And many who gathered there beat their chests as a sign of mourning and went away. But those who knew Him—especially the women there—stood at a distance and watched.

After Jesus died, one of the religious leaders named Joseph, who had disagreed with the rest of the leaders' actions, asked for Jesus' body. He took it, wrapped it in burial cloth, and put it in an unused tomb that had been cut into the rock. He had to do it before sundown because the Passover Sabbath was about to begin. The women who had been at the cross followed and saw where the tomb was. Then they went home and prepared burial spices and perfumes so they could take them to the tomb after the Sabbath.

DISCUSSION QUESTIONS

- How did the Roman guards treat Jesus while He was being held overnight? How did Jesus react to them?
- What did the council ask Jesus? How did He answer them?
- What did they think when He said He was the Son of God? Did they think that was possible? Why did they consider this to be evidence against Him?
- What accusations against Jesus did the leaders claim when they took Him to Pilate? What did Pilate think of these charges?
- What did Herod think about seeing Jesus? What did he want to see? What did he decide to do with Jesus?
- What did Pilate want to do with Jesus? What did the religious leaders do to change his mind?
- Who was set free in Jesus' place? What was he in prison for? Why do you think it's significant that a guilty prisoner was set

free while Jesus was condemned to die?

- What did Jesus say to the women who were weeping for Him? What did He say about the soldiers who were crucifying Him?
- What did the people who were mocking Jesus say He should do? What did the sign placed above Jesus say?
- What did the criminals who were executed with Jesus say to Him? How much faith did it take for the criminal to say "when you come into your kingdom" to a dying man? What had he realized that the disciples didn't yet know? How did Jesus respond to the criminal who had faith? What promise did He give?
- What natural phenomena occurred in Jerusalem while Jesus was being crucified? What do you think was the significance of these events?
- Who took care of Jesus' body after He died? Why do you think he did this?
- Do you remember what God told Adam and Eve the consequence would be if they ate the forbidden fruit? What did their sin cost? In what way did Jesus pay the price for their sin?
- What attitudes did Jesus demonstrate during His trial and execution? Toward whom did He show restraint? Toward whom did He show love and forgiveness? In what way are these attitudes an example for us? When do we have opportunity to show them to others?

QUESTIONS FOR FAMILIES/CHILDREN

- What did the guards do to Jesus? Did Jesus fight back? Why or why not?
- Did the religious leaders think Jesus might really be the Son of God? Why did it make them mad when Jesus said He was?
- Did Pilate think Jesus was guilty of anything? What did Herod think? What did Pilate want to do with Jesus?

- Who was released instead of Jesus? Who was crucified with Him? What did the criminals say to Jesus? What did one of them say that showed he had faith? What did Jesus say to the one who had faith?
- What did Jesus say about the soldiers who were crucifying Him? Did He want God to forgive them or punish them? Why?
- Is it hard for you to forgive people when they do bad things? Why or why not?
- What did the sign above His head say? Was it true? What kind of king was Jesus?
- What happened to the sunlight while Jesus was being crucified? What happened to the curtain in the temple?
- Who helped bury Jesus after He died? Why do you think the man wanted to do this?
- What does it mean for us that Jesus died in our place? What does He promise to give us instead of death?

MEMORY VERSES

From now on, the Son of Man will be seated at the right hand of the mighty God.

LUKE 22:69

Father, forgive them, for they do not know what they are doing.

LUKE 23:34

KEY APPLICATION

We must trust that Jesus' death was for us.

48

RESURRECTED

The Beginning of the New Creation

THEME

Jesus rises from the dead, validating His sufficient sacrifice.

PASSAGE/REFERENCE

Matthew 28:1-15; Luke 24:9-32

BACKGROUND

In spite of several warnings about what would happen to Jesus, the disciples still didn't understand that He had to die and rise again. In fact, His death seems to have caught them by surprise. Between Friday and Sunday, they must have wondered how they could have been so wrong about Jesus. How did He do such miracles if He wasn't from God? But why did He make such inflated claims about Himself if He was from God? It didn't make sense. But on the morning after the Sabbath, the bigger picture started to unfold.

PRE-STORY DIALOGUE

What do you do when your world comes crashing down around you? Many people have had such an experience. And although the worst-case scenario often looks like the end of hope, it can really be the beginning. God often brings beauty out of ashes (see Isaiah 61:3) or turns mourning into dancing (see Psalm 30:11). In this case, He brought life out of death. As you listen to this story, think about the worst-case scenarios in your life. Have you faced a terminal illness or known someone who has? Suffered a broken relationship? Lost your job or your hopes or your dreams? Even if you haven't seen God intervene yet, it doesn't mean He hasn't or He won't. When He gets involved, nothing is too difficult to overcome. Not even a dark, sealed tomb could hold Him.

TELL THE STORY

The morning after the Sabbath, Mary Magdalene and another Mary went to the tomb. There had been a violent earthquake, and an angel had come from heaven and rolled back the stone covering the entrance. He sat on the stone, shining like lightning and wearing snow-white clothes. The guards who were there to prevent Jesus' followers from taking His body were terrified.

The angel told the women not to be afraid and said he knew they were looking for Jesus. "He is not here; he has risen, just as he said." The angel showed them where Jesus' body had been and told them to go tell the disciples that Jesus would be in Galilee before they even arrived at their homes there. So the women, full of joy, hurried away to go tell the disciples.

On their way back, Jesus suddenly met them. They grabbed His feet and worshipped Him, and He told them not to be afraid. He told them the same thing the angel had said: Tell the disciples to go to Galilee, and they would see Him there.

While this was happening, some of the guards went into the city and told the chief priests about all that had happened. The religious leaders met and came up with a plan, then paid the soldiers a lot of money to spread a story that the disciples had come during the night and stolen the body. (They even had to say they were sleeping while this happened.) The leaders said they would keep the soldiers out of trouble if they spread this story, so they took the money and did as they were told.

When the women found the eleven remaining disciples and some other followers of Jesus, they explained what had happened. But no one believed the women because it all sounded like nonsense. But Peter ran to the tomb to see, and he found some strips of linen lying there. He left wondering what had really happened.

Later that day, two disciples were walking to a village called Emmaus, about seven miles from Jerusalem. They were talking about everything that had happened, and Jesus came up beside them and walked with them. But He didn't let them recognize Him. He asked them what they were talking about. One of them, Cleopas, couldn't believe there was someone who didn't know what had been happening in Jerusalem; it was the talk of the town.

Jesus asked them what had been going on, so they started telling Him about the man named Jesus, a prophet who spoke powerful words and did amazing miracles. Then they explained how He had been tried and crucified by the religious leaders and Romans. "We had hoped that he was the one who was going to redeem Israel," they said. Then they told Him about the strange events of that day—how the women had gone to the tomb, found it empty, and seen an angel who said Jesus was alive.

"How foolish you are, and how slow of heart to believe all that the prophets have spoken!" Jesus exclaimed. "Did not the Christ have to suffer these things and then enter his glory?" Then He explained everything in the Hebrew Bible that had been written about Himself.

When these travelers arrived at Emmaus, Jesus acted as if He were going farther, but they begged Him to stay with them. When they were eating their evening meal, Jesus took the bread, said a prayer of thanks, and gave these two disciples some of it. Then their eyes were opened and they recognized Him. Yet as soon as they did, He disappeared.

They remarked that their hearts had been burning while He was talking with them and explaining the Scriptures to them.

DISCUSSION QUESTIONS

- When did the women go to the tomb? What did the women see there?
- Who spoke to them? What did he say to them? What were they instructed to tell the disciples?
- Who did the women meet on their way to see the disciples? How did they respond to this encounter? What instructions did they receive?
- What plot did the religious leaders devise to cover up the Resurrection? How well do you think this plan worked?
- How did the disciples react to the women's news? If you had been one of them, how would you have reacted?
- Do you think doubts are common for people who are learning about who Jesus is? Do doubts disqualify us from ever believing in Him?
- Who did two disciples encounter on the road to Emmaus? Why do you think this traveler hid His identity from them?
- Why did Jesus call these disciples "slow of heart"? What did He ask them about their understanding of the Christ? What did He show them in the Scriptures?
- What happened when the two disciples and Jesus had a meal together? What did they notice from the time He had been teaching them?
- What does this story teach us about how well we understand Scripture on our own, apart from God opening our eyes? Why do you think the disciples on the Emmaus road had never realized that the Christ must suffer and die, even though it was foretold in Scripture? Do you think it's common today for us to have blind spots in our

interpretation of Scripture? Why or why not?

- What does this story teach us about situations that are impossible? In what ways does it encourage you in your circumstances in life?
- What does it mean for us today that Jesus is still alive? How does that apply to our lives? How does that encourage and strengthen us?

QUESTIONS FOR FAMILIES/CHILDREN

- Who came to the tomb on the third day? What did they see? Do you think they were afraid? How would you have felt if you saw what they saw?
- What did the angel tell the women to do? Who did they see on their way back to the disciples? What did they do when they saw Him?
- Did the disciples believe what the women told them? Why or why not? Would you have believed them?
- What story did the religious leaders come up with to explain why Jesus wasn't still in the tomb? Were they telling the truth?
- Who did the travelers on the road to Emmaus meet? Did they know who He was?
- What did Jesus explain to these disciples on the road? When did they finally recognize Him?
- What does this story teach us about situations that are impossible? Is anything impossible for God?
- What does it mean for us today that Jesus is still alive? Can we still talk to Him? Can He still speak to us and help us?

MEMORY VERSES

He is not here; he has risen, just as he said. Come and see the place where he lay. Then go quickly and tell his disciples: "He has risen from the dead."

MATTHEW 28:6-7

Did not the Christ have to suffer these things and then enter his glory?

LUKE 24:26

KEY APPLICATION

Our hope for our own resurrection is assured by Jesus.

49

RESTORED TO SERVE

After Denials and Doubts

THEME

Jesus restores His sinning, fearful followers.

PASSAGE/REFERENCE

John 20:24-29; 21:1-19

BACKGROUND

The night before the Crucifixion, Peter had sworn to stick with Jesus through thick and thin. Then he promptly denied Jesus three times before the night was over. We're told that when morning came, he fled and wept bitterly. What was he doing between Friday and Sunday? We don't know, but the angel at the tomb was careful to tell the women who came at sunrise to go "tell his disciples *and Peter*" (Mark 16:7, emphasis added)—as though it was especially important for this disciple to hear the good news. As for Thomas, he missed out on Jesus' first appearance to the disciples and was very skeptical. Jesus had plenty of mercy for both of these men.

PRE-STORY DIALOGUE

Our beliefs don't just happen by accident. We choose them. Our choices are helped by the things we've been taught by others, but no one dictates our beliefs for us. We have to make a decision. As you listen to this story, notice the decisions made by the disciples who are mentioned by name. Who believed eagerly? Who believed reluctantly? What would you have believed if you were in their place? And, more importantly, what do you choose to believe now?

TELL THE STORY

Thomas, one of the disciples, wasn't with the others when Jesus first visited them. So when they told him they had seen the Lord, he doubted. "Unless I see the nail marks in his hands and put my finger where the nails were, and put my hand into his side, I will not believe it," he told them.

One week later, all the disciples were together behind locked doors. But Jesus suddenly appeared among them and said, "Peace be with you!" Then He turned to Thomas and told him to put his finger in the scars in his hands and side. "Stop doubting and believe," He said.

"My Lord and my God!" Thomas exclaimed.

Jesus answered, "Because you have seen me, you have believed; blessed are those who have not seen and yet have believed."

Later, Jesus appeared to His disciples again by the Sea of Tiberias (the Sea of Galilee). Some of them went out on the water to fish, but they caught nothing that night. Early in the morning, they saw someone standing on the shore. It was Jesus, but they couldn't see clearly enough to know it was Him. He called out and asked them if they had caught any fish yet.

"No," they answered. So Jesus told them to throw their net on the right side of the boat. When they did, there were so many fish that they couldn't haul the net in. Then the disciple Jesus loved (John) immediately knew who was standing on shore. "It is the Lord!" he said. Peter jumped in the water and started swimming toward Him. The other disciples followed in the boat, towing the net full of fish. They were only about a hundred yards out. When they got to shore, they found Jesus there cooking some fish over a fire. He told them to bring some of the fish they had just caught.

Simon Peter climbed back on the boat and helped drag the net to shore. It had 153 large fish in it, but even with so many, the net didn't tear. Jesus invited them to come eat breakfast. No one dared ask who He was; they already knew it was Jesus. He gave them some bread and fish to eat. This was the third time He had appeared to them after rising from the dead.

After they ate, Jesus asked Simon Peter: "Do you truly love me more than these?"

Peter answered, "Yes, Lord, you know that I love you."

"Feed my lambs," Jesus said.

Then Jesus asked him the same question two more times, and they repeated the conversation. The third time Jesus asked, Peter was hurt. "Lord, you know all things; you know that I love you." Again, Jesus told him to feed His sheep. Then He prophesied how Peter would die one day and told him, "Follow me!"

DISCUSSION QUESTIONS

- Which disciple doubted Jesus' Resurrection after the others had seen Him? What did he say would have to happen for him to believe?
- How did Jesus cause Thomas to live up to his own words? How did Thomas respond when he saw Jesus? What did Jesus say about his kind of faith? What kind of faith did He bless after that? Who does that blessing apply to today?
- What were some of the disciples doing the next time they encountered Jesus? Did they recognize Him at first? What caused them to recognize Him?

- What happened when the disciples recast their net according to Jesus' instructions? How did they react when they realized it was Him?
- How was this encounter with Jesus similar to the time He called Peter, James, and John to be His disciples (see session 30)? Why do you think Jesus chose a setting like this to appear to these disciples?
- What was Jesus doing when the disciples got to shore? What did He invite them to do?
- What question did Jesus ask Peter three times? What answer did Peter give each time? What instructions did Jesus give after Peter answered?
- Why do you think Jesus asked Peter this question and listened to Peter's answer three times? What else had Peter done three times recently? How did his answers make up for his earlier failure in the high priest's courtyard?
- How would you describe Jesus' attitude toward Peter in this conversation? Did He indicate that Peter's denial nullified the prophecy He had once given Peter—that he would be a leader in the church (see Matthew 16:18)?
- How do you think Jesus treats us when we've failed? Is He willing to forgive our doubts, denials, and other sins? Do you need to ask Him to forgive any of your sins?
- Based on this story, what would you tell someone who said that Jesus was resurrected spiritually but not physically? What evidence is given to show that He had a physical body after the Resurrection?

QUESTIONS FOR FAMILIES/CHILDREN

- Which disciple said he wouldn't believe Jesus had risen unless he touched Jesus' scars? What did Jesus do to convince him?
- Do you think Jesus understands when we doubt Him? What

did Jesus say about those who believe in Him even when they can't see Him?

- What were some of the disciples doing the next time Jesus appeared to them? How many fish had they caught when they saw Jesus? What happened when they threw their net where Jesus told them?
- What did Jesus invite them to do when they got back to shore?
- How many times had Peter denied Jesus the night before the Crucifixion? How many times did Jesus ask Peter if he loved Him? Why do you think Jesus asked him three times?
- What did Jesus tell Peter to do for His sheep? What do you think He meant?
- Do you think this meant that Jesus had forgiven Peter for saying he didn't know Him? Does Jesus forgive us when we make mistakes? Does He still let us serve Him after we've failed?
- Is there anything you need to ask Jesus to forgive you for?

MEMORY VERSE

Then Jesus told him, "Because you have seen me, you have believed; blessed are those who have not seen and yet have believed."

JOHN 20:29

KEY APPLICATION

When we fail God, we have a loving Restorer in Jesus.

50

REACH THE WORLD
A God-Sized Mission

THEME

Jesus sends His people worldwide with His good news.

PASSAGE/REFERENCE

Matthew 28:16-20; Mark 16:15-18; John 20:21-23; Acts 1:3-8

BACKGROUND

The disciples had been training with Jesus for three years. He had already sent them out on short-term missions to heal the sick and proclaim the kingdom of God. But now He was leaving the entire mission of the kingdom in their hands. They wouldn't be alone; His Spirit would be with them always, leading and empowering them. Still, it was a huge mission for eleven men plus a few other followers who had been with Jesus. But this mission had a long history; God had given a global assignment to Adam and Eve and a global blessing to Abraham. This assignment was not a new plan for God.

PRE-STORY DIALOGUE

Jesus gave His disciples a task that was too big for them. But that isn't unusual for God; He wants His people to depend on Him in everything. As you listen to this story, notice what Jesus asked His disciples to do. What kind of mission did He give them? How far and how long was it supposed to continue? Then ask yourself how that mission applies to believers today. What role do we have in fulfilling the assignment Jesus gave to His disciples?

TELL THE STORY

When the disciples went to Galilee after the Resurrection as Jesus had told them to do, they saw Him there and worshipped Him. But some weren't sure it was really Him at first. Then Jesus came to them and said, "All authority in heaven and on earth has been given to me. Therefore go and make disciples of all nations, baptizing them in the name of the Father and of the Son and of the Holy Spirit, and teaching them to obey everything I have commanded you. And surely I am with you always."

Jesus also said this another way: "Go into all the world and preach the good news to all creation. Whoever believes and is baptized will be saved, but whoever does not believe will be condemned." He told the disciples that certain signs would accompany those who believe. They would be able to drive out demons, speak in new tongues, and have their lives miraculously preserved in spite of snakebites and poisons. They would be able to lay their hands on sick people and see them healed.

At one point after the Resurrection, Jesus told His disciples, "As the Father has sent me, I am sending you." He breathed His Spirit on them and told them they had the authority to forgive or not forgive the sins of others.

DISCUSSION QUESTIONS

- Who has all authority in heaven and earth? Why does that matter to those who are sent on Jesus' mission?

- Where were Jesus' followers told to make disciples? What was involved in making disciples? Where would Jesus be while His followers were doing this? For how long?
- To whom were the disciples to preach the good news? What happens to those who believe and are baptized? What happens to those who don't believe?
- What signs did Jesus say would accompany those who believe?
- According to Jesus, what's the connection between the way God sent Him into the world and the way Jesus sends His followers into the world? If Jesus is the example, what attitudes will His disciples have on their mission? What sacrifices will they need to be prepared to make? What message will they proclaim? What works will they do?
- What authority did Jesus give His disciples when He breathed His Spirit on them?
- Based on this story, how would you describe the mission given to the disciples? If you were one of the disciples, how would you have felt about receiving this assignment?
- How do you think this assignment applies to believers today? What can we do to carry out this mission?
- Do you remember the blessing God gave to Abraham? How far did it extend? In what ways does the Great Commission given to Jesus' disciples fulfill that blessing?
- Do you think the goal of this mission is simply for people to make a decision or obey God? Or is the goal for them to enter a relationship with Him? Why?

QUESTIONS FOR FAMILIES/CHILDREN

- Who is in charge of everything in heaven and earth? Why was it important for Jesus to tell the disciples this?
- Where did Jesus tell the disciples they would make other disciples? What kind of people were included in those

instructions? What were the disciples supposed to teach people to do?

- Where did Jesus say He would be when the disciples were on their mission? For how long?
- Where were the disciples supposed to preach the good news? What kinds of signs did Jesus say would be seen around people who believe?
- How did the Father send Jesus into the world? What kind of mission did He have? How does that compare to the way Jesus sent His disciples into the world?
- Do followers of Jesus have the right to forgive people? Why is that important?
- Do you think Jesus wanted only His disciples to carry out this assignment, or did He mean it for all believers for all time? What can we do to help with this mission?

MEMORY VERSES

All authority in heaven and on earth has been given to me. Therefore go and make disciples of all nations, baptizing them in the name of the Father and of the Son and of the Holy Spirit, and teaching them to obey everything I have commanded you. And surely I am with you always, to the very end of the age.

MATTHEW 28:18-20

KEY APPLICATION

Jesus recruits us to actively join His mission to the world.

51

JESUS ASCENDS

Awaiting His Return

THEME

Jesus returns to His Father in heaven.

PASSAGE/REFERENCE

Acts 1:3-14

BACKGROUND

Jesus had told the disciples He would be going away, and even that He would prepare a place for them so they could join Him one day. Then He would return for them. We saw in the last session that Jesus gave His followers an assignment to carry out until He returned. He made it clear that no one would know the day or hour of His return, but that those who belong to Him should look forward to that day and be busy preparing for it. In another part of the New Testament, we are told that Jesus serves as our high priest in heaven and is currently praying for us. Even now, He is working on our behalf.

PRE-STORY DIALOGUE

Do you look forward to Jesus' return? For those who love Him, it seems like an easy question to answer. But many people are anxious about His return because of the trauma and change it will bring, and others are skeptical that He's coming back at all. As you listen to the story, think about what it must have been like to see Him ascend. Then consider these questions: How do you feel about seeing Him come down from heaven? Do you look forward to it? Do you hope He waits because you still have a lot to accomplish or know people who don't believe in Him yet? Know that however long it takes, He will keep His promise. He is coming for those who love Him.

TELL THE STORY

Jesus appeared to His disciples and others many times over a period of forty days and convinced a lot of people He was really alive. He taught them about the kingdom of God. At one meal, He told the disciples not to leave Jerusalem because the Father was going to give them a gift: the Holy Spirit. They were to wait for this gift before they began carrying out His mission. Just as John baptized with water, Jesus' followers would be baptized with the Holy Spirit.

Before Jesus ascended, the disciples met with Him and asked Him if it was time for Him to restore the kingdom to Israel. He told them they didn't need to know times or dates that the Father had set by His own authority. Their job after being filled with the Spirit was to be His witnesses in Jerusalem, Judea, Samaria, and out to the ends of the earth.

After Jesus said this, He was taken up to heaven right before their eyes. A cloud came and hid Him from their sight. They stood there gazing into the sky as He was ascending, and suddenly two men dressed in white were standing there with them. These angels asked the disciples why they were staring into the sky. "This same Jesus, who has been taken from you into heaven, will come back in the same way you have seen him go into heaven," they said.

The disciples returned to Jerusalem from the Mount of Olives, where they had seen Jesus ascend, which was only a short distance from the city. They went upstairs to the room they were staying in, and they began praying together constantly. The women who had followed Jesus, as well as His mother, Mary, and her other sons, joined them.

DISCUSSION QUESTIONS

- How long did Jesus show Himself to people between the Resurrection and His ascension? What kinds of things did He talk about during that time?
- Why did Jesus want the disciples to wait in Jerusalem? Do you think they realized what they were waiting for?
- What did the disciples ask Jesus about the kingdom? What do you think they were expecting Him to say? How did Jesus answer them?
- Where did Jesus say they would be His witnesses?
- What did the disciples do when they saw Jesus ascend into heaven? Who came to stand with them? What did these visitors say?
- Do you think the disciples understood how long it would take for Jesus to return? What do you think they expected?
- How do we know Jesus isn't returning in the same way He came the first time: as a human baby who grows up among us?
- What did the disciples do when they returned to Jerusalem?
- What does this story teach us about the direction history is headed? Is it random, or is there an ultimate goal?
- How expectant should we be about Jesus' return? Should we plan for the future or live for the short term, knowing that He'll come back soon?

QUESTIONS FOR FAMILIES/CHILDREN

- How long did Jesus stay on earth after His resurrection? What did He do to prove that He was still alive?
- What did Jesus tell His disciples to wait for? Why was this an important gift for them to receive?
- Where did Jesus say His disciples would be His witnesses?
- What did the disciples do when they saw Jesus go up into heaven? What would you have done if you had seen Jesus ascending?
- Who came and stood with the disciples? What did these visitors say?
- In what way is Jesus going to come back again? Do you look forward to His return? Why or why not?

MEMORY VERSES

You will receive power when the Holy Spirit comes on you; and you will be my witnesses in Jerusalem, and in all Judea and Samaria, and to the ends of the earth.

ACTS 1:8

This same Jesus, who has been taken from you into heaven, will come back in the same way you have seen him go into heaven.

ACTS 1:11

KEY APPLICATION

Jesus is our Intercessor and High Priest right this moment.

52

SPIRIT DESCENDS

Promised Power from Above

THEME

Jesus sends His Spirit to His followers.

PASSAGE/REFERENCE

Acts 2:1-21,38-47

BACKGROUND

The night before He was crucified, Jesus told His disciples that even though He was leaving them, He would not leave them *alone*. His presence would be with them. He repeatedly said He would be sending a Helper, a Comforter, a Counselor—or, more specifically, the Holy Spirit. In fact, this Spirit would no longer be with them; He would be *in* them. Since the fall of humanity in the Garden of Eden, the history of God's presence with His people had gone from sporadic appearances to a tent in the wilderness, then to a temple in Jerusalem, then to one holy human incarnation of God, and now to the people of God themselves.

PRE-STORY DIALOGUE

Does Jesus feel distant? He isn't. Though we can't see Him physically or hear His voice audibly, His Spirit is with us and in us. God's desire to dwell with human beings was fulfilled when He sent His Spirit into those who believed in Jesus. And the promise of His Spirit is just as valid for us today. As you listen to this story, think about what it was like for these early disciples to be filled with God's Spirit. Then ask God to show you how His Spirit can fill you, too.

TELL THE STORY

Jesus' followers were together on the day of Pentecost, and all of a sudden a rushing wind came blowing into the house where they were meeting. Something looking like tongues of fire came in and rested on each one of them. They were all filled with the Holy Spirit and started to speak in other languages.

Jerusalem was filled with Jews who had traveled from every nation to celebrate the feast, and when they heard all the commotion, they were bewildered. They gathered around, and everyone heard these disciples speaking in their own languages. This shocked them because the disciples were Galileans. How could they be speaking in all the languages from the far reaches of the empire? "We hear them declaring the wonders of God in our own tongues!" they exclaimed. They were amazed and wondered what it all meant.

Some people there who didn't understand what was going on made fun of these babbling disciples and suggested that they had had a little too much to drink. But Peter stood up and spoke to the crowd. "These men are not drunk, as you suppose," he said. After all, it was only nine in the morning. Peter quoted a prophecy from the book of Joel: "In the last days, God says, I will pour out my Spirit on all people." That scripture told how people would prophesy and see visions and have God-given dreams. Men and women, young and old—anyone would be qualified to prophesy. God had said He would do all kinds of signs and wonders in heaven and on earth "before the coming of the great and glorious day of the Lord. And everyone who calls on the name of the Lord will be saved."

After Peter preached some more and explained about Jesus' crucifixion and resurrection, he told everyone that they needed to repent and be baptized in the name of Jesus so they would be forgiven of their sins. Then they would receive the gift of the Holy Spirit too. This promise would be good not only for the people in the crowd but for their children—for future generations near and far—and "for all whom the Lord our God will call." Peter warned them and pleaded with them to be saved, and about three thousand people did just that.

The disciples devoted themselves to the apostles' teaching, fellowship, meals together, and prayer. Everyone was in awe of what was happening, and the apostles (disciples) were doing all kinds of miracles, signs, and wonders. The believers stayed together while God was doing this amazing work, many of them selling their possessions and helping each other out. They shared everything. They met together in the temple courts every day and enjoyed being together in each other's homes. They praised God and experienced the favor of all the people. And God kept adding to their numbers, with people being saved daily.

DISCUSSION QUESTIONS

- Why were so many people in Jerusalem?
- What happened where the believers were gathered? What did they hear? What did they see?
- What happened when they were filled with the Holy Spirit? How did the crowds in Jerusalem react to this? What was surprising about it?
- Why do you think God chose to work through such unexpected people? How clear was it that God rather than human ability was at work?

- What were the believers talking about in all the languages they were speaking?
- Why do you think it was significant for this event to be witnessed by people from all ethnic and language groups across the empire?
- What did some people accuse the disciples of? Why do you think they thought this? How did Peter respond to the accusation?
- How did Peter explain the wonders that were happening? What had Scripture prophesied about these things? Who qualified to receive God's Spirit? Who would be able to prophesy and have visions and dreams?
- According to Peter's message, who can be saved? How? Whose name should they call on? What should they do for forgiveness of sins?
- According to this story, how does someone receive the Holy Spirit? Who does the promise of the Spirit apply to?
- How many people heeded Peter's words and believed in Jesus on the day of Pentecost?
- How does this story describe the fellowship of believers? What did they devote themselves to? What were the apostles doing?
- What was the mood like around Jerusalem in the following days? What attitudes did the community of believers demonstrate?
- In what ways did God bless their fellowship? How did people perceive them?
- If you saw a community that displayed these characteristics, would you want to be a part of it? Why or why not? What do you think is necessary for a group of people to have these characteristics?
- Have you ever responded to Peter's plea to be saved by calling upon the name of the Lord, repenting, being baptized, and receiving God's Spirit? If not, would you consider doing that now?

QUESTIONS FOR FAMILIES/CHILDREN

- What happened when the followers of Jesus were gathered together on the day of Pentecost? What did they see and hear? What would you have thought if you saw something like that?
- What were these disciples able to do when God's Spirit came upon them? Why did this amaze all the people?
- According to the Old Testament verses Peter quoted, who would receive God's Spirit and be able to hear from Him? Who would God pour out His Spirit on?
- Who should people call on to be saved? How did Peter explain that we can be forgiven of our sins?
- How many people believed in Jesus after Peter finished preaching?
- What were the believers like after this? What did they spend their time doing? What did they see God doing? How did they treat each other?
- If you saw a group of people acting like this, would you want to be part of it? Why?
- What can we do to be saved? What can we do to receive the Holy Spirit? Have you ever done these things? Do you want to?

MEMORY VERSES

In the last days, God says, I will pour out my Spirit on all people. Your sons and daughters will prophesy, your young men will see visions, your old men will dream dreams. . . . And everyone who calls on the name of the Lord will be saved.

ACTS 2:17,21

They devoted themselves to the apostles' teaching and to the fellowship, to the breaking of bread and to prayer. . . . And the Lord added to their number daily those who were being saved.

ACTS 2:42,47

KEY APPLICATION

We must yield to the Holy Spirit living in us.

ACKNOWLEDGMENTS

WALK THRU THE BIBLE is grateful for the people who helped make *Story Thru the Bible* a reality. Avery Willis presented to us the idea of a small-group resource containing fifty-two Bible stories that would give individuals and families a God-centered worldview. The team that initially developed and clarified the major themes of each story included Phil Tuttle, John Houchens, Rich Leland, Steve Keyes, and David Hodge. The assistance of John Van Deist throughout this process was invaluable.

It has been a joy working with the team of servant leaders at NavPress, including Mike Miller, Barry Sneed, Mike Linder, Kris Wallen, and Jamie Chavez. We are excited to continue our partnership with The Navigators. Our ministries have a close bond through a common mission of encouraging people to live God's Word.

We want to offer a special thanks to Chris Tiegreen, senior editor at Walk Thru the Bible and the writer of this book. For more than a decade, Chris has written devotionals and books that have deepened the walk of hundreds of thousands of Christians worldwide. But to those of us at Walk Thru the Bible, he is a friend and team member who consistently exhibits the grace and humility of our Lord Jesus.

LEADER'S TIPS AND NOTES

1. CREATION

Key Points to Include:

- God is the origin of everything that exists.
- God created by speaking things into existence.
- There is an order and sequence to the way God created.
- Everything as originally created was "very good."
- Human beings are made in God's image and are of highest value in His creation.

More Information:

- Romans 1:20 tells us that God's nature is clearly seen in the things He made. If your group has time, discuss how God's invisible qualities are displayed in creation.
- A discussion about the Creation story in Genesis can easily get sidetracked into whether or not God created the world in seven literal days. Remember the purpose of this story is to tell us that God is the creator of all things, that He created with design and purpose, and that He created us specially to know Him and be good stewards over His creation.

2. FALL

Key Points to Include:

- Adam and Eve had everything they needed in Eden. God allowed them much freedom and gave them only one restriction.
- The serpent tempted Eve by causing her to question what God had said. Some of what the serpent said was true, and some of it was a

distortion of what God had said.

- Sin caused Adam and Eve to hide from God, and it changed their relationship with Him.
- Even in His judgments against the serpent, Eve, and Adam, God already had a plan for redemption.

More Information:

- Genesis 3:15 is the first prophecy specifically about Jesus in the Bible.
- Satan used the same tactics when he tempted Jesus in Matthew 4:1-11: He questioned the truth of what God had said. He also appealed to desire and ambition as he had done with Eve.
- Some people find it confusing that God would prevent Adam and Eve from eating of the tree of life when His ultimate goal for human beings is for us to live forever with Him. But to allow them to have eternal life in their fallen condition would have been tragic. God had another plan to redeem us and give us eternal life as a "new creation" (2 Corinthians 5:17).

3. FLOOD

Key Points to Include:

- God was grieved (sorrowful and anguished) over humanity's sin.
- The story of the Flood shows two aspects of God's character: His judgment of disobedience and His desire to save.
- Noah had to go out on a limb to obey God; he had to build an ark based on God's voice and not on any evidence of rain.
- God made a promise to Noah to which He remains faithful today.

More Information:

- Genesis 6:6 says that God's heart "was filled with pain." Many people think of God as unemotional or above feelings. Consider discussing this observation with your group, asking what this shows us about God and how we should relate to Him. If He feels pain (or joy, anger, delight, or any other emotion) and we are made in His image, is it then appropriate for us to relate to Him on an emotional level? If we were to bring our emotions in line with His, what would grieve us? What would make us happy? What would anger us? What would give us a sense of peace?

- Though God told Noah to take one pair of each kind of animal onto the ark, He told Noah to take seven pairs of certain kinds of "clean" animals (7:2-3). These would become sacrificial animals that Noah and his family could offer to God after the Flood without endangering the species.
- God referred to "the days of Noah" in Isaiah 54:9-10 as an example of how He would forgive Israel; Jesus referred to "the days of Noah" in Matthew 24:37 and Luke 17:26 when He foretold His second coming, saying that people would be as surprised at His return as they were when the Flood came; and Peter referred to "the days of Noah" in 1 Peter 3:18-22 to compare our salvation in Christ with God's rescue of Noah.

4. NATIONS

Key Points to Include:
- God had repeatedly given people a commandment to spread out and fill the earth.
- Building the tower of Babel was an attempt to remain in one place and reach God on humanity's own terms.
- The ability to speak a common language was a key to achieving things. Once that ability was taken away, people separated into distinct groups.

More Information:
- The kind of tower built by the residents of Shinar was most likely a ziggurat, a terraced pyramid designed as a temple or shrine. Many scholars believe it was also useful as a refuge from floods, a purpose that might have been at the forefront of many minds in the generations after Noah.
- When the Holy Spirit descended upon the believers in Jerusalem at Pentecost, He essentially reversed the curse of Babel. He gave those gathered the ability to speak in other languages, and He gave the many ethnic groups gathered in Jerusalem the opportunity to hear the gospel in their own native language (see Acts 2:4-11).
- Eventually, the separation into distinct language groups and cultures enriches the kingdom of God. One day, people from "every nation,

tribe, people and language" will worship Jesus together (Revelation 7:9).

- God isn't opposed to cities and towers or to people gathering together; after all, Revelation ends with a picture of the city of God, and His people are united in Him. The story of the tower of Babel shows us that God is opposed to human efforts and the attempt to build a civilization apart from Him. And the mission of filling the earth and subduing it had not been accomplished yet, so creating a tight, local civilization defied God's plans.

5. ABRAHAM

Key Points to Include:

- In obedience to God, Abram left behind all that was familiar and went forward without knowing where he was going.
- God's promised blessings to Abram are a further extension of His original instructions to Adam and Eve.
- God's promise to make Abram "a great nation" did not seem possible because Abram was seventy-five years old and still had no children (Genesis 12:2).
- Abram worshipped God at each new place he settled.

More Information:

- Though the title of this session is "Abraham," his name is still Abram at this point in God's story and his wife's name is Sarai. At a key point later in their lives, God will change their names to Abraham and Sarah as their identity is shaped by His promise.
- In the New Testament, both Paul and the writer of Hebrews pointed often to Abraham as an example of faith. Referring to the story in this session specifically, the writer of Hebrews says, "By faith Abraham, when called to go to a place he would later receive as his inheritance, obeyed and went, even though he did not know where he was going. By faith he made his home in the promised land like a stranger in a foreign country; he lived in tents, as did Isaac and Jacob, who were heirs with him of the same promise. For he was looking forward to the city with foundations, whose architect and builder is God" (11:8-10). His leaving the old life behind—becoming a

stranger in a foreign land and looking forward to a more lasting home—is an inspiring metaphor for the life we are all called to live.

6. ISAAC

Key Points to Include:
- God's promise to Abraham appeared to be impossible, but nothing is impossible with God.
- Even though Abraham did not understand how God would fulfill His promise and tried to accomplish it by his own efforts, he ultimately believed God.
- In God's command to sacrifice Isaac, it was more important for Abraham to obey God than to hold on to what God had promised—to treasure the Giver rather than the gift.

More Information:
- Though the title of this session is "Isaac," the story really centers around Abraham and the promise God had given him. Isaac is considered an important patriarch, but the Bible speaks of him primarily as Abraham's son and Jacob's father. Very little of God's story focuses on Isaac himself.
- In this story, Sarah is the one who laughed at God's promise. But in Genesis 17, Abraham also laughed when God reminded him of the promise and suggested an alternate plan (see verses 17-18). Even so, the Bible commends both Abraham and Sarah for having great faith.
- Isaac was circumcised because God had made circumcision a sign of the covenant between Him and Abraham's family in Genesis 17:10-11.
- Abraham believed God's promise, and God considered him righteous because of his faith. This became an important point for New Testament writers in proving that God saves us by grace through faith. Paul wrote much about Abraham's faith in Romans 4, for example. For more on Abraham's faith, read Hebrews 6:13-15 and 11:11-12,17-19.
- Abraham's offering of Isaac is a dramatic picture of what God would one day do with His own Son, Jesus: offer Him as a sacrifice for our sins. The mountain where Abraham offered Isaac is the same

mountain on which Jerusalem was later built and where Jesus was eventually crucified.

7. JACOB

Key Points to Include:

- Jacob was not completely innocent — in fact, he clearly caused a lot of his own trouble — but he was chosen by God, and God defended him and remained faithful to him.
- Jacob's family situation was a mess and he had many worries about how things would work out, but God took care of him and gave him great promises.
- God initiated the encounters with Jacob.
- Jacob wrestled with God with persistence and insisted on being blessed, and God honored him for it.
- Jacob was delivered from the things he was most worried about.

More Information:

- In John 1:43-51, Nathanael heard about Jesus from Philip but was very skeptical. When Nathanael finally met Jesus, Jesus spoke a prophetic insight about him, which convinced him of who Jesus was. Jesus assured Nathanael he would see greater things and then said, "You shall see heaven open, and the angels of God ascending and descending on the Son of Man" (verse 51). His point was to connect Himself with Jacob's dream and assert that He was the true Bethel, the house of God and gate of heaven.
- Jacob's name means "one who supplants," a reminder of the times he had deceived people. The new name God gave him — Israel — can mean "struggles with God" or "rules with God." In asking his name, the man who wrestled with Jacob may have been asserting authority over him and, in a sense, getting him to confess his old nature. Jacob's new name became the name of the nation of Israel. *Jacob* and *Israel* were often used interchangeably later in Scripture, particularly in the prophetic writings.

8. JOSEPH

Key Points to Include:

- Joseph's dreams were true, but for many years it seemed that they weren't.

- The Bible does not record a single negative reaction by Joseph to the injustices he experienced.
- God was with Joseph in everything he went through and made sure he ended up in exactly the right places.

More Information:

- Many people have noticed remarkable symbolism of Jesus in Joseph's life. Jesus was rejected by His brothers (Jewish leaders), who were offended by His claims (dreams) of glory; was put into the ground for a short time and presumed dead by many; had His blood-soaked robe stripped from Him; has had a ministry to Gentiles for many years; and eventually will be recognized by His brothers. (As Scripture promises, Jews will one day accept the Messiah they once did not want to bow down to.)
- Joseph named his firstborn Manasseh, which means "made to forget," because God's great blessings had caused him to forget his troubles. He named his second son Ephraim, which means "twice fruitful," because God made him fruitful in the land of his suffering. Both names are a testimony to how God redeems the painful situations in our lives.
- The New Testament parallel to Genesis 50:20 is Romans 8:28, a very encouraging verse to many. We don't understand how God works all things together for our good, but even in cases of terrible injustice—when people like Joseph's brothers really are responsible for things that should not have happened—God is Lord over all the details of our lives.

9. MOSES

Key Points to Include:

- God heard the cries of His people and had compassion on them.
- God chose Moses for an important task, and even though Moses didn't feel prepared for it, God's choice was good—and nonnegotiable.
- God knew all the obstacles ahead of time and promised Moses everything he would need for his task.
- When we are afraid to do what God calls us to do, we can still move forward in faith that He is with us.

More Information:

- God had told Abraham that his descendants would be enslaved and mistreated for four hundred years (see Genesis 15:13). God's response to Israel's prayers may have appeared to be a long delay, but it was exactly on schedule according to the ancient prophecy.
- The New Testament martyr Stephen gave a concise summary of the time from Abraham to Moses in his defense before the Jewish court. Read Acts 7:1-34 for the portion of Israel's history that takes us through this session's story.

10. PASSOVER

Key Points to Include:

- God's deliverance of Israel through the last plague is rich with symbolism involving a lamb and a blood sacrifice.
- The Israelites had to "cover" themselves with the blood of a lamb in order to be saved.
- God demonstrated complete power over His enemies, which included not only Pharaoh and the natural phenomena in the plagues but also death itself.
- God wanted the events and symbolism of the first Passover to always be remembered and celebrated in future generations.

More Information:

- The first nine plagues involved darkness over the land, the Nile River, frogs, flies, locusts, and more. Egyptian deities included a sun god, a river god, and a multitude of lesser spirits over plants and animals. It is believed that each of the plagues demonstrated God's power over a specific god of Egypt.
- Jesus was crucified on the eve of Passover, and His last supper with the disciples seems to have been a celebration of the Passover meal. This is not a coincidence, of course, as the New Testament specifically refers to Jesus as the Lamb of God who takes away the sins of the world and whose blood saves us from slavery and death. The Passover is seen by Christians as a dramatic picture of the deliverance God has provided for us through the blood of His firstborn, spotless Son.

11. RED SEA

Key Points to Include:

- As with Israel, whatever or whomever has enslaved us in the past does not give up easily.
- The Israelites were in an extremely vulnerable position with no visible means of rescue. The situation looked impossible.
- God leads His people rightly—even when it appears that He has led us into a difficult situation.
- God defends His people. He fights battles on behalf of those He has called. We are called to stand firm.

More Information:

- Many people see a picture of baptism in Israel's deliverance through the Red Sea: God first passes *over* our sins as we are covered by Jesus' blood; then as we pass *through* the waters, we leave bondage behind and enter into new life.
- The deliverance at the Red Sea became the subject of many later psalms (for example, see Psalm 66:6; 74:13; 77:19; 78:13,52-53; 106:7-11; 136:10-15), and its symbolism was used by Israel's prophets (Isaiah 10:26; 43:2,16; 51:10; 63:11-13). It is considered by many to represent the birth of Israel as a nation.

12. TEN COMMANDMENTS

Key Points to Include:

- God's presence was not to be taken lightly; it required preparation and a sense of being set apart for Him.
- God's covenant with Israel expressed specific commitments and expectations for both parties.
- God's highest priority for His people is worship. He wants us to love Him above all else.
- The commandments God gave were not for the purpose of limiting His people but to benefit them. Living consistently with His character makes life more fulfilling. The Bible generally presents God's laws as aspects of a relationship with Him rather than simply a list of dos and don'ts.

More Information:

- Many rabbis throughout the centuries have seen the covenant at Sinai as a marriage betrothal—an engagement ceremony between God and His people, complete with a contract of expectations for each party. (This is reinforced by Jeremiah 2:2.) Christians understand the fulfillment of this betrothal to be the marriage of the Lamb (Jesus, the Bridegroom) and His bride in Revelation 19 and 21.

13. TWELVE SPIES

Key Points to Include:

- God did not send the spies into the Promised Land to decide whether they could take it; He sent them to scout it out before they entered.
- This passage compares unbelief in God's promises with rebellion and contempt for Him.
- Much of what the Hebrew people experienced was conditional on whether or not they believed God's promise.
- Even though God forgave the Israelites, their unbelief still resulted in serious consequences.

More Information:

- Fear of other people is often portrayed in the Bible as an enemy of faith. In the next generation when Joshua was preparing to lead the people into the Promised Land, God repeatedly had to encourage him to be strong and courageous, even though Joshua had been one of only two spies to demonstrate faith and courage in this session's story.
- The writer of Hebrews used this event as an extended example for Christians who are growing weak in their faith. He compared life in Christ with the Promised Land and urged his readers not to harden their hearts as they did in their time of testing in the desert (see especially Hebrews 3:7-19).

14. JOSHUA

Key Points to Include:

- Rahab is not the kind of person we would expect to find as a hero in a Bible story, but she is exactly the kind of person God often chooses to use.

- Unlike the spies forty years earlier, the two men sent to spy on Jericho sought strategic information and returned with a faith-filled report.
- The key to taking Jericho was to follow God's strategy.
- God's strategies are often unusual, unexpected, and something we would never come up with on our own.
- God is able to overcome any difficulty that stands between us and the purposes He has called us to fulfill. What He promises, He fulfills—no matter what obstacles get in the way.

More Information:

- Rahab is mentioned in Hebrews 11:31 and James 2:25 as an example of faith. Even though she was a prostitute, she was considered righteous because she recognized what God was doing and chose to side with His people.
- The instructions to devote everything in Jericho to the Lord demonstrate the principle of firstfruits—the practice of giving back to the Lord the first portion of crops, income, victories, and so on. This practice was taught frequently throughout the books of the law.

15. GIDEON

Key Points to Include:

- Even though Israel was responsible for its own predicament through its disobedience and idolatry, God still responded to His people with mercy when they cried out to Him.
- Gideon was not a likely hero, but God chose him as an example of His faithfulness in spite of our weaknesses.
- Gideon's first assignment—to destroy an altar to Baal and build an altar to God—was a powerful statement against the spiritual decline of the nation.
- God not only wanted to defeat Israel's enemy but to receive glory in the battle and have His people's hearts turned back toward Him.
- As with Jericho, God's strategies are not what we would come up with on our own.
- Even though Gideon had moments of fear throughout the story, God never tired of encouraging him.

More Information:

- Gideon would have identified with Paul's famous statement in
  2 Corinthians 12:9 about the Lord's attitude toward our frailties:
  "My grace is sufficient for you, for my power is made perfect in
  weakness." If there's time after your discussion of this story, read
  2 Corinthians 12:9-10 and discuss personal experiences with this
  principle.

16. RUTH

Key Points to Include:

- When the story begins, Naomi was as hopeless as a Jewish woman
  could get.
- Ruth's loyalty to Naomi was unusual and very selfless.
- Even though the story doesn't say so specifically, it implies that God
  arranged for Ruth to end up in Boaz's field.
- Ruth's appeal to Boaz during the night was a very risky plan that
  required a lot of faith. If Boaz had not responded positively, if her
  suggestive appearance where he slept had been misinterpreted, or if
  the other men nearby woke up and saw her there, her reputation
  could have been ruined and she could have become an outcast.
- God brought a lot of good out of Naomi's tragic situation: joy to the
  whole family, a great grandson who would become Israel's greatest
  king, and the lineage that the Messiah would come from.

More Information:

- Because of their origins, the Moabites carried quite a stigma in the
  eyes of Jews. (You can read the story in Genesis 19:30-38.) Ruth
  would have been looked down upon by many in Israel simply
  because of her ethnicity, which is perhaps one reason Boaz was so
  careful to look after her safety in the fields.
- Inheritance was a vital issue in the Promised Land, so God's law
  had provisions for situations when a man died without heirs. The
  law of the kinsman-redeemer required a brother or a near relative of
  the dead man to father children through his widow and count those
  children as the dead man's heirs rather than the redeemer's own.
  This is what Naomi and Ruth sought, and why Boaz needed to ask
  a closer relative before agreeing to marry Ruth and reclaim Naomi's
  land for the family.

- Boaz shows up in Jesus' genealogy in Matthew 1:5 and Luke 3:32—an opportunity missed by the unnamed man who declined to redeem.
- Many see in the story of Ruth a picture of what Jesus does for us. It begins with a woman with no hope—a foreigner outside of God's inheritance—who approaches the redeemer in faith. By accepting her, he brings her into the family of God and gives her a lasting legacy.

17. SAUL

Key Points to Include:
- God's judgment against the Amalekites was based on a long history of their violent opposition to His people.
- Saul thought it was enough to do the gist of what God commanded. He seemed to think he had obeyed.
- Saul's lack of diligence to heed God's word in this story and on one other occasion (see 1 Samuel 13:5-14) cost him his kingdom.
- Though it may appear on the surface that this story emphasizes strict outward obedience, the real issue is the kind of heart we have toward God. That becomes clear later when God chooses David as the next king.

More Information:
- Even though Saul said he had killed all Amalekites except the king, Israel continued to encounter them for centuries to come. David later had several confrontations with Amalekite warriors, and the villain in the book of Esther (centuries later) was a descendant of Agag. Clearly the Amalekites had not been thoroughly destroyed.

18. DAVID

Key Points to Include:
- The ark represented God's presence. Israel had carried it with them through the wilderness and into the Promised Land.
- God desires heartfelt worship, even if it's undignified. God did not bless Michal because she criticized someone's heartfelt worship.
- God promised David an everlasting kingdom—a promise that would be fulfilled through the Messiah, a descendant of David.

- The idea of a temple was more than a building project for David. It would be a place to host God's presence—where God could be worshipped and where He would be accessible to human beings. The temple was an expression of David's desire to honor God.
- David's zeal was for God's presence and God's reputation. At many points in his life, David demonstrated what it's like to have a God-centered focus.
- God's highest priority for us is to love Him.

More Information:
- For background about the greatest commandment, read Deuteronomy 6:4-6 and Matthew 22:36-40.
- Samuel the prophet called David "a man after [God's] own heart" in 1 Samuel 13:14, pointing out that this is where Saul was lacking. This phrase is quoted by Paul in the New Testament when he reminds a Jewish congregation of Israel's history and God's true purposes (see Acts 13:22).
- David made some major mistakes, most notably his affair with Bathsheba and the murder of her husband to cover it up. But even after his failure, he turned to God quickly. Being a person after God's heart doesn't imply being perfect, but it does mean always turning to Him, even in times of failure.
- David wrote Psalm 27, which speaks of his desire to "dwell in the house of the LORD" and "to seek him in his temple" (verse 4), as well as Psalm 30, which is labeled as a dedication song for the temple. These were apparently written in faith, as the temple would not be built until the next generation.

19. SOLOMON

Key Points to Include:
- Solomon's building project was a fulfillment of a promise God had given to David. It began as something heavy on David's heart and is never specifically portrayed as something God initiated and ordered, though God blessed it and used it as part of His plan for His people.
- The temple was seen as a contact point between heaven and earth—a place where God's people worshipped Him and where God met His people with His presence.

- The dedication of the temple is described in terms of a covenant between God and His people that involved expectations for both parties.
- Many nations would be drawn to God's presence in the temple. It was not built for the sake of Israel alone.
- God's presence at the temple and His favor on Israel were in some ways conditional on the king's and the people's obedience.

More Information:

- The story of Solomon is told in 1 Kings and 2 Chronicles. The 2 Chronicles version was written later but contains more detail and is the version from which the story in this session was taken.
- The story of the temple dedication mentions specific places within the temple that can be confusing for the reader. It's important to know that the temple was constructed with an outer court, an inner court called the Holy Place, and an inner sanctuary within the Holy Place called the Most Holy Place. This inner sanctuary is where the ark was placed. After the initial installation, this "Holy of Holies" would be off limits to anyone except a high priest during extremely special observances.
- Solomon's temple was finished around 960 BC and destroyed by the Babylonians around 587 BC. The temple in Jerusalem during Jesus' time was a rebuilt and modified version of the original.
- The New Testament tells us that God inhabits believers in the same way He inhabited the temple—that believers individually and the church corporately are now the temple of God (see 1 Corinthians 3:16-17; 6:19-20; 2 Corinthians 6:16-18; Ephesians 2:19-22).

20. JOB

Key Points to Include:

- Job was a human being, so he wasn't perfect. But he was innocent of any of the reasons that normally cause God to discipline His people.
- God was the one who brought up Job as an example, not Satan. And God kept Satan "on a leash" by limiting what he could do to Job.
- Much of what Job's friends said was theologically correct, but not when applied to that person in those circumstances. They were examples of people who have all the "right" answers but don't

understand what God is doing in a situation.
- God did not rebuke Job for asking questions or for being confused about his circumstances.
- God gave Job double what he lost—except for children. Just as he had ten children before his trials, he had ten afterward. Many people believe this is because his first ten were not permanently lost; they were still alive with God. So in essence, Job's number of children doubled just as his possessions did.

More Information:
- The literal meaning of the word *Satan* is "adversary." Often in the Old Testament, Satan is portrayed as a prosecuting attorney who has access to the courts of God and accuses God's people.
- In Leviticus 26 and Deuteronomy 28, God explained the conditions for receiving blessings and curses. He described all the ways He would bless His people for obedience and all the ways He would curse them for disobedience. In other words, He presented the norm for dealing with His people—at least how He would deal with them corporately as a nation—and, surprisingly, it was largely consistent with the perspective of Job's three friends. But the principles of "blessings for obedience" weren't intended to be a rigid formula for individual lives. One of the lessons we learn from the book of Job is that suffering is universal and doesn't always indicate God's attitude toward someone. Hardships are never a reliable measure of a person's righteousness.
- Romans 8:18-25 and 2 Corinthians 4:16-18 are good background reading for understanding suffering from a New Testament perspective.

21. ELIJAH

Key Points to Include:
- God was the one who disciplined His people with a drought and famine, but He used a prophet to declare both the beginning and end of the drought.
- Elijah's challenge would have resulted in his immediate death if God had not answered as dramatically as He did.
- The purpose of this incident was not simply to judge Ahab and

Jezebel's idolatry but to turn the hearts of the Israelites back toward God. The focus is worship of the true God.

- Even though God had already told Elijah that rain would come, the prophet needed to pray persistently for rain to come. God's declarations in Scripture are usually not a fatalistic prediction but an invitation to pray for His purposes.

More Information:

- Deuteronomy 11:13-17 (as well as the blessings and curses of Deuteronomy 28) explains why God used a drought and famine to discipline His people during this time of rampant idolatry.
- Elijah's name literally means "The Lord is God." His name was his message, which the people clearly understood when they began chanting, "The LORD—he is God!" (1 Kings 18:39).
- If Elijah had expected Ahab and Jezebel to realize the true God and repent for their idolatry, he was sadly disappointed. In fact, the showdown at Mount Carmel enraged Jezebel, who vowed to find Elijah and kill him. Elijah fled, grew very depressed, and had to have an encounter with God to regain his strength and carry on.
- James 5:17-18 refers to this story as an example of how powerful and effective our prayers can be. It describes Elijah as "a man just like us" who shut and opened the heavens with his prayers.

22. JONAH

Key Points to Include:

- Jonah disobeyed God and tried to flee his assignment.
- God wouldn't let Jonah escape. He gave him a second chance.
- The fish was God's provision to keep Jonah alive and to give him an opportunity to change his mind.
- God wanted Jonah to share His heart and understand His compassion.
- The major theme of Jonah is not about obeying God, although that's an important theme; it's about God's love for those who do not know Him.

More Information:

- Jesus had a lot to say about loving those who are difficult to love. See Matthew 5:43-46 for an example.
- Compare the story of Jonah with God's covenant with Abraham in Genesis 12:1-3 and the Great Commission in Matthew 28:19-20. God's heart for the nations is a theme woven throughout Scripture.
- Jesus compared Jonah's time in the belly of the fish with His own time in the grave (see Matthew 12:40). In interesting symbolism, both events were followed by a mission to Gentiles and the conversion of many.

23. ISAIAH

Key Points to Include:

- Isaiah lived hundreds of years before Jesus was born.
- The prophecies about the Messiah in Isaiah describe someone who is human but also clearly more than human.
- The Messiah comes as a ruler and as a servant, in suffering and in victory. Before Jesus came, these contrasting pictures were difficult to reconcile as one Messiah, but He showed how they fit together in Him.
- The law of Moses required a blood sacrifice of an unblemished offering in order to forgive sin. Jesus became that offering by shedding His blood on the cross.

More Information:

- Isaiah is quoted in the New Testament more than any other Old Testament prophet.
- Many of Isaiah's prophecies have an immediate application and an application for the distant future. For example, the immediate context of the virgin (or young woman) who conceives implies a sign that would signify something about Israel's enemies at the time. But ancient rabbis and the New Testament writers also saw this as a reference to the Messiah's birth.
- The Suffering Servant has a dual meaning in Isaiah: Israel and Jesus. In the New Testament and other Christian literature, Jesus became the representative of Israel and of all mankind when He took our sins to the cross so we could be raised with Him. Even in those places

where the Suffering Servant implies Israel, it points to Jesus as the fulfillment of Israel.

24. DANIEL

Key Points to Include:
- Daniel and his friends were captives against their will, but they served God in whatever situation they found themselves.
- God blessed Daniel and his friends in their adverse circumstances. He gave them favor in the eyes of people and blessed them with health, wisdom, and position.
- Daniel and his friends faced a choice between obeying God and obeying men, and even though they chose to obey God, they respected the human authorities over them.
- Daniel left the ultimate responsibility for the situation in God's hands. If God had not defended him, he would have been at the mercy of the Babylonian authorities.
- God honored Daniel and his friends for their faithfulness. He can use anyone, but He looks especially for people of high character and integrity.

More Information:
- Daniel and his friends all had Hebrew names that referred to God, but the Babylonian names they were given all referred to the pagan gods of Babylon and identified them by those deities.
- The memory verse is taken from an episode that occurred after the time of the story in this session. When the king had a perplexing dream, Daniel's wisdom and understanding were put to the test. This was the kind of moment God had prepared him for.

25. ESTHER

Key Points to Include:
- God doesn't prevent His people from having enemies. He does, however, prevent the enemies of His people from thwarting His plans for them.
- Esther demonstrated both fear and faith. Courage is not the absence of fear; it is doing the right thing in spite of one's fear.

- God puts His servants in strategic places to step forward at opportune times.

More Information:

- Esther is the only book of the Bible that never mentions God. In this story, just as in our lives, we are left to ourselves to discern His involvement in human events. Even so, His intervention is clear to those who read between the lines.

- Many people mistakenly believe that Mordecai refused to bow down to Haman because God forbade showing such honor to a human being, but that doesn't seem to be the case. God's law forbids worship of anything or anyone other than God, but it never forbids bowing down to honor or respect someone. In fact, this show of honor happens quite often in Scripture without any negative implications (see, for example, Genesis 23:12; 33:3; 43:28; Exodus 18:7). Mordecai's refusal seems more related to Haman's background as an Amalekite and a natural enemy of the Jews.

- The last chapters of the book of Esther describe the origins of the Feast of Purim, the Jewish holiday that celebrates God's deliverance of His people from Haman's plot. This feast continues today and is the most joyous celebration on the Jewish calendar.

26. NEHEMIAH

Key Points to Include:

- Nehemiah prayed and repented on behalf of his people, even though his sin was not the reason they had been taken captive so many years before.

- God used Nehemiah as an answer to his own prayer.

- The enemies' tactics against Nehemiah covered a wide range. They were at times subtle and at times obvious; sometimes external and sometimes internal; and included intimidation, slander, taunts, accusations, temptation, lies, blackmail, and death threats. Nehemiah refused to be swayed by any of these.

- The people grieved over their neglect of the law, but they rejoiced over their opportunity to have a fresh start in keeping it.

More Information:
- Notice how often Nehemiah prayed during this process. The first chapter contains one of the most sweeping, heartfelt prayers in Scripture, and even in the midst of conversations and conflicts Nehemiah would turn to God and voice his concerns and requests.
- Building or repairing a wall in ancient cities was a difficult task, as raiders and saboteurs would often try to burn it or tunnel under it. Heavily manned guard posts were always needed. This physical reality sheds light on Nehemiah's daunting task, but it also provides a great spiritual illustration: God's work on earth is almost always opposed by fierce enemies. God's people are called to withstand attacks and continue in faith.

27. JESUS' BIRTH

Key Points to Include:
- Jesus is both human and divine—born of God the Father and a human mother.
- For both Mary and Joseph, parenting Jesus was an awesome privilege and a sobering (and eventually painful) responsibility.
- The fact that God used common people like Joseph and Mary and announced Jesus' birth first to shepherds shows that salvation is for all kinds of people.
- Jesus came to save us from our sins and to be "God with us" (Matthew 1:23).

More Information:
- Some of the familiar elements of the Christmas story—the wise men and Herod's rage that a rival king was born, for example—are not included in this session because they seem to have occurred sometime after Jesus' birth. If you would like to add them to your telling of the story, you can find them in Matthew 2.

28. JESUS' BAPTISM

Key Points to Include:
- Though many people thought John might be the Messiah, John made a clear distinction between himself and Jesus.

- John identified Jesus as someone who would take away sins and bring God's Spirit to people.
- John was confused by Jesus' request to be baptized because Jesus did not need to be cleansed of sin. But Jesus saw His baptism as necessary to "fulfill all righteousness" (Matthew 3:15).
- All three members of the Trinity were noticeably present at the baptism.

More Information:
- Though sorrow is often involved in repentance, the biblical term *repent* does not simply mean to be sorry for sin. It can mean to change direction (turn around) or to change how one thinks.
- The Bible doesn't spell out the reasons Jesus was baptized, but most explanations emphasize either His purpose as a righteous role model for us or His role in fulfilling righteousness on our behalf. In other words, He was baptized either as our example or our substitute—or both.
- For more key references to baptism, see Matthew 28:19; Mark 16:16; Acts 2:38,41; and Galatians 3:27.

29. JESUS' TEMPTATION

Key Points to Include:
- God allowed Jesus to be tempted; the Spirit led Him into the wilderness for that purpose.
- Satan questioned the truth God had just spoken to Jesus—that He was God's Son. This was also one of Satan's strategies in the Garden of Eden; he questioned the truth of what God had already said.
- Jesus answered Satan by quoting Scripture.
- Satan quoted Scripture too.
- The third temptation offered Jesus a way to fulfill His mission to reclaim the world from Satan's influence, but this wasn't God's way to win the world.

More Information:
- Many people wonder how Satan could genuinely offer the kingdoms of the world to Jesus, because God is Lord over the whole earth. But in a real sense, Satan has influence in authority of the world's systems

and kingdoms. For some key verses related to this, see John 12:31;
2 Corinthians 4:4; Ephesians 2:2; and 1 John 5:19.
- Important background verses related to temptation—Jesus' and
ours—include 1 Corinthians 10:13 and Hebrews 2:17-18; 4:14-16.

30. JESUS CALLS THE DISCIPLES

Key Points to Include:
- Jesus was already drawing big crowds.
- The fishermen had been working all night—the normal time for
deep-water fishing—and hadn't caught anything.
- Jesus' timing and His command were the keys to the fishermen's
success.
- Jesus' power made Simon aware of his own sinfulness.
- Jesus had such a powerful impact on Simon (Peter), James, and John
that they left everything behind to follow Him.

More Information:
- Jesus often used a boat as a platform in order to manage the pressure
of crowds. See Mark 3:9 and 4:1 for other examples.

31. JESUS HEALS THE PARALYTIC

Key Points to Include:
- Jesus drew a crowd everywhere He went.
- The friends of the paralyzed man demonstrated bold and persistent
faith.
- Jesus responded to *their* faith—not just the faith of the paralytic but
also of his friends.
- The paralytic's greatest need was the forgiveness of sins. Jesus was
concerned about his paralysis, too, but as a secondary need.
- By exercising the authority to forgive sins, Jesus was claiming
divinity.
- Jesus proved He had authority to forgive sins by demonstrating that
He also had authority to heal.

More Information:
- Capernaum was the home of Simon Peter, James, John, and Andrew,
as well as Matthew the tax collector. Archaeologists believe they have

discovered the house of Peter there. This city was considered Jesus' home during part of His ministry.
- Roofs were made of clay and thatch and were usually flat, making it possible for people to stand on top of one and dig a hole in it.

32. NICODEMUS'S SECOND BIRTH

Key Points to Include:
- Nicodemus knew that Jesus was sent by God, but he may have been afraid to acknowledge that publicly. He may have come to Jesus at night because many of his fellow Pharisees opposed Jesus, or he may have done so simply to avoid the large crowds who followed Jesus.
- Jesus said that being born again is a requirement for seeing and entering the kingdom of God.
- The way to be born again is through faith—believing in Jesus.
- Those who love darkness—who hold on to their sin and don't want to see the truth—do not come to Jesus. But those who love truth and are willing to deal with their sins will come to Him and be saved.

More Information:
- Pharisees were a religious/political group who were experts in the law of Moses and in Israel's oral traditions. Most of them interpreted the law very rigidly and had high expectations for a Messiah who would come and overthrow the Roman Empire and establish God's kingdom.
- The term "born again," or "born from above," was already commonly used among Pharisees, and Nicodemus was probably already very familiar with it. But it applied to Gentiles becoming Jewish converts; a Gentile becoming a Jew was said to be "like one reborn." When Nicodemus asked how one could be born when he is old, he was using the same metaphor Jesus used—essentially asking, "How can I become a Jew when I'm already Jewish?" Jesus assured him that being Jewish wasn't enough; a spiritual conversion of the heart was necessary.
- John 3:8 is a play on words; *Spirit* and *wind* are the same word in Greek, the original language of the New Testament.
- For the background story of Moses and the serpent, read Numbers 21:4-9.

- The biblical word for *believe* means more than just mentally agreeing with a truth; it means to rely on and trust in someone or something. This is the kind of belief Jesus called for.
- Later in the gospel of John, Nicodemus openly supported Jesus (see 7:50-52) and helped bury Him after His crucifixion (see 19:38-40).

33. WOMAN AT THE WELL

Key Points to Include:

- Many people would have considered Jesus' conversation with the woman inappropriate for several reasons, but that didn't stop Him from doing it.
- Jesus kept redirecting the conversation to target the woman's deepest needs.
- Jesus offers to quench our spiritual thirst and meet our real needs in a way that is ultimately satisfying and fulfilling.
- God actively looks for people who will worship Him honestly from their heart and deep in their spirit.
- Real "food" is doing the will of God. Serving Him can energize and strengthen us.
- God looks for a harvest of people and invites us to participate in that harvest.

More Information:

- The woman at the well had three spiritual strikes against her in Jewish culture, which made Jesus' conversation with her extremely surprising to His disciples: (1) she was a Samaritan; (2) she was a sinner; and (3) she was a woman. (Women, while respected, were not generally entrusted with deep spiritual truth.) Most Jews, and especially most rabbis, would have avoided a one-on-one conversation with her for any one of those facts—and much more so for all three.
- Women generally came to get water from a well in the morning or evening and then often in groups. This woman's odd timing and lack of company may indicate that she was an outcast because of her moral reputation.

34. STORM STILLED

Key Points to Include:
- The disciples were out on the lake because they followed Jesus' instructions. He was not caught by surprise by the storm.
- Even when we panic in a crisis, Jesus knows exactly what to do.
- In our difficult circumstances, there's a battle between fear and faith in our minds and hearts. Jesus tells us to trust Him even when we're afraid.
- Jesus is not just a teacher, a good man, or a prophet. He has authority even over nature.

More Information:
- Galilean fishing boats were usually small and had no covered areas. For anyone to be able to sleep on a boat like that during such a storm was remarkable.

35. CROWD FILLED

Key Points to Include:
- Jesus had compassion on the crowds who came to see Him.
- Jesus can take the little we give Him and do with it more than we can imagine.
- Jesus didn't give the people only what they needed; He gave them all the food they wanted with plenty left over.
- Our primary act of obedience is to believe in Jesus and trust Him.
- Jesus doesn't just give us life; He *is* our life.
- Those who believe in Jesus can trust Him to save them, keep them, and raise them up from death.

More Information:
- This was not the only time Jesus fed a large crowd miraculously. Both Matthew and Mark, who record this story of feeding the five thousand, also tell of another time when Jesus fed four thousand men plus all the women and children who were there (Matthew 15:32-38; Mark 8:1-9).
- The people spoke to Jesus about how their forefathers ate manna in the wilderness. This was how God sustained them after they left Egypt and wandered in the desert; breadlike substance fell from

heaven every day, and they gathered it up and ate it. Jesus told them He was the true bread from heaven. You can read the story of manna in Exodus 16.

- When Jesus fed the multitude, some people said He was "the Prophet who is to come into the world" (John 6:14). They were referring to a prophecy in Deuteronomy 18:15-19 in which Moses said God would one day send a prophet like him. The Jews in Jesus' day were looking for the "prophet like Moses," as they called him, whom many assumed would be the Messiah.

- Jesus' words about being bread from heaven led to a great controversy later in John 6. He not only referred to Himself as manna but also spoke of people "eating" His flesh and "drinking" His blood—a picture of the Lord's Supper (see verse 56). These strange words caused many of His followers to leave Him (see verse 66).

36. LAZARUS RAISED

Key Points to Include:

- Jesus sometimes delays answers to our requests in order to allow our need to deepen and to show God's glory in our situation.
- Martha and Mary both felt that Jesus had let them down. Jesus understands when we feel that way, even though He has a good plan we haven't seen yet.
- Jesus grieves with us when we are hurting, even when He has a perfect solution planned for us.
- Those who believe in Jesus will never truly die. He is resurrection and life.
- Our worst enemy—death itself—has to bow to the power of Jesus.

More Information:

- Many Jews believed a soul could stay with a dead body for up to three days, which may be why John points out that Lazarus had been dead for four days. There was no mistaking the fact that he was truly dead.
- The raising of Lazarus was the last straw for many of the religious leaders. This is when the plot to kill Jesus began in earnest (see John 11:53). The leaders were afraid so many people would follow Jesus that the Romans would consider Judea to be a political problem and take complete control. And not only did they plot to kill Jesus, they

also wanted to get rid of the evidence of this miracle by killing Lazarus too (see 12:10-11).

37. ZACCHAEUS PRAISED

Key Points to Include:

- Even though Zacchaeus was hated by many, Jesus saw him as valuable. In fact, he was exactly the kind of person Jesus came to save.
- Zacchaeus demonstrated faith and a desire to know Jesus by going to great lengths to see Him. Jesus rewarded his perseverance and zeal.
- Jesus often shows grace to those we might consider to be the least likely candidates.
- Restitution was an important part of Zacchaeus's repentance. It didn't earn forgiveness for him, but it did reflect a changed heart.

More Information:

- When one person defrauded another, the law of Moses required the offender to pay restitution of the original amount plus one-fifth (see Numbers 5:5-6). Stealing livestock was an exception; the offender had to restore four or five times the number of cattle or sheep stolen (see Exodus 22:1; 2 Samuel 12:6). Zacchaeus went above and beyond the normal law of restitution and took the worst penalty for thievery upon himself.
- Jesus' mission to seek out and save those who most need it is expressed in various ways throughout the Gospels. See Luke 5:29-32 and the three parables in Luke 15 for more examples.

38. DEMONIAC DELIVERED

Key Points to Include:

- The tormented man who encountered Jesus was beyond hopeless in the eyes of his community.
- Every spirit ultimately has to bow to Jesus.
- Jesus wants us to be free from all that oppresses us.
- When we are under spiritual attack or any kind of oppression from the Enemy, we can ask Jesus to intervene. We can exercise His authority over Satan and live in freedom.
- The power of Jesus is often frightening to those whose lives are interrupted by it.

- Everyone who has truly encountered Jesus has a testimony to tell and is qualified to tell it.

More Information:
- Both in biblical practice (as when Jacob wrestled with God) and in popular tradition at the time of Jesus, asking for and using someone's name implied a sense of authority or claim over them. Though Jesus didn't get an exact answer—there were many names of many spirits in this man—He was able to exercise control over those spirits anyway.
- A Roman legion usually had more than five thousand soldiers in it.
- Jesus' instructions for the ex-demoniac to "go and tell" make him the first missionary presented in the Gospels—a clear sign that anyone who has been touched by Jesus is qualified for some kind of ministry.
- Many times when Jesus healed or delivered someone, He told that person not to tell anyone, probably because people would have tried to push Him into a role He had not come to fulfill. We saw an example of this in John 6, where the people were coming to try to make Him king. But in Gentile territory, there was no fear of messianic expectations getting out of control. It's one of the only times before the end of the Gospels that Jesus urged someone to go and tell.

39. LEARNING TO PRAY

Key Points to Include:
- Jesus wants His disciples to know how to pray.
- Jesus used the familiar term *Father* to address God and instructed us to do the same.
- We are not limited to only the requests mentioned in the model prayer, but they do let us know what our priorities should be when we pray.
- Our private prayers are our sincerest prayers. This is the kind of attitude God wants us to have, even when we pray with others around.
- God doesn't give us formulas or tell us to recite the right words so He will hear us. Prayer is heart-to-heart communication with someone who already knows our needs.

- Persistence is a very important aspect of prayer.
- We can trust God not only to answer our prayers but also to answer them with good things.

More Information:

- In Middle Eastern culture, hospitality customs required the man to provide food for his visitor, and any resident's response would have been seen as a reflection on the entire community. The sleepy friend should have been just as interested in feeding the visitor as the host was.
- The verb tenses for *ask*, *seek*, and *knock* all imply a continuous process—keep asking, keep seeking, keep knocking.
- Luke's version of this passage says God will surely give the Holy Spirit to those who ask Him, but Matthew's version is more general. God will give "good gifts" to those who ask Him (Matthew 7:11).
- Jesus also taught about persistence and attitudes in prayer in Luke 18:1-14. The two parables in that passage are good background for the story in this session.

40. SEEKING THE LOST

Key Points to Include:

- The three stories of "lost things" was Jesus' response to people who didn't understand His mission or God's compassion.
- All three parables make the same point but in different ways.
- God's purpose in sending Jesus was not to categorize people as righteous or unrighteous but to reclaim those who don't know Him.
- The prodigal son committed terrible offenses and sank as low as a Jewish man could go, but he didn't wander beyond the reach of God's grace.
- God accepts those who return to Him and lavishes His love on them regardless of their past.
- The older son thought his place in the family was based on his good behavior and faithfulness, but the father based his relationships with his sons only on his love for them.
- Those who follow Jesus need to understand His mission and are invited to be a part of it.

More Information:

- By requesting his inheritance before his father's death, the son was essentially wishing his father was already dead.
- Jesus' portrayal of the son — both his behavior (consorting with prostitutes) and its consequences (serving Gentiles and tending pigs) — made him an extremely vile character in the eyes of the Jews listening to Jesus. This was as low as a Jewish man could sink.
- In Middle Eastern culture, an older man in robes does not run. To run through the town like this would be considered undignified and humiliating. But the father's joy causes him to completely disregard his reputation.
- The older son may have had in mind Deuteronomy 21:18-21, which would have required his younger brother to be stoned for his offenses.

41. REVEALING THE KINGDOM

Key Points to Include:

- The values, attitudes, and characteristics highly favored in the kingdom of God are not always the same as those valued in the world. The kingdom of God and the kingdom of the world have distinct cultures.
- There will be a time when those in the kingdom and those outside of it are separated forever.
- God's kingdom is to be valued more than all else.
- Those who enter the kingdom will shine like the sun. Those who do not will weep and gnash their teeth with regret.
- Humility is a requirement for the kingdom of heaven. We can only enter the kingdom through faith.
- We do not become angels when we enter heaven, but Jesus did say that like the angels, we do not marry in heaven.
- Jesus is currently preparing a place in heaven for those who love and believe in Him.
- We are to represent the kingdom on earth and pray for God's kingdom to be made manifest here. But there are aspects of the kingdom that we will not experience in full until heaven.

More Information:

- Parallel stories in Matthew, Mark, and Luke use different terms for the kingdom. In Matthew, it's usually "the kingdom of heaven," whereas in Mark and Luke it's always "the kingdom of God." This is probably due to the fact that Matthew wrote to a largely Jewish audience, many of whom believed it was presumptuous to write God's name. Although Matthew did use "kingdom of God" occasionally, he wrote it much more sparingly than the other gospel writers did.

42. DECLARING THE KING

Key Points to Include:

- Many people speculated about who Jesus was, but even His disciples weren't sure He was the Messiah until God revealed it to them.
- Jesus didn't fit many people's expectations of a Messiah. Peter's confession was a revelation from God, not a natural conclusion of human reasoning.
- Jesus guaranteed that His church would be victorious.
- Those who follow Jesus have been given the right to exercise at least some degree of His authority on earth.
- The disciple who voiced a profound revelation from God about Jesus being the Messiah is the same disciple whom Jesus rebuked for speaking the thoughts of Satan.
- Jesus' death and resurrection were God's plan, but to human eyes, the events at the Cross appeared to be contrary to God's will.

More Information:

- Peter's name means "rock," so Jesus was making a play on words when He said, "You are Peter, and on this rock I will build my church" (Matthew 16:18). Many Christians believe the "rock" is the truth Jesus declared. Some, particularly within the Catholic church, believe Peter himself is the rock on which the church would be built. Regardless of one's interpretation of this wordplay, Peter became a foundational apostle and leader of the early church, and his declaration of Jesus as the Christ became a foundational truth of the Christian faith.
- The "binding and loosing" function of the church refers to the authority believers have in declaring and establishing on earth what God has already declared and established in heaven.

43. HEAVEN OR HELL

Key Points to Include:
- The rich man seems to have had no regard for the poor man outside his house.
- God cares about justice and has compassion on the poor.
- There are only two places one can go after death: heaven or hell.
- There is a divide between heaven and hell that cannot be crossed.
- Those who believe in Scripture's testimony, specifically about Jesus, will be saved. According to the story, that determines where one spends eternity.
- Those who do not already believe what Scripture says are unlikely to believe even when they see a miracle as dramatic as someone rising from the dead.

More Information:
- Lazarus was a fairly common name, and the man in this story has no connection with the Lazarus whom Jesus raised from the dead.
- Abraham himself was a rich man, so this story clearly isn't teaching that wealth is evil and poverty is good. The key to heaven is believing the testimony about Jesus — in this story, as the Old Testament foretold Him, but for us, as all of Scripture describes Him. Even so, there is a clear theme in this story of God's compassion for the poor and broken.
- The reference to "Moses and the Prophets" is another way of saying "the Law and the Prophets," a common term for the entire Old Testament.

44. WASHING THEIR FEET

Key Points to Include:
- Jesus knew the time was coming for Him to be crucified, so He gave His disciples a visual illustration of how He had humbled Himself. He went from exalted Lord to a human in the flesh to exalted Lord again.
- We do not need to be "cleaned" — washed of our sins — again and again. Those who have believed have already been forgiven. But we do need to maintain our cleanliness just as a clean person might wash his or her feet.

- Being a servant is a vital aspect of the Christian life.

More Information:
- Jesus' teaching in Matthew 20:20-28 is a good background for this story. In addition, Paul's words in Philippians 2:5-11 use the symbolism of this story to describe Jesus' ultimate service and sacrifice. Just as Jesus took off His robe and put on the garments of a servant to wash His disciples' feet, He took off His divine nature and became human on our behalf.

45. LAST SUPPER

Key Points to Include:
- Jesus knew what was about to happen, and He willingly went ahead with the plan.
- The Jewish leaders were looking for a way to get rid of Jesus, and they needed Judas's help to do it.
- The first Passover at the time of the Exodus was a picture of an even greater deliverance that would occur at the Passover in this story.
- The sacrifice of Jesus' body and blood secures our freedom from sin and death if we believe.
- Jesus instructed His disciples—and all who would follow—to remember His sacrifice by eating and drinking His "body" and "blood," the bread and wine of the Passover meal.
- At this Passover meal, Jesus established with His followers a new covenant that was different from the covenant God established with Israel through Moses.

More Information:
- Session 10 gives the Old Testament background to this story and provides a necessary understanding of Jesus as the true Passover Lamb.
- There was a genuine political reason for the religious leaders to fear Jesus' popularity. Messianic movements created a context for unrest, and unrest could prompt Rome to intervene in a more heavy-handed way: with military force and possibly an order to nullify Israel's local government.

46. PRAYED, BETRAYED

Key Points to Include:

- Jesus knew His disciples would face much temptation in the days to come and that they should pray not to enter temptation.
- Jesus did not look forward to the pain of the Cross, but He wanted to do God's will. That was His highest priority. And He was willing to endure anything to restore fallen humanity.
- The disciples seemed to expect this crisis moment to be the catalyst for a change in government from corrupt leaders to Messiah Jesus. And in a sense it was—but not in the way they thought.
- Everything can appear out of control and still be perfectly in line with God's will.
- Peter was absolutely convinced he would never leave or forsake Jesus—and absolutely wrong about his own strength.
- Crisis moments lead to a choice between fear and faith.

More Information:

- Most Christians seem to pray more that they would be able to resist temptation rather than that they would be able to avoid it. But Jesus teaches in this passage (see Luke 22:40) and the Lord's Prayer ("Lead us not into temptation but deliver us from the evil one" [Matthew 6:13]) that we can ask God to keep us from tempting situations.
- Though Jesus prayed to avoid the Cross altogether if possible, He didn't go to it reluctantly or simply because it was the right thing to do. He genuinely looked forward to the result it would accomplish. Hebrews 12:2 tells us He endured the Cross "for the joy set before him."
- Jesus had told Peter that Satan wanted to sift him like wheat, but He also said He had prayed for Peter. His comments in Luke 22:31-32 indicate that He already knew Peter would fail and already had a plan to restore him—a great encouragement to those of us who experience similar failures. Jesus is not surprised by them and is willing to restore and forgive.

47. TRIED, CRUCIFIED

Key Points to Include:

- Most of the accusations against Jesus were untrue or distortions of the truth.
- Jesus could have defended Himself effectively but chose not to.
- Jesus demonstrated patience with His accusers, compassion for those who mourned for Him and believed in Him, and forgiveness toward those who crucified Him.
- During the Crucifixion, God demonstrated that this was a critical moment for the world. He also showed that through Jesus people have direct access to God through faith.
- Jesus' death was an offering to satisfy the penalty for humanity's sins. That offering applies to anyone who believes in Him.

More Information:

- Tradition allowed the release of one prisoner at Passover to symbolize the deliverance of the first Passover event in Egypt. In this case, the leaders and the crowds elected Barabbas over Jesus. Barabbas seems to have been a zealot, a revolutionary who had helped lead a failed insurrection against Rome (and killed someone in the process). Ironically, Barabbas was fighting for freedom, which Jesus came to provide. And fittingly, Barabbas's name means "son of the father," an accurate description of the prisoner who took his place, as well as an accurate description of all who would believe in the sacrifice that holy prisoner made.
- Who was responsible for Jesus' death? History's emphasis often blames either Pontius Pilate for the sentence or the Jewish leaders for instigating it. The truth is that the human race, represented by both Jews and Gentiles, conspired to crucify Him. It was a joint effort by those He came to redeem, a picture of the truth that "all have sinned" (Romans 3:23).
- The curtain that was ripped in two was the veil covering the Most Holy Place in the temple. This phenomenon represented the fact that God gave all human beings, not just the high priest, access to His presence through faith.
- We're told in the gospel of John that Joseph of Arimathea was joined by Nicodemus, the Pharisee who had once approached Jesus at night

to ask Him questions (see session 32). These two men willingly defiled themselves by touching a dead body and rendered themselves ritually unclean to celebrate Passover with their families. According to a special provision of Moses' Law, they would be able to celebrate the feast a month later when they had been purified.

48. RESURRECTED

Key Points to Include:

- The first people to know of the Resurrection were the women who came to tend to Jesus' body on the morning after the Sabbath.
- An angel rolled the stone away and was visible to the guards and the women who visited.
- The disciples were slow to believe the report of the Resurrection, even though it had been foretold by Jesus Himself.
- The religious leaders devised a cover-up plot to keep the Resurrection a secret, and they paid numerous soldiers to spread lies about what had happened.
- Jesus appeared to many people after His resurrection, explaining to some of them how He had been revealed in Scripture from ages past.
- Nothing is impossible with God.

More Information:

- In the chaos of Resurrection morning, the gospel writers give slightly different accounts of what happened. For example, Luke says Joanna was among the women who went, but others mention only the Marys. John says both Peter and "the other disciple" (John himself) went to the tomb, while some of the gospels mention only Peter. For a fuller account, it's best to read all four Gospels, which together paint a fascinating picture of the events of that morning.
- Luke records that the disciples considered the women's report "nonsense" (24:11), and we know from the gospel testimonies that some said they would only believe when they saw it for themselves. Mark 16:14 tells us what Jesus thought of that kind of skepticism: "He rebuked them for their lack of faith and their stubborn refusal to believe."

49. RESTORED TO SERVE

Key Points to Include:

- Jesus was resurrected physically. People touched Him, He ate food, and He interacted with others as someone who was physically present.
- Jesus understands our doubts and gives us grace for them, but He calls us to the kind of faith that believes even when we can't see.
- Just as He showed the disciples where to catch fish, Jesus shows us how to bear fruit even when we've been fruitless in the past.
- Jesus doesn't give up on us but restores us when we fall. He loves us and uses us in His plans in spite of our failures.

More Information:

- The gospel of John mentions that the disciples counted 153 fish when they pulled their net to shore. Interestingly, an ancient document refers to 153 known languages in the world at the time of Jesus. (There were more, but only this number were known to many of Jesus' contemporaries.) The number of fish may have been God's way of saying the gospel is for people of all languages and nations—and God's nets are strong enough for them all.
- The question of whether the Resurrection was a spiritual or physical event was a big one in the culture of the early church. In Luke's gospel, Jesus makes a point of emphasizing His physical body: "Touch me and see; a ghost does not have flesh and bones, as you see I have" (Luke 24:39).

50. REACH THE WORLD

Key Points to Include:

- Jesus told His disciples in several different ways that the good news was for the whole world.
- The task of the Great Commission is more than just getting decisions for Christ. The goal is to make disciples—people who love, follow, and learn to live like Jesus.
- Jesus promised that those who carry out His mission would experience His power and that He would be with them.
- Jesus sent His disciples out with the same Spirit, the same attitudes, the same goals, and the same approach that the Father sent Him.

- God's goal is not just for people to change their behavior by obeying Him but for sinful human beings to be restored to fellowship with Him. The goal of the Great Commission is for people to come into a relationship with God.
- God had a global vision from the very beginning, instructing Adam and Eve to fill the earth and subdue it, and telling Abraham that all the peoples of the world would be blessed through him.

More Information:

- You can read about the covenant God made with Abraham and how it applies to the peoples of the world in Genesis 12:1-3.
- On several occasions after the resurrection, the gospel writers refer to people who worshipped Jesus: the women at the tomb (see Matthew 28:9), the disciples in Galilee (see Matthew 28:17), the witnesses of the Ascension (see Luke 24:52), and Thomas when he touched His scars (see John 20:28). Even though Scripture is clear that only God is to be worshipped, Jesus did not rebuke anyone for doing this. This is an implicit claim to be God, contrary to the argument of many that Jesus never made that claim.

51. JESUS ASCENDS

Key Points to Include:

- Jesus proved He was physically alive to many people through many appearances.
- The disciples were not to carry out their mission until they had been empowered by the Holy Spirit.
- The disciples' mission would begin in Jerusalem and then extend outward to the ends of the earth.
- No one knows the timing of Jesus' return.
- Jesus is going to come back in the same way He left: by appearing in the air.

More Information:

- What is Jesus doing in heaven? According to the writer of Hebrews, He serves as our high priest and is currently praying for us at the throne of the Majesty (see Hebrews 7:23–8:2).

- After several decades passed and Jesus had returned, many in the early church began to wonder if He would keep His promise. Peter assured the early believers that He would but that God's timing is not the same as ours. Read 2 Peter 3:8-10 for a reminder of the promise and one reason that Jesus hasn't come yet; then read verses 11-14 for instructions about how we should live while we wait for Him.

52. SPIRIT DESCENDS

Key Points to Include:
- God worked through unexpected, common people. It was clear that His power was needed for otherwise incapable people to do such things.
- God demonstrated on the day of Pentecost that the good news of salvation was for all people of all languages.
- This outpouring of the Spirit was part of God's plan that was predicted centuries earlier by His prophets.
- The promise of the Holy Spirit is for all who believe.
- The Holy Spirit's presence and work inspired awe and radically changed the people who experienced Him.

More Information:
- The night before He was crucified, Jesus told the disciples repeatedly that He would send His Spirit to them. You can read about the various ways He expressed these promises in John 14:16-17,25-26; 15:26; and 16:7-15.
- Pentecost, also known as the Feast of Weeks or the Festival of Firstfruits, was fifty days after the end of Passover. It was a harvest festival that celebrated not only the harvest but also God's giving of the law at Mount Sinai. The connections with the law and with the harvest made it a significant day for God to pour out His Spirit on human beings, representing both a new covenant and its firstfruits. Pentecost was one of the three major feasts on the Jewish calendar that brought Jews to Jerusalem from afar.
- Galileans were considered by many to be the hillbillies of the region — the least likely people to be cosmopolitan and multilingual.
- The unusual communal flavor of these days after Pentecost was at least partly due to the fact that many people who experienced this

amazing move of God were from out of town. No one wanted to leave while God was working so dramatically, but most new believers were far from their homes and jobs. They needed support, and the Spirit-inspired generosity of local believers provided it.

ABOUT WALK THRU THE BIBLE

For more than three decades, Walk Thru the Bible has created discipleship materials and cultivated leadership networks that together are reaching millions of people through live events, print publications, audiovisual curricula, and the Internet. Known for innovative methods and high-quality resources, Walk Thru the Bible serves the whole body of Christ across denominational, cultural, and national lines. Through strong and cooperative international partnerships, it is strategically positioned to address the church's greatest need: developing mature, committed, and spiritually reproducing believers.

Walk Thru the Bible communicates the truths of God's Word in a way that makes the Bible readily accessible to anyone. It is committed to developing user-friendly resources that are Bible centered, of excellent quality, life-changing for individuals, and catalytic for churches, ministries, and movements; and it is committed to maintaining global reach through strategic partnerships while adhering to the highest levels of integrity in all they do.

Walk Thru the Bible partners with the local church worldwide to fulfill its mission, helping people "walk thru" the Bible with greater clarity and understanding. Live seminars and small-group curricula are taught in more than forty-five languages by more than eighty thousand

people in more than seventy countries, and more than one hundred
million devotionals have been packaged into daily magazines, books,
and other publications that reach more than five million people each
year.

Walk Thru the Bible
4201 North Peachtree Road
Atlanta, GA 30341-1207
(800) 361-6131
www.walkthru.org

Use orality even more.

Truth That Sticks
Avery T. Willis Jr. and
Mark Snowden

Seventy percent of the
unreached people in the world
are oral learners. How will
you reach them with the truth
of Jesus Christ? Discover the
TruthSticks strategy, a method
of creating disciples with
biblical storytelling in small
groups.

978-1-61521-531-7

Walk Thru the Bible
Magazine Rack

Closer Walk Reading Scripture reveals what God says about Himself and what He has to say about you— His plans and purpose for you. *Closer Walk* is a daily devotional guide, accompanied by excerpts from great teachers of the faith, for reading through the entire New Testament in one year.

Daily Walk God speaks every day! Are you listening? Unique insights, overviews, charts, and other special features have made *Daily Walk* a dependable Bible study tool for over 25 years. With its systematic reading plan, your life will be revolutionized as you read through the entire Bible in just one year.

Tapestry *Weaving God's Wisdom into a Woman's Heart.* Just as one tapestry's delicate beauty is different from another, your relationship with God is unique and unduplicated. *Tapestry* draws you into His presence and offers guidance, encouragement, and a realistic presentation of what it means to be a Christian woman in today's complex world.

indeed *Exploring the Heart of God.* If you desire to know God's heart more deeply, *indeed* is the devotional you want. By focusing on one short passage each day, new insights and new applications are revealed that show your part in God's great plan. For those who want to meditate deeply on the wisdom of Scripture, *indeed* will help you mine those treasures.

YW is a magazine of daily devotionals designed to help students navigate the Bible, to get to know God through it, and to answer His call to live the adventure. This adventure, stamped by the Holy Spirit and pioneered by Jesus Christ, is dangerous yet wonderful, day-to-day yet holy. Invite your students to step into the journey with us.

WALK THRU THE BIBLE
TAKE A WALK. CHANGE THE WORLD.

To order, visit our website:
www.devotionals.org